STANISLAVSKY AND RACE

Stanislavsky and Race is the first book to explore the role that Konstantin Stanislavsky's "system" and its legacies can play in building, troubling and illuminating today's anti-racist theatre practices.

This collection of essays from leading figures in the field of actor training stands not only as a resource for a new area of academic enquiry, but also for students, actors, directors, teachers and academics who are engaged in making inclusive contemporary theatre. In seeking to dismantle the dogma that surrounds much actor training and replace it with a culturally competent approach that will benefit our entire community, the "system" is approached from a range of perspectives featuring the research, reflections and provocations of 20 different international artists interrogating Stanislavsky's approach through the lens of race, place and identity.

Stanislavsky and … is a series of multi-perspectival collections that bring the enduring legacy of Stanislavskian actor training into the spotlight of contemporary performance culture, making them ideal for students, teachers and scholars of acting, actor training and directing.

Siiri Scott is a Chicago actor/director and serves as the Head of Acting and Directing and a Professor of the Practice in the Department of Film, Television and Theatre at the University of Notre Dame, USA.

Jay Paul Skelton is a lecturer on the MA/MFA Actor Training and Coaching programme at The Royal Central School of Speech and Drama, UK, and has taught at RADA, Rose Bruford, Kingston University and the University of Notre Dame London Global Gateway.

STANISLAVSKY AND RACE

Questioning the "System" in the 21st Century

Edited by Siiri Scott and Jay Paul Skelton

Routledge
Taylor & Francis Group

LONDON AND NEW YORK

Designed cover image: © Design by Colin Chan; Stanislavsky image used by permission of Bridgeman Images.

First published 2023
by Routledge
4 Park Square, Milton Park, Abingdon, Oxon OX14 4RN

and by Routledge
605 Third Avenue, New York, NY 10158

Routledge is an imprint of the Taylor & Francis Group, an informa business

British Library Cataloguing-in-Publication Data
A catalogue record for this book is available from the British Library

Library of Congress Cataloging-in-Publication Data
Names: Scott, Siiri, editor. | Skelton, Gerald Paul Jr., editor.
Title: Stanislavsky and race : questioning the "system" in the 21st century / edited by Siiri Scott and Gerald Paul Skelton, Jr.
Description: New York : Routledge, 2024. |
Series: Stanislavsky and ... | Includes bibliographical references and index.
Identifiers: LCCN 2023014243 (print) | LCCN 2023014244 (ebook) |
ISBN 9781032362342 (hbk) | ISBN 9781032362335 (pbk) |
ISBN 9781003330882 (ebk)
Subjects: LCSH: Method acting. | Stanislavsky, Konstantin, 1863-1938--Criticism and interpretation. | Race. | Racism.
Classification: LCC PN2062 .S63 2024 (print) | LCC PN2062 (ebook) |
DDC 792.02/8--dc23/eng/20230712
LC record available at https://lccn.loc.gov/2023014243
LC ebook record available at https://lccn.loc.gov/2023014244

ISBN: 978-1-032-36234-2 (hbk)
ISBN: 978-1-032-36233-5 (pbk)
ISBN: 978-1-003-33088-2 (ebk)

DOI: 10.4324/9781003330882

Typeset in Galliard
by Taylor & Francis Books

We dedicate this book to our fellow students, theatre artists and colleagues with gratitude, humility and hope for the future

CONTENTS

ILLUSTRATIONS

Figures

Boxes

CONTRIBUTORS

Sylvan Baker is an artist, academic, practitioner and researcher working across the fields of Applied Theatre and arts in social justice for over 30 years. He is a Senior Lecturer in Community Performance and Applied Theatre at the Royal Central School of Speech and Drama, London, teaching on the BA Contemporary Performance Practice, specialising in Drama, Applied Theatre and Education (DATE), and on the MA Applied Theatre courses. Beyond Central, his practice has taken place in the UK and globally in sites across Brazil and the US. He has delivered projects in a diverse range of communities and contexts from *favelas* to hospitals, and has a specific interest in participatory collaboration, transitional justice and interventions in sites of conflict. His current research projects work with young researchers with experience of the UK care system, and separately with neurodivergent young people to develop resources to support positive adolescent mental health.

Marissa Chibás is a Los Angeles-based writer, filmmaker, actor, educator, Sundance fellow and recipient of the TCG Fox Fellowship for Distinguished Achievement. She is on the Theater School faculty at California Institute of the Arts, Los Angeles where she is Director of Duende CalArts, an initiative at CalArts Center for New Performance that produces innovative Latinx and Latin American artists. Marissa is the Robert Corrigan Chair in the School of Theater. Her work as an actor has been seen on Broadway and on major stages throughout the world and her solo show, *Daughter of a Cuban Revolutionary*, has toured the United States, Europe and Mexico. Her acting book *Mythic Imagination and the Actor* was released by Routledge Press in 2021. For more information, visit www.marissachibas.com.

Conrad Cohen is a Scottish and Jewish actor, director and educator, and is Teachers Programme Manager at the Royal Shakespeare Company. He is currently working towards an MFA in Actor Training and Coaching at the Royal Central School of Speech and Drama, where he is also a Visiting Lecturer. Since training as an actor at the American Academy of Dramatic Arts, he has performed in and directed productions in New York and throughout the UK. A qualified teacher with a PGCE from the University of Northampton, he is a Member of the Chartered College of Teaching and has experience leading departments in secondary education. Whilst specialising in teaching drama, acting and theatre, he also has a BSc (Hons) in Mathematics from the University of Nottingham. For more information please visit conra dcohen.com.

James Cooney has a BA in Acting from the Liverpool Institute for Performing Arts (LIPA) and an MA in Actor Training and Coaching from the Royal Central School of Speech and Drama (RCSSD). He has worked as an actor for the Royal Shakespeare Company (RSC), Shakespeare's Globe and The Old Vic, amongst other UK theatre companies. As an actor trainer he has worked with RCSSD and the RSC Education department, as well as freelance work with schools and individuals across the UK. He draws from different acting approaches underpinned by a pedagogy of belonging he developed whilst training.

Gemma Crooks is an actor trainer, artist and researcher. In 2019 Gemma became the Head of Acting at ARTS1, where she co-developed the acting pathway for post-16 students. She works as an acting practitioner on the MA Theatre Lab programme at the Royal Academy of Dramatic Art. As a freelance acting practitioner, she works within UK drama schools and universities teaching and directing contemporary and classical texts. Gemma is part of a two-woman collaborative research practice that looks at the creation of new works and Black British narratives. Her collaborative practice-based research led to the exploration of reframing actor training through her co-created model S.P.H.E.R.E. Gemma holds a BA in Acting from Birmingham Conservatoire, an MFA in Actor Training and Coaching from The Royal Central School of Speech and Drama and Foundation Studies in Laban from Laban Guild International Studies. She holds joy and celebration at the centre of her life and her work.

Zuri Eshun has appeared in a number of film, television and theatre productions both in the US and UK. She has been seen in *Intimate Apparel, Insecure* and *Random Acts of Flyness*, to name just a few. She has also recently finished her directing debut of *This Is Modern Art* at the Decio Theatre in the US. Zuri studied performance at the University of Notre Dame and received her MFA in Acting at the East 15 Acting School of London. During her graduate training, Zuri started The Culture Collective, an on-campus performance group and learning resource focused on developing BIPOC artists. Aside from her work in theatre, Zuri is an accomplished writer and percussionist. A native of Dallas, Texas, Zuri now lives in Chicago, where she actively pushes for BIPOC artists' engagement on a collegiate level.

Dominic Hingorani is Professor of Performing Arts and Head of Department at the University of East London and Co-Artistic Director of Brolly Productions CIC, a global majority-led cross arts performance company who create new roles in the repertoire for under-represented artists and develop diverse artists, participants and audiences for the Arts and Heritage. His research is by practice and publication and focuses on art form innovation and specifically addresses issues of representation, inclusion and diversity. Dominic's work for Brolly as writer and director includes *The Stopping Place* (2021) The *Powder Monkey* (2019); *her* (2017) *Clocks 1888: the greener* (2016) and *Guantanamo Boy* (2013). https://www.brollyproductions.com

Michelle Jasso is an award-honored, LA-based, Latine performer with credits encompassing opera, cabaret, theatre, television, commercial and voiceover. Within her stage repertoire of over 25 leading and supporting roles, favorites include the title role in Puccini's *Suor Angelica*, Sally Bowles (*Cabaret*), The Witch *(Into The Woods)*, The Beggar Woman (*Sweeney Todd*, Bay Area Theatre Critics Circle award), Elizaveta Grushinskaya in *Grand Hotel* (2019 Jeff Award) and Soyla Reyna (*American Mariachi*). She has appeared regionally with Chicago Shakespeare Theater, Music Theater Works, Porchlight Music Theatre, TheatreSquared, Opera Grand Rapids, Portland Opera, and The Industry in Los Angeles. Jasso was on the Broadway national tour of *The King's Speech* at the time of the Broadway shutdown. She has appeared on *Chicago PD*, *The Chi*, and in the Latinx web series *Border'd*, the first full season of which premiered on OTV in November 2021. She is a member of SAG-AFTRA, Actors' Equity, and AGMA.

Erica Jeffrey is an artist, educator and practice-based researcher. She trained on the MFA Actor Training and Coaching programme at The Royal Central School of Speech and Drama. Erica has coached actors at several distinguished conservatoires and collaboratively led an MA Acting course. Her practice centres on cultivating a joyful, transformative and inclusive training method for contemporary actors. Erica utilises the S.P.H.E.R.E. framework to establish a reflexive pedagogy towards innovation.

Kristine Landon-Smith is a theatre practitioner and lecturer in higher education. Her work in industry and HE has included three years as Lecturer in Acting at the National Institute of Dramatic Art, Australia; 23 years as Co-Artistic Director of Tamasha, UK; four years as Senior Producer for

BBC Radio Drama; and freelance appointments as a director and lecturer within industry and HE settings. A recognized leader in the Black/Global Majority sector in the UK, she focuses on artist training in intracultural theatre practice, the creation of new work with and from diasporic heritage artists, and the development of audiences for this work. She currently freelances as an educator and director in mainly the UK and Australia, and her industry work has been focusing on applied theatre and her multilingual practice, which explores how to bring different nationalities and languages together in existing texts.

Sandra Marquez is an award-winning Chicago-based actor, director and educator. She was the first self-identified Latinx artist to join Steppenwolf Theatre Company's storied ensemble where her acting credits include *The Seagull, A Doll's House Part 2, The Doppelganger, Mary Page Marlowe* and *The Motherfu&*er with the Hat*. Her directing credits with the company include *La Ruta* by Isaac Gomez, which marked the first all-Latina cast on a Steppenwolf stage, and the critically acclaimed and sold-out world premiere of *I Am Not Your Perfect Mexican Daughter*. She played Clytemnestra in four productions billed as Court Theatre's Iphigenia Cycle: *Iphigenia in Aulis* (Chicago and The Getty), *Agamemnon* and *Electra*. Also a longtime ensemble member at Teatro Vista, she served as Associate Artistic Director (with Artistic Director Edward Torres) from 1998–2006. She has had roles on *Chicago Med, Chicago Justice, Prison Break, Boss, Timer*, Amazon Original *Night Sky*, as well as other shows and films. Currently, she is an Associate Professor of Acting and Directing and the Co-Director of Graduate Studies for the MFA in Acting Program at Northwestern University where she enjoys teaching and mentoring young people. She maintains a persistent aim to uplift voices of the unheard at every opportunity.

Diego Moschkovich is a theatre director, theatre pedagogue and a translator. Diego studied at Sergei Tcherkasski's Studio at the St. Petersburg State Theatre Arts Academy (Russia) and has an MFA in Russian Culture and Russian Language at the University of São Paulo (Brazil). His latest work in the MAT Museum Archives was published in Brazil in 2021 as the book *The Late Stanislavski in Action: Experimenting on a New Method*. Part of this work has recently been published in English in Stanislavski Studies. Diego's PhD research, "Towards a Theatre with Moving Walls: Stanislavski's Last and Unfinished Revolution", is currently being carried out at the Drama Department of the University of São Paulo (Brazil). Moschkovich translated the first Russian to Portuguese translation of Meyerhold's *On Theatre*, as well as Maria Knebel's *Action-Analysis* and Sergei Tcherkasski's *Stanislavski and Yoga*. Diego worked as an assistant-director and translator to Anatoli Vassiliev in his "Masters in Residence" program held at the Grotowski Institute. Currently, Moschkovich directs the Laboratory for Dramatic Technique in São Paulo, Brazil, a laboratory for investigating practically different performance drama-based procedures in Brazilian contemporary theatre.

Monica White Ndounou is an Associate Professor of Theater at Dartmouth College and the founding Executive Director of The CRAFT Institute and The International Black Theatre Summit. CRAFT administers the Pay-It-Forward All-Career Level Mentorship Program and various initiatives designed to create culturally inclusive ecosystems throughout the world of arts and entertainment by transforming formal training and industry practices while promoting equitable access. She is past President of the Black Theatre Association (BTA) (2016–2018), past Vice President of Advocacy for the Association for Theatre in Higher Education (ATHE) (2019–2021) and served on the board of The August Wilson Society and The Black Seed's founding National Advisory Committee. She is the author of several publications as well an actor, director and alumnus of The Black Arts Institute. She is a creator and co-curator of Echoes of Us, produced by the African Diasporic Network and a co-founder of CreateEnsemble.com, a digital platform for creative artists of color.

James Palm trained at East 15 School of Acting and the Royal Central School of Speech and Drama, achieving an MA in Advanced Theatre Practice. James also has a PGCE in Drama from the University of Reading. James was awarded a PhD in 2014: "Acting Towards the Possibility of Good Faith". James practices a humanist, existential methodology of acting and pedagogy. As an actor, James has worked at Shakespeare's Globe, Young Vic, BAC, The Gate and in television and radio. James is currently the Short Courses Programme Leader at the Royal Central School of Speech and Drama.

Tlaloc Rivas is a Chicano theatre-maker, playwright and director focused on new work and reimagined works for the stage. He currently brings his expertise and experience as an educator at the David Geffen School of Drama at Yale University. He is the co-founder of the Latinx Theatre Commons, the recipient of the Sir John Gielgud Fellowship in Classical Directing, the NEA/TCG Career Development Program for Directors and a Usual Suspect of New York Theatre Workshop. Advanced training includes the SITI Company Intensive at Skidmore College, the María Irene Fornés Institute, La Mama Umbria Summer Intensive, NALAC Leadership Institute, Mabou Mines Resident Artist Program, Cornerstone Theatre Company Summer Institute, and Anti-Racism training with Equity Quotient and artEquity. Tlaloc also serves on the boards of The New Harmony Project and Latiné Musical Theatre Lab NYC. He is a member of Dramatists Guild and the Society of Stage Directors & Choreographers. Education: B.A. (with Honors) University of California, Santa Cruz; MFA Professional Directors Training Program,

University of Washington School of Drama; Postdoctoral Presidential Fellow, Carnegie Mellon University. www.TlalocRivas.com

Siiri Scott is the Head of Acting and Directing at the University of Notre Dame and teaches advanced courses in the Department of Film, Television, and Theatre. In addition to training actors for over 25 years, she is a Chicago theatre director and voice-over artist and teaches professional masterclasses on dialect design and acting pedagogy in the US and the UK. An award-winning audiobook narrator, Siiri is also a company member with the Japanese Noh Theatre Nohgaku and Irish Theatre of Chicago. Publications include: "Vulnerability in Performance: Daring to be Ourselves" centering the relationship between the instructor, the student, and the environment. She specialises in anti-racist theatre practices and methodology with the intent of supporting inclusivity both in the classroom and the rehearsal room.

Jay Paul Skelton currently teaches a range of theory- and practice-based courses on the MA/MFA Actor Training and Coaching programme at The Royal Central School of Speech and Drama and the University of Notre Dame London Global Gateway. He has also taught at RADA, Rose Bruford College, Kingston University and St Mary's Twickenham amongst others. He holds an MFA in Directing from The Theatre School at DePaul University, and both an MA in Classical Theatre and a practice-based PhD from Kingston University. In addition, Jay has written, produced or directed over 100 productions in London, Edinburgh, New York, Chicago and Boston.

Evi Stamatiou is a practitioner-researcher of actor training. During her two decades of international experience as an actor and creative, she has won international awards and the Arts Council of England and the Stavros Niarchos Foundation have funded her work. She is a Senior Lecturer in Acting for Stage and Screen and Course Leader of the MA Acting for Stage and Screen at the University of East London. She has a PhD from the Royal Central School of Speech and Drama, University of London. She is a Senior Fellow of the Higher Education Academy. She is the incoming chair of the Acting Program at the Association for Theatre in Higher Education and a convener of the Performer Training Focus Group at the Theatre and Performance Research Association. She has published in academic books and journals, currently writing the monograph *Bourdieu in the Studio: Towards Decolonising and Decentering Acting Training*, and co-editing with Lisa Peck the volume *Critical Acting Pedagogies: Shifting Epistemologies with Intersectional Approaches*.

Amy Steiger is a director, actor, scholar and Associate Professor of Theater at St. Mary's College of Maryland. She holds a PhD in Performance as Public Practice from the University of Texas at Austin, and her interests include community-based theatre processes, critical pedagogy in acting classrooms, theatre performance as research and the potential of theatre training as anti-racist, pro-LGBTQ+ practice. Amy's publications include "Moving Forward, Living Backward, or Just Standing Still?: Newspaper Theatre, Critical Race Theory, and Commemorating the Wade-Braden Trial in Louisville, Kentucky," in *Pedagogy and Theatre of the Oppressed Journal*, "Whiteness, Patriarchy and Resistance in Actor Training Texts" for *Howlround*," "Paradoxical Sleep and Flights of Imagination: Sleep Rock Thy Brain and the Performance of Research" in *Journal of Dramatic Theory and Criticism*, and "Re-Membering Our Selves: Acting, Critical Pedagogy, and the Plays of Naomi Wallace" in *Theatre Topics*.

Joe Wilson, Jr is a Professor of the Practice of Theatre at Wheaton College and Producer and Director of the Wheaton X Series. Joe is the Founder/ Producer of *America Too*, held at Trinity Rep in Providence, Rhode Island every Fall. He has been a member of the Resident Acting Company at Trinity for 18 seasons. In 2020, Joe was honored by the Rhode Island Council for the Humanities with its Public Scholar Award. He also received the 2020 Providence NAACP's Medgar Evers Award for Public Service and was inducted into the City of Providence 2020 MLK Hall of Fame for Outstanding Service. Joe served on the Board of Directors for the Manton Avenue Project in Olneyville, and the Center for Reconciliation at the Cathedral of Saint Paul in collaboration with the Episcopal Diocese of Rhode Island. Mr. Wilson has a BA in Political Science from the University of Notre Dame, and an MFA in Acting from the University of Minnesota/Guthrie Theatre. Besides being a member of the resident acting company, he is on the boards of Providence's Manton Avenue Project, South Side Community Cultural Center and Center for Reconciliation. He is the recipient of the 2014 Volunteer of the Year Award from the Manton Avenue Project for recognition of his contributions as a guest artist, teacher, and board member. In addition, he is the recipient of the Sissieretta Jones Award for Cultural Literacy and the Arts, 2012 from the Rhode Island Black Heritage Society awarded to excellency in the arts (acting) presented "in recognition of those who have made outstanding contributions to the African American Community of Rhode Island." He was also a Featured Artist in "Black Lavender," Brown University, Providence, Rhode Island, 2009–2010: an exhibit curated by Robb Dimmick and sponsored by the Rhode Island Council for Humanities, highlighting the historical contributions of black gay men in Rhode Island. Mr. Wilson is a native of New Orleans, LA, and is a proud member of the Actor's Equity Association and SAG/AFTRA. Joe has recently accepted an appointment by the newly elected Mayor, and will serve as the Director of Art, Culture and Tourism for The City of Providence starting in January 2023.

ACKNOWLEDGEMENTS

We would like to thank all of the individuals, organisations and institutions that made this publication a reality.

Our work would not have been possible without the support of The S Word at the Stanislavsky Research Centre in the UK, and the Institute for Scholarship in the Liberal Arts, the Nanovic Institute for European Studies and the Initiative for Race and Resilience at the University of Notre Dame in the US. We are also grateful to the Department of Film, Television, and Theatre at the University of Notre Dame in the US and the staff at its London Global Gateway (Alice Tyrell, Charlotte Parkyn, Tom Finch, Joanna Byrne and Bridget Keating) for their support of the original webinar, subsequent symposium and this publication; to Nicole M. Brewer, Dr Broderick V. Chow, Pamela Jikiemi, Dr Stephen Atkins, Dan Barnard and Nathan Benjamin for their participation in the project during its earlier incarnations; to Lucy Baron, Gabriel Ozaki and Jo Ann Norris for editorial and logistical support; and to Quinlan Earley for doing double duty, including meeting with our contributors and creating graphics as needed.

We are indebted to Paul Fryer, the editor of the *Stanislavsky and ...* series, for his unending patience, guidance and wisdom during the process.

Our additional thanks go out to Anne García-Romero, Pamela Robertson Wojick, Kevin Dreyer, James Collins, Stacey Stewart, Lawrence Rosenblum and Colin Chan, for seeing the project to the finish line.

We are especially grateful to Dr Jessica Hartley for setting us on this path in the first instance.

INTRODUCTION

Siiri Scott and Jay Paul Skelton

It is late afternoon on 13 September 2019.

We (Siiri and Jay) are participating in the final day of a symposium on race and actor training co-hosted by The Royal School of Speech and Drama and Shakespeare's Globe in London. We are shoulder to shoulder with students, colleagues, scholars and practitioners in the tiny seating area of the Wanamaker Theatre, the Globe's indoor performance space. Our primary focus is a 90-minute "long table"[1] discussion on the future of anti-racist theatre and its impact on training, rehearsal and performance practice. The moderator, Dr Sylvan Baker, invites everyone – as a conclusion not only to the session but also to the symposium as a whole – to write our individual intentions on the large sheet of paper covering the table. In other words, after two days of rumbling[2] with racism in our respective studios, rehearsal rooms and offices, what concrete anti-racist actions were each of us going to undertake moving forward?

We see this book as one of our concrete actions toward anti-racist practice.

The question of the centralisation of Stanislavsky, a white, cisgendered, heterosexual male born over a century ago, and his "system", a two-pronged approach to the physical and psychological aspects of performance, in international actor training and professional practice is the focus of this response. It is also personal for us, as our own creative and pedagogic lives have been dedicated to perfecting the form and technique without critical engagement.

Stanislavsky's "System" as the *Lingua Franca*

Stanislavsky's "system" has been the *lingua franca* of actor training and professional practice in the Western world – and growing in influence across the globe – for almost a century.[3] It certainly was a common language for us in

DOI: 10.4324/9781003330882-1

our graduate school training in the 1990s at The Theatre School at DePaul University in Chicago where Siiri trained as a performer and Jay trained as a director. We were immersed in the lexicon of units, actions, given circumstances, objectives, super-objectives, emotion memory, sense memory, "Real I", "Dramatic I" and other elements of the "system" through practical, theoretical and sociological experiences. The actor training program for Siiri was entirely experiential and the methodology was filtered by individual instructors' understanding of the "system" and their own pedagogical approaches. Jay's key reference during his studies – and well into his professional career – was the book *On Directing* (1972) written by Harold Clurman, one of the founders of the Group Theatre, the members of which are largely credited with disseminating the "system" (and its variants) in the US during the 20th century. We had only a nascent understanding at the time that we were being asked by our instructors to inhale the common oxygen that the majority of contemporary actors and directors breathe; namely, standard Western training, rehearsal and performance methodologies as influenced by Stanislavsky's "system" regardless of our individual identities, experiences, interests or ways of learning.

In a class we took together, we were taught by a Stanislavsky-influenced acting instructor who happened to be elderly and Russian, which helped us believe we were in the room with someone who might have sounded like Stanislavsky. We received her comments, criticisms and (rare) compliments with utmost seriousness, so it was especially troubling when Siiri, as a biracial postgraduate actor in training, asked this instructor for guidance in playing a role intended explicitly for a white person and was told, "You're an actor, go and act." (We should note here that Jay is white.) It was clear that neither the teacher nor the practice she believed in, and offered to us, supported the needs of the Global Majority[4] actor; and in this case, even the question about race was deemed irrelevant to a methodology that focuses on the "reality" of a given response.

In other words, we choose to centre Stanislavsky and the "system" in this volume in order to destabilise and deconstruct our individual experiences and inherited methods in the furtherment of anti-racist practice. In the following pages, we are joined by others as they offer their personal processes and share their pluralist reconciliations (or renunciations) as we collectively seek to forward what Nicole Brewer refers to as "conscientious training", which takes

> the foundational principles of acting – listening and responding, actionable choices, voice work, presence, specificity, script analysis, relationships, movement, and vulnerability – and changes how these tenets are taught by removing the harmful erasure of non-white cultural identifiers and shift[...] to a communal ideology designed to minimize bias, racism, and discrimination and meet the needs of a diverse population.
>
> *(Brewer, 2018)*

The "system" (in quotes and using the lower case as Stanislavsky preferred) operates on the principle that historian and biographer Jean Benedetti states is the "understanding of the way we behave in our daily lives" (1998, p. 2). Stanislavsky separated the elements of a performer's process into what could be considered "accessible" concepts, processes and exercises to support what he referred to as "the creation of the life of the human spirit in a role and the communication of that life in an artistic form" on stage (Stanislavski, *An Actor's Work*, p. 19). He further suggested that the performers' "prime task is not only to portray the life of a role externally, but above all create the inner life of the character […] bringing our own individual feelings to it, endowing it with all the features of your own personality".

The underlying principle that Stanislavsky advanced was the relationship between an actor "being" real in order to "seem" real for an audience, a premise long contested (see *Paradoxe sur le comédien*, or *Paradox of the Actor*, by Denis Diderot published in 1830), but that was laid as doctrine in the advancement of the "system". He might have initially undertaken his inquiry into creating a "grammar" of performance to help overcome his crippling self-consciousness as a young amateur actor in the late 19th century, but he ultimately became "the first practitioner in the twentieth century to articulate systematic actor training" (Carnicke, 2010, p. 2). In the ensuing years, Stanislavsky's methodology became the Western performer's way of knowing, the way of being "professional" in the rehearsal room and the way of being "real" in performance. We were recipients of that legacy as we navigated our own theatre training and pursued our respective careers. In other words, we were both so steeped in the "system" that it was difficult for us to identify alternatives in our practices and pedagogies as they expanded and developed over 30 years.

The genesis and dissemination of the "system" took place in environments created and supported by structures informed by white supremacy and racist ideology that were in place before Stanislavsky became interested in performance. He was born in Moscow in 1863 into significant privilege as Konstantin Sergeievich Alekseyev, the son of a wealthy thread manufacturer. Russia was under Tsarist rule. It was only two years after the institution of serfdom in Russia had been abolished. Alekseyev later changed his stage name to Stanislavsky, inspired by a ballerina he admired with the same surname, to shield his amateur theatrics from his society-conscious parents. However, in his youth, he and his siblings were able to pursue their performance-related interests since "the family money was available to the children to buy or rent costumes and props, musical scores, and anything else they needed" (Ignatieva, 2014, p. 12). As a young man, Stanislavsky was installed in the family business, but he used both his salary and his inherited wealth to finance his dream of becoming a professional actor. The Moscow Art Theatre (MAT), founded in 1897 with Vladimir Nemirovich-Danchenko (also the son of an aristocratic Russian family) was a predominantly white company, unsurprising given the demographics of the country, and largely supported by the intelligentsia of Russian society; indeed, "it was from them, and especially the liberal professions among them – doctors, lawyers, writers, teachers – that, in the early years, the MAT would generally draw its audiences" (Shevtsova, 2020, p. 3).

The development of the "system" inside and outside the context of the MAT ensemble and its collaborators consequently did not include people of colour nor incorporate influences directly from racialised peoples, though there are some connections. Mikhail Chekhov (whose mother was Jewish) and Yevgeny Vakhtangov, two notable figures who emerged from the MAT, worked intermittently with the Habima Theatre, one of two Jewish theatres operating in Moscow during the early 20th century, but it remains uncertain as to how much these relationships informed Stanislavsky and his "system" at the time or how much of the Jewish narrative was visible for those at the MAT (Schedrin, 2020). (However, Conrad Cohen argues how the transformation of the "system" into the "American Method" can be seen as a particularly "Jewish journey" in Chapter 6). Russian poet, playwright and novelist Alexander Pushkin, who inspired Stanislavsky to establish the "given circumstances" of the play to be the primary material to which any performer must respond truthfully, was the great-grandson of Abraham Petrovitch Gannibal, an African general from Logone, or modern-day Cameroon (Green, 2018). In addition, Stanislavsky's interest in yogic principles is well-documented,[5] but it was inspired by his reading of *Hatha Yoga* by Ramacharaka Yogi, a pseudonym of William Walker Atkinson, a white American who popularised Eastern concepts for Western audiences. It's clear there was inclusion within the narratives of the MAT, yet how much the development of the "system" benefited from ongoing cultural exchange is a subject for further research.

Stanislavsky instead positioned himself as a universalist in that he "believed that his evolving "'system' was essentially a means of applying natural and biological laws to the conventions of the theatre" (Merlin, 2003, p. 20). He sought to explain in his own "home-grown vocabulary" aspects of human behaviour such as empathy, "memory, linguistics, non-verbal communication and reception theory" that the theatre artist could recognise and employ for the purposes of performance (Benedetti, 1998, p. xiv). The translation of these laws into a practical approach to actor training and performance could, according to Stanislavsky, be applicable to "artist actors of all nations" (1968, p. 2). However, through the lens of anti-racist practice, this position erases difference for the assertion of universality based on whiteness. As Alison Nicole Vasquez states in her chapter "Representation Matters" in *Stages of Reckoning* (2022), "Many practitioners use the pursuit of [...] truthful interpretation in Stanislavski's method as a 'universal' way to address questions about human thought and behavior, but this may be making assumptions on the universality of the exploration to be done" (p. 131) and allowing little space for cultural differences to inform the process. The application of his "system" thus can become, as noted by several contributors to this volume, a process of ignoring – or actively refusing as seen in Siiri's exchange with our acting instructor – the cultural specificity of the individual performer, and effectively neutralising race and culture in favour of the dominant white aesthetic. (In contrast, Kristine Landon-Smith offers a means by which to celebrate the cultural specificity of the performer through "intracultural practice" in Chapter 7.)

Stanislavsky was a reflective, practice-based researcher. He feared stagnation and experimented constantly from his earliest days as an amateur actor to his final days under virtual house arrest by the Soviet government under Stalin. He absorbed and synthesised lessons from his students and colleagues over three decades as they pursued their own practices, which were often undertaken in direct response to his original approach. Stanislavsky came to understand that the "system" would never – nor should – be fixed in theory or practice. In fact, in his last class at the Opera-Dramatic Studio[6] on 25 May 1938, just under three months before he suffered a fatal heart attack, Stanislavsky urged his students to continue questioning the "system":

> Start directly by criticising the method I propose. I don't consider it to be ideal, without mistakes. Of course, it is one of the many stages in the research [...] [W]hat has this method shown in practice? What was good and what was bad about it? What could be wrong or too difficult in it?
>
> *(Moschkovich, 2021)[7]*

It was in this spirit that our first concrete joint action toward interrogating our own practices and pedagogies through an anti-racist intervention was to invite four international theatre artists to an online discussion about the "system" as part of the growing need to "criticise" the actor training curriculum. "Stanislavsky and Race: Questioning the 'System' in the 21st Century", sponsored by The S Word in partnership with the University of Notre Dame London Global Gateway, took place in November 2020 and featured Nicole M. Brewer, Broderick V. Chow, Pamela Jikiemi and Dominic Hingorani as panellists. It soon became clear that our 90-minute conversation, overflowing with personal insights, provocative arguments and passionate calls for change, was only the starting point for a longer campaign to fully air and develop the number of points raised.

The S Word and the University of Notre Dame London Global Gateway, with generous funding from the main US campus of the University of Notre Dame, agreed to support our desire to expand on the ideas exchanged in the online panel and include more voices in the discussion. The result was a two-day symposium, also titled "Stanislavsky and Race: Questioning the 'System' in the 21st Century", which was live-streamed in November 2021 and featured emerging and seasoned practitioners, pedagogues and scholars from across the globe. It was heartening to find that were we not alone in examining our individual Stanislavsky-based practices and that there were others seeking to build an anti-racist approach to actor training in myriad ways.

The majority of participants in this last symposium agreed to share – and expand upon – their original presentations for inclusion in this edited collection. We also reached out to several working artists of the Global Majority, many of whom had been previously unpublished, and invited them to offer additional reflections on the issues, ideas and practices featured in three key dialogic chapters in this book. We are excited to introduce them to you, and We are grateful for each contributor's willingness to share their thoughts and experiences as we all take concrete action toward anti-racist practice in our individual acting studios, rehearsal rooms, film sets and performance spaces.

Race as a Shifting Lens

We don't seek to define "race" in specific terms but rather employ it as a lens through which our readers can view Stanislavsky's "system" and its effects. Geraldine Hong, in her 2018 study, *The Invention of Race in the European Middle Ages*, states that "race *has* no singular or stable referent: that *race is a structural relationship for the articulation and management of human differences, rather than a substantive content*" (p. 19, italics in original). Hong refers to the work of race scholar Anne Stoler, who affirms "the concept of race is an 'empty vacuum' – an image both conveying [the] 'chameleonic' quality [of race] and [its] ability to ingest other ways of distinguishing social categories" (quoted in ibid., pp. 19–20). We have learned from our own experiences and observations – and from the experiences and observations of our generous and culturally diverse contributors – that race is, indeed, a deeply entrenched yet fluid theoretical construct that impacts performers at every stage of their training and careers. For example, both Joe Wilson, Jr. (in Chapter 2) and Sandra Marquez (in Chapter 5) reflect specifically on a range of experiences from their student days to their individual memberships as adults in well-respected theatre ensembles in the US. The pervasiveness of racism in every aspect of the "theatre industrial complex" specifically in the US is addressed in the "living document" *BIPOC Demands for White American Theatre*, created by #WeSeeYou, a collective of theatre artists, producers, instructors and administrators. It includes 31 pages of demands that touch on virtually every aspect of training, performance and business practice in the interest of supporting the physical and psychological well-being of Global Majority participants (#WeSeeYou, 2020). (Monica White Ndounou responds to this call for harm reduction in Chapter 9 of this volume by rejecting Stanislavsky outright in favour of Black- and Global Majority-based practices and practitioners.) Indeed, as author and activist Ngũgĩ wa Thiong'o writes, "The real politics of the performance space may well lie in its external relations; in its actual or potential conflictual engagement with all the other shrines of power" (1997, p. 13).

Theatre, as established internationally by #WeSeeYou and a number of individuals, collectives and organisations, is subject to the same racial barriers and inequities that reveal and redefine themselves in society over time. In the theatre industrial complex, the construct of race can tell performers – and writers and directors and producers – what, for example, a "realistic" family looks like, and who, as another example, should be cast as enslaved peoples. Global Majority actors can also be othered by lighting designers, costume designers, makeup and hair artists through micro- and macro-aggressions, and once the show is finally open, by theatre critics who are armed with their own biased aesthetics (see actor James Cooney's experience in Chapter 7 of being "white-washed" by a prominent British theatre reviewer). The result is that Global Majority performers experience both the system (writ large) and Stanislavsky's "system" (the *lingua franca*) in and on racialised bodies, and they do so while navigating white supremacist culture – without the privilege of walking away from what sociologist Pierre Bourdieu (2008, p. 52) refers to as their *habitus*, or "a system of structured, structuring dispositions", that derive from an individual's upbringing, whether they find themselves at the end of the rehearsal period, the close of the stage curtain or the stopping of the camera. (Diego Moschkovich and Evi Stamatiou, in Chapters 3 and 4, respectively, further explicate the concept of *habitus* and apply it specifically to the "system" in the furtherment of anti-racist practice.) We therefore invited our contributors to explore their experience of the "system" – and the system of actor training and professional performance practice – from their individual positionalities and culturally specific knowledge and experiences rather than provide a fixed definition of race to which they needed to ascribe themselves and their narratives.

It became apparent very quickly how difficult it was for each author to untangle the theoretical construct of "race" from the physical and psychological harm of "racism". As Ta-Nehesi Coates writes in *Between the World and Me*:

> Americans believe in the reality of 'race' as a defined indubitable feature of the natural world. Racism – the need to ascribe bone deep features to a people and then humiliate, reduce, and destroy them – inevitably follows from this inalterable condition [...] But race is the child of racism, not the father.
>
> *(2015, p. 7)*

The assumption that Global Majority student-performers absorb and integrate training in the "system" in the same way as their white classmates is a racist one. There are two complementary forces that serve to distance students of colour from their work. First, the Western canon of theatrical literature did not imagine multiracial bodies and experiences in roles beyond those of servants and/or enslaved persons. And second, when in an effort to create a "diverse" classroom environment, we cast, for example, a South Asian woman as Hedda Gabler and ask her to use the "system" to create her character, she is in a precarious position. The "system" asks the performer to imagine herself as a character in the world of the play, but the assumption in the text – and the majority of those in the Western canon – is that both the actor and character are white. The young performer in question is thus constantly aware of her *habitus* and the environment in which she is working. In predominantly white institutions, she might be the only person of colour in the room. Her teacher or director may not recognise the nuanced complexity of her position yet is responsible for adjudicating the actor's choices. This actor may try to use the "system" with varying degrees of success. The achievement of "truthful human behaviour" in her performance – as defined by Stanislavsky and interpreted in different ways by different instructors and practitioners – will be viewed through the lens of her race by the racism inherent in the dominant white culture that permeates the space.

It also emerged that each contributor found practice and pedagogy inextricably intertwined, at times pointing to the "system" as perpetrator of a white supremacist ideology, but more often seeing the culture of white supremacy imbued in the teaching itself. For example, in Chapter 1, Zuri Eshun, one of three panellists questioning trust in the "system" in particular and the system of actor training in general, describes the additional labour she needed to expend as a student to navigate techniques and instructors informed by a white aesthetic. Historically, classrooms, acting studios and rehearsal rooms have overlooked – whether consciously or unconsciously – race and racism in a misguided effort to treat everyone as equals, perhaps mirroring Stanislavsky's position of universality. However, these efforts inadvertently created – and continue to create – exclusive, inequitable environments as described in several chapters in this volume. It is subsequently unsurprising to note that *Teaching Stanislavski*, a large-scale study published in 2010 and focused on the teaching of Stanislavsky in the UK across several levels of education, does not engage in the consideration of race in the dissemination of the "system". However, the study does recognise that curriculum content often neglects to locate Stanislavsky historically and expresses concern over "a pedagogical style encouraged by a practitioner who was working over eighty years ago and who chose to structure his writing as a fictional description of classroom practice" (Dacre, 2010, p. 8).

Stanislavsky chose to write about the "system" and its pedagogy through the eyes of a fictional student named Kostya Nazvanov (reportedly a combination of a young Stanislavsky and Yevgeny Vakhtangov, one of his favourite pupils) attending classes held by Arkady Tortsov, a well-respected teacher and director and an obvious stand-in for the author. A pedagogy infused with white supremacy is immediately revealed in the narrative. The opening pages include Tortsov asking Nazvanov, a white student, to attempt the role of Othello and, as described by Amy Steiger in her essay, "Whiteness, Patriarchy, and Resistance in Actor Training Texts", "[Nazvanov's] representation of Othello includes more than one application of blackface makeup – of which there are extensive descriptions – stereotypical eye-rolling, and racist pre-conceptions of the character's physicality" (2019, para. 6). The student's attempt at Othello fails, but not necessarily for the reasons we might recognise through our contemporary lens. Steiger (who in Chapter 8 of this volume offers a means of resistance to white supremacist ideology embedded in the concept of "professionalism") continues:

> While Torstov encourages critical capacity in the young actor and recognizes the racist culture in which his perceptions have been shaped, the critique centers on the lack of specificity in the actor's work and his minimal engagement with Shakespeare's writing rather than a complex analysis of racism and representation in theatre.
>
> *(Ibid., para. 7)*

It is no wonder that actors in training, when encouraged by well-meaning instructors to read Stanislavsky's account of a fictional student being guided through the "system" by its creator, voice their concerns about the practice *and* its pedagogy in the same breath. The result of this callout by students of the Global Majority, as attested by some of the contributors to this collection, is being labelled "difficult" or "problematic" or expressing what poet and professor Cathy Park Hong refers to as "minor feelings". Hong defines "minor feelings" as "the emotions we are accused of having when we decide to be difficult", and when externalised, "are interpreted as hostile, ungrateful, jealous, depressing, and belligerent, affects described to racialized behavior that whites consider *out of line*" (2021, p. 57, italics in original). The response to such callouts by Global Majority theatre artists have often been met with passive indifference at best and aggressive suppression at worst. Yet, "paradoxical as it may seem", as Brazilian educational theorist Paolo Freire suggests, "precisely in the response of the oppressed to the violence of their oppressors that a gesture of love can be found" (1996, p. 30). If, collectively, we are going to create spaces that value multiracial collaboration, inclusivity and equity – spaces that reflect Brewer's conception of "conscientious training" – we need to identify barriers in ourselves and in the structures to which we subscribe, dissolve those encumbrances, dismantle dogma and replace it with a culturally competent approach that will benefit not only our students, but our entire community. As bell hooks writes, "Progressive professors working to transform the curriculum so that it does not reflect biases or reinforce systems of domination are most often the individuals willing to take the risks that engaged pedagogy requires and to make their teaching a site of resistance" (1994, p. 21).

A Note on Language

We hope the work in *Stanislavsky and Race* provokes the reader to examine their own positions, practices and pedagogies. As we consider the conversations happening around the globe, we find that language is one tool amongst many that can help move us toward concrete anti-racist actions. If Stanislavsky has been the *lingua franca* of our actor training studios, rehearsal rooms and professional stages, how can we broaden our artistic vocabulary to speak to pluralist spaces? The international theatre artists in the pages of this book offer their suggestions and provocations as an invitation to consider our own in the furtherment of anti-racist practice and pedagogy.

We, as co-editors, chose neither to interfere with each contributor's expression of their individual knowledge and experience nor impose our own conventions on their work. The reader will notice that grammar, syntax and spelling will differ from chapter to chapter depending on the authors' preferences. We felt that language restrictions served only to resurrect the precise legacies of colonialism that *Stanislavsky and Race* strives to deconstruct. For example, authors who currently reside in the US use different vocabulary and spellings in contrast to those located in the UK or elsewhere. In this introduction, we reflect British spellings to reflect the origins of the two symposiums that led to this collection and the home of The S Word, the sponsor of those symposiums and part of the Stanislavsky Research Centre based at the University of Leeds in England. However, with full transparency, we chose to honour the publisher's desire for consistency in punctuation, most notably in the use of double quotes and the absence of the Oxford comma throughout each chapter. We, as co-editors, also chose not to capitalise "white" and "whiteness" in an effort to centre the Global Majority; however, some of contributors do use "White/Whiteness" to underscore the concept of white as a racialised group. In addition, the reader will also notice the use of "Latine" and "Latinx" interchangeably as alternatives to the gendered terms "Latino" and "Latina" except where the speaker or writer wishes to call attention to specific identities. (The reader will encounter this fluidity in the roundtable discussion that forms Chapter 5.)

An Invitation

A nuanced exploration of race, identity and language in relation to Stanislavsky's "system" suggests that addressing the needs of the Global Majority performer is essential to creating anti-racist theatre practices. Each chapter regards Stanislavsky's "system" as foundational and part of the framework of our current construction/conception of acting methodology. However, the contributors' examinations seek not to revere Stanislavsky's approach to performance but to critically engage with the "system" from the perspective of 21st-century artists and scholars from a variety of countries, ethnicities and lived experiences. All of the authors are transparent about their backgrounds and consider their own positionalities in their work.

We invite our readers to imagine 21st-century theatre spaces where restrictive voices do not impose tradition for the sake of tradition. We recognise this perhaps stands in contrast to the purpose of the conservatoire, derived from its etymology as "to conserve". This volume aims to expand our collective expectations about what theatre training/practice might look like and sound like if we include a plurality of voices and welcome differences. To that end, the chapters offer examples of innovative pedagogy, provocative theories, sample scripts and lesson plans, and envision classrooms, rehearsal spaces and professional stages that embrace cultural authenticity to re-envision the future of acting training within an anti-racist theatre framework. Using inclusive language, the contributors offer suggestions for decolonising our own vocabulary and training techniques whilst centering the Global Majority theatre artist in the process.

Lastly, as editors, we recognize the limitation of a single volume, even with multiple authors, as incapable of capturing the plurality of individuals working with the "system" and the ways in which the approach is renewed, reframed or rejected. We regret that everyone will not be reflected in these pages, but we hope that readers at any point in their educational or professional journeys will feel compelled to take their own specific and concrete actions toward anti-racist practice.

Notes

1 The Long Table, conceived by Lois Weaver, a member of the theatre collective Split Britches, used the setting of a dinner table as a means to generate public conversation. It allows "voices to be heard equally, disrupting hierarchical notions of 'expertise'" ("Long Table", n.d.).
2 The act of "rumbling" is derived from lecturer and author Brené Brown concept of a "rumble", which she defines in part as "'a discussion, conversation, or meeting defined by a commitment to lean into vulnerability" (2018, p. 10).
3 See *Stanislavsky in the World* edited by Jonathan Pitches and Stefan Aquilina (2017) for a collection of essays that detail Stanislavsky's growing global influence.
4 We choose to use the term Global Majority as suggested by Revolution or Nothing, a UK-based network of Black and Global Majority scholars in theatre, dance and performance studies. We remain, like our colleagues, "conscious and cautious of the very tensions inherent in any and all labels of identifications" and accept that the term, "while not perfect, attempts at signalling a political, collective and positive identification" unrelated to whiteness (Revolution or Nothing, 2020).
5 See *Stanislavsky and Yoga* by Sergei Tcherkasski (2015) and "Stanislavsky and Ramacharaka: The Impact of Yoga and the Occult Revival on the System" by R. Andrew White in *The Routledge Companion to Stanislavsky* (2014).
6 Stanislavsky founded the Opera-Dramatic Studio, operating in his own home, in 1935 to continue his research into his "system". He often asked his students to take notes for him as he was increasingly frail in the final three years of his life.
7 The quote is taken from Diego Moschkovich's *The Late Stanislavsky in Action: Rehearsals for a New Working Method* (2021) that contains the full translation of previously unpublished stenograms of Stanislavsky's work at the Opera-Dramatic Studio.

References

Benedetti, J. (2008[1998]) *Stanislavski and the Actor*. London: Methuen.
Bourdieu, P. (2008) *The Logic of Practice*. Translated from the French by R. Nice. Stanford, CA: Stanford University Press.

Brewer, N. (2018) "Training with a Difference", *American Theatre* (4 January). Available at: https://www.americantheatre.org/2018/01/04/training-with-a-difference/ (Accessed: 10 February 2023).

Brown, B. (2018) *Dare to Lead*. London: Vermilion.

Carnicke, S. M. (2020) "Stanislavsky's System: Pathways for the Actor", in A. Hodge (ed.), *Actor Training*, 2nd edn. London: Routledge, pp. 1–25.

Clurman, H. (1972) *On Directing*. New York: Simon & Schuster.

Coates, T. (2015) *Between the World and Me*. New York: Spiegel & Grau.

Dacre, K. (2010) "Introduction", in *Teaching Stanislavski*, The Standing Conference of University Drama Departments in conjunction with the Higher Education Academy Subject Centre for Dance, Drama and Music, pp. 3–9. Available at: https://www.advance-he.ac.uk/knowledge-hub/teaching-stanislavski (Accessed: 27 February 2023).

Freire, P. (1996) *Pedagogy of the Oppressed*, rev. edn. Translated from the Portuguese by M. Bergman Ramos. Harmondsworth: Penguin.

Green, C. (2018) "How Alexander Pushkin was Inspired by His African Heritage", *JSTOR Daily*, 1 February. Available at: https://daily.jstor.org/how-alexander-pushkin-was-inspired-by-his-african-heritage/ (Accessed: 22 January 2023).

Hong, C. P. (2021) *Minor Feelings: A Reckoning on Race and the Asian Condition*. London: Profile Books.

hooks, b. (1994) *Teaching to Transgress: Education as the Practice of Freedom*. New York: Routledge.

Ignatieva, M. (2014) "Stanislavsky as Amateur: The Alekseev Circle and the Society of Art and Literature", in R. A. White (ed.), *The Routledge Companion to Stanislavsky*. London: Routledge, pp. 11–25.

"Long Table" (n.d.) *Split Britches*. Available at http://www.split-britches.com/long-table (Accessed 4 March 2023).

Merlin, B. (2003) *Konstantin Stanislavsky*. London: Routledge.

Moschkovich, D. (2021) *O último Stanislávski em Ação: ensaios para um novo método de trabalho* [The Late Stanislavsky in Action: Rehearsals for a New Working Method]. São Paulo: Perspectiva.

Pitches, J. (2017) "A System for All Nations? Stanislavsky's Transmission in the World", in J. Pitches and S. Aquilina (eds), *Stanislavsky in the World*. London: Bloomsbury Methuen Drama, pp. 12–24.

Revolution or Nothing (2020) *White Colleague Listen* An Open Letter to UK Theatre, Dance and Performance Studies*. Available at https://medium.com/@revolutionornothing/white-colleague-listen-2d098d6a4a5d (Accessed: 4 March 2023).

Schedrin, V. (2020) "The Birth of Jewish Theatre", *The Theatre Times*, 12 July. Available at: https://thetheatretimes.com/the-birth-of-jewish-theatre/ (Accessed: 7 February 2023).

Shevtsova, M. (2020) *Rediscovering Stanislavsky*. Cambridge: Cambridge University Press.

Stanislavski, K. (2008) *An Actor's Work*. Translated from the Russian and edited by J. Benedetti. London: Routledge.

Stanislavski, C. (1968) *Stanislavski's Legacy*, translated from the Russian and edited by E. Reynolds Hapgood. London: Methuen.

Steiger, A. (2019) "Whiteness, Patriarchy and Resistance in Actor Training Texts: Reimagining Actors as Embodied Public Intellectuals", *HowlRound*, August. Available at: https://howlround.com/whiteness-patriarchy-and-resistance-actor-training-texts (Accessed: 4 March 2023).

Vasquez, A. N. (2022) "Representation Matters", in A. M. Ginther (ed.), *Stages of Reckoning*. London: Routledge, pp. 129–148.

wa Thiong'o, N. (1997), "Enactments of Power: The Politics of Performance Space", *TDR (1988-)*, 41(3), pp. 11–30. doi:10.2307/1146606 (Accessed 6 March 2023).

#WeSeeYou (2020) *Our Demands*. Available at https://www.weseeyouwat.com/demands (Accessed 6 March 2023).

1

RE/GAINING TRUST

The "System" and the System of Actor Training

Sylvan Baker, Zuri Eshun and James Palm

We invited three international colleagues to discuss Stanislavsky's "system" and the system of actor training in a pre-recorded transatlantic session that was shared during the Stanislavsky and Race symposium in November 2021. This chapter is an edited transcript of that session.

SYLVAN BAKER: Thank you both for joining me in this conversation about the "system" and the system of actor training from our positions as artists, teachers and scholars. I hope we might throw some light – and perhaps encounter some disagreement – on a range of issues that are facing the institutions where we each deliver our respective practices. These issues revolve around identity and equity, and where these two pillars of social justice come face to face with the practices, like Stanislavsky's "system", that are the bedrock of our disciplines.

JAMES PALM: I'm James Palm, and I am currently the head of acting at Bird College in Southeast London.

ZURI ESHUN: I'm Zuri Eshun, and I'm a professional actor from the United States. I did my masters training in London at East 15 Acting School, and I am the co-founder of the Culture Collective, a university-based BIPOC initiative where we look at playwrights of colour, educate university students about them and showcase their work through performance. It's mainly a resource for Black and Brown students at the undergraduate training level.

SYLVAN BAKER: Zuri, could you say a bit more about the term BIPOC and your understanding of it from the context that you're working in?

ZURI ESHUN: BIPOC stands for Black, Indigenous and People of Colour. It is an inclusive term that enables us to call attention to the unique experiences of non-white members of various communities and spaces, the arts

DOI: 10.4324/9781003330882-2

being one of them. As an African American woman, most of my work centres around the "B", or Black people and Black stories. While the term BIPOC has allowed a space for honest and open dialogue about the people it encompasses, from an American perspective, it can sometimes be misused as a way to dodge "being offensive" or as a tactic to not credit a specific group's contributions.

SYLVAN BAKER: James, as a precursor to our wider conversation, could you share what draws you into the debate we're going to have around how practices like Stanislavsky's "system" can be delivered with equity and justice in the 21st century?

JAMES PALM: I think, for me, it's been a question of questioning myself and my own practice, questioning colleagues within the institution where I work and questioning colleagues far and wide about what we are all doing in rooms. It seems that, in the past, trust has been given to people because of their apostolic lineage, meaning who they worked with and the institutions in which they worked. But now, for very good reasons, these lineages, practices and methods, including Stanislavsky's "system", are being questioned. Over the last couple of years, students have been standing up and saying, "No, I take issue with what I see as a harmful or racist practice." So what do we do? Where do these issues of trust, practice and pedagogy intersect?

I personally think trust was initially put in the lineage rather than in the individual or the practice. In other words, "The people teaching me must be trustworthy, and their practice must be trustworthy because of their lineage, right?" I also believe this outlook has been reinforced by the whole culture of conservatoire training. We need to change these things, but how does that affect what we do, or the relationship between ourselves, our courses and our institutions?

SYLVAN BAKER: I should acknowledge my positionality as an applied theatre scholar and practitioner within this conversation. Applied theatre is a general term for activities that are based around the application of theatre and performance, but not so much in a conventional theatre setting or within a theatre ecology. I'm not necessarily working with people who want to be performers or have training in performance, but there is the hope that in using ideas, practices and theories from theatre and performance, they may be invited as participants to discover how theatre changes things or makes things explicit in ways that alternative, arguably less creative or participatory, routes may not. So, to a certain extent, I sit as an outsider to the open secret that is actor training.

I not only see actor training as an outsider, but I also bring to it a certain degree of cynicism because I don't understand it. As an outsider, it feels arcane and secret. I just wanted to make it clear that, though I work in a conservatoire and I do get to work intermittently with those who are actor trainers or are undergoing actor training, it isn't the centre of my practice. My practice comes at these issues of identity and equity from the social justice or wider societal angle.

Zuri, James has said that trust is at the core of the issues in actor training right now. If we are honest with ourselves – and objectively look at our institutions as well – that trust has been lost for a large majority – if not all – of the student population. How do you think that has occurred? Is inclusivity part of the solution for that loss of trust or is it something else?

ZURI ESHUN: Trust, during my undergraduate training, was something earned by the teachers I had the pleasure of working with. It wasn't something that was assumed or something that was ever discussed. It was definitely something that was earned by whomever we were working with throughout the years. When I transitioned into graduate training, trust was just assumed in the room. We thought it would be a space we could play in, work in and learn in, and there wouldn't be any negativity or hostility. It was assumed that we were all on the same page. However, these assumptions turned out not to be true throughout my training. As a student, this assumption of trust you enter training with dissipates throughout your education, so you feel you can't trust the art or training when you leave. Unfortunately, there were times when trust amongst the students was lost, and then trust amongst the professors was lost because certain situations weren't handled appropriately.

I had the pleasure of attending East 15 Acting School, and the graduate training program is definitely international, so there were a lot of American students. But there were also a lot of students from various countries where race was something they'd never encountered, or if they had, it was from a media standpoint rather than from an actual experience. It created a lot of classroom issues simply because of cultural differences. However, these issues weren't just amongst international students, but also amongst American students because of cultural differences in the classroom. And because the proctor of that class may not have been informed on those cultural differences, it led to many situations in the classroom that might not have happened had the entire program been white or one whole other thing. It makes the education for an actor of colour difficult because you are not only navigating graduate training, but you now have to learn how to keep yourself safe in a space where you're not understood.

SYLVAN BAKER: So there's something massive about one's sense of legibility as a Black student. I'm not going to extrapolate it across those groups we've already spoken about because I don't want to speak for areas where I don't have enough experience, but there's definitely something about having to make an internal choice – as a student and as a Black student – that the only way to pass through this training is to go from the perspective of being white. How can I, as a student, be confident that the professors teaching me understand my worldview, understand my sociality and care about my sociality? And what does that difference in point of view, in approach or in orientation of value do to the training? James, I know that you've thought about this at length. What do you think about this question of how and, perhaps, when this conservatoire ecology lost the trust of its students?

JAMES PALM: I'm not sure. It's the reason I'm posing this question of whether it's gaining trust or *regaining* trust. I'm making a massive generalisation, but I imagine most instructors have undergone some form of performance training and look to relay it to their students. I think a culture of "What I'm teaching must be right because it was taught to me, and I know who taught it to the person who taught me" has existed for some time. What I see now is the centering of the individual within these methods, and the teacher or director not standing as the indisputable font of all knowledge. So there is a tension between the teaching of apostolic lineage and actually doing things in the room with people, whether it's working with text or improvising or devising.

In the UK, we're experiencing an ideological crisis in actor training conservatoires due to students questioning the methods and behaviours they've experienced. I remember having some conversations a few years ago when I started a PhD. I was approaching tutors and directors in conservatoires here and asking if I could come and watch a class. There were some "Ummms" and "Ahhhs" and "Well, someone's presence in the room changes the dynamic and we have trust as a group." I was naturally quite suspicious. I think now, given the current crisis, we can speculate why these classes weren't open to observation.

I was personally very used to people just walking into a theatre studies class since I did a postgraduate certificate in education (PGCE) many years ago and taught as a secondary school teacher. I wasn't worried about what could be perceived as an intrusion. I also found it ironic that when I was doing this research, I emailed institutions in the US and said, "I'm coming over and this is the research I'm doing," and I was welcomed with open arms.

I read a paper about the conservatoire being likened to what Erving Goffman called "the total institution". It was about a study of a psychiatric hospital in Washington, DC in the 1950s, and the conservatoire is likened in this study to a "quasi-institution". I think the phrasing is "the total institution relies on the individual's thought reform or religious conversion to a certain way of thought and a certain way of thinking" (Goffman, 1961). The number of hours spent in training and the insularity of classes dedicated to particular methodologies is unusual compared with other disciplines.

SYLVAN BAKER: I have tried from the outside to make material my understanding of what actor training is, and, from the point of view of my own practice, the fact there seems to be such a reliance on the concepts of mastery and apprenticeship. I think, to paraphrase Brazilian educator Paulo Freire, the possibility for an oppressive banking pedagogic structure in the classroom is inherent.

I understand that notion around the resistance to being transparent about processes to sometimes near Masonic levels. I've spoken to actors who have all been trained in the same techniques and asked a very basic question: "Well, what's that like? And how does it happen?" And then seeing glances crossed between them, wondering whether I can be trusted or whether they can tell me about how they were trained. I know that might sound melodramatic, but it's something that is there.

So what's struck me – that seems to link both of your opening conversations – is that *awareness*. There is something in Zuri's comments about a Black student having to come into an institution and do a different kind of work just to navigate passage through it. And in James's account, in wanting to examine what might be going on within a process for a range of reasons, it triggered a suspicion at the resistance to openness. Why then was trust not the subject of discussion sooner? For those who are in conservatoire training institutions or have been through them, how can these structures become fit for purpose in our current times?

I'm going to introduce another question that is linked to this. It comes from my limited understanding around the act of training in the practice of naturalism and how Stanislavsky sits within it. It's my understanding that a lot of training around Stanislavsky is inexplicably linked to Anton Chekhov because there was a relationship between the two artists in real time. If that's the case, as a Black student studying Chekhov, how can that relate? What is that doing to the field? And what's it doing to the student who is being told the only way they can be "natural" on stage is if they pretend to be not themselves?

ZURI ESHUN: The Chekhov unit was extremely difficult for me, especially after our training. It's a unit that I had to go in and work with my professors on constantly. And it's not for being unable to connect to the material because, at the core of it, there is something that you can link yourself to. However, it wasn't something that I was naturally drawn to. So when we worked on it in our classes, it was assumed that this was something that we were all relating to or that we all held in very high regard. In my theatre practice and upbringing in theatre, it was the exact opposite. But if Stanislavsky is informing Chekhov and vice versa, and I was never meant to be a part of that conversation, I can only *sometimes* fit into what's going on.

And it didn't stop at Chekhov. It continued into what this institution had decided is the standard in theatre. So when we were working in our course, we had a Chekhov unit, an Ibsen unit, a Shakespeare unit and our contemporary theatre units, which, in this program, featured only white

British playwrights. None of those plays, despite my exposure to some fantastic work, were designed in a way where I fit into the narrative. So, for me, it's complicated. It's extra work that I have to do – to go in and fit myself into this world and then do all the work required of the actor.

What happens then is you realise throughout the training that you might have to go outside of the university to do something that you might fit into, which for the student is difficult because of the logistics of being an actor: you're paying for the train, you're paying to go to rehearsal, you're paying for food while you're at rehearsal or you're sometimes getting a paycheck but that paycheck is going toward just getting to rehearsal. You are paying extra money – outside the funds you're spending on your training – to practise in a way that will benefit you. It's frustrating to experience that because what you're being told in school is, "This is the standard we've set. These are the playwrights, methods and practitioners we believe are at the core of acting. Regardless of race and cultural background, this is the information you need to know that is necessary to graduate – and that's also necessary for you to become a professional actor, and none of that includes non-white playwrights or non-white theatre practitioners. So you go into the world believing someone has told you the core of theatre and actor training, and they've also said to you that you, in a way, don't belong there. It's why I started Culture Collective at East 15. It was simply a way to educate students on campus about other playwrights. We would go over Katori Hall, August Wilson, Ntozake Shange, and Suzan-Lori Parks. I would bring in all these works and let students devise pieces, and we would do a showcase at the end of each year.

I also realised I wasn't the only student experiencing that sense of needing to do extra work. I had my twin sister in my program, and they put us in separate classes so we didn't train together, which made sense because we could influence each other's learning. But it also created a really terrible feeling of being alone. If something happened in class, there was no one for me to turn to. It was the experience of many BAs, too, in that there was usually only one or maybe two students of colour per course and you never got to work with that other person. You're separated in that practice. So even if you feel like you don't fit into the practice or if the methods being used aren't built for you, there's no one in the room to back you up. If you then ask a question in class, you look like a lone wolf or like you're trying to disrupt the classroom structure. And it makes it seem like you're resisting the work when you're just trying to bring attention to the fact that you're not included in it. This person never meant for me to sit down and read this book, read this play, or even participate in it. I become a bit unenthused about doing the work aside from looking at it as, "Okay, I need to do this so I understand the technique," rather than, "I need to do this because there's something about the work that pulls me in."

SYLVAN BAKER: I've spoken to colleagues in the discipline of dance, particularly contemporary dance, and heard similar narratives. Ballet is often held as the foundation of technique for most dance, but the way in which it was developed was for a white body. And there is a strong argument to say that Black bodies, for example, don't look the same aesthetically as white bodies. I've had Black dance colleagues recounting being told to tuck their bottoms in and stand in a different way because their physiognomy is different. So not only are they forced to do that, they're also finding – because their bodies were not designed to deliver the technique in a way that was considered aesthetically correct by their tutors- that they are becoming injured.

James, what are your thoughts on Stanislavsky, Chekhov, naturalism and a standard that has been decided by others that many students may not conform to? Why is it that we can't do naturalism through, for example, Suzan-Lori Parks?

JAMES PALM: I think the relationship between Stanislavsky and Chekhov is a really important part of literary history, and a massively important watershed as far as the way people were trained to act. I have a memory of reading in Sharon Marie Carnicke's *Stanislavsky in Focus* (2009) about Stanislavsky's frustration with the fact that this technique was married with naturalism or, I think as he called it, "Russian realism".

I remember doing *Uncle Vanya* by Chekhov as a 21-year-old and loving it, but I don't think I've ever taught it. I still prefer Elisaveta Fen's 1950s translations of the play to the contemporary versions by Brian Friel, Simon Stephens and other playwrights. Fen's translations are richer and more poetic; they give such a sense of period and culture that's so removed from anything I've ever experienced. I was brought up in Essex in the 1970s, which was very far removed from provincial Russia of the late 19th century. Now that I'm in my fifties, I love these plays even more than I did when I was in my twenties.

However, as pedagogues, we might need to accept that our passions might have less currency in contemporary actor training. I think there are those who teach acting that would struggle with this idea. Acting, for me, is a continuum of choices, so when we're looking at a performance, all we're seeing is a continuum of choices. How do we arrive at those choices given a particular context? Is Chekhov a necessary part of this process? A few years ago, I was teaching in a London conservatoire and saw the second-year students walking round the building in fake beards and suits. "Ah, it's the Chekhov term," I thought. It's unlikely that these students will play any of those roles for another twenty years – if ever. It's clear why doing these plays during training is of value since there are so many layers of culture, behaviour, politics and gender to unravel. However, if actor training is vocational, why look at plays that are so far removed from the realities of employment? I understand that many people will passionately disagree with this. Perhaps there's a way of approaching these plays from a methodological perspective that's more relevant.

SYLVAN BAKER: Is that not a little bit like saying students of English literature can't consider themselves literate unless they've done Shakespeare? Is that an unfair comparison?

JAMES PALM: No, I don't think it is an unfair comparison. I don't think it's essential. But I also have this voice in the back of my head screaming, "James, they must do Shakespeare!" Perhaps my concern is that if I don't *advocate* for Shakespeare, I'll be viewed by colleagues as a charlatan or ignorant.

I will say Stanislavsky unlocked Shakespeare for me as an actor in training. As a young actor, applying a Stanislavkian approach to *Richard II* made everything fall into place. The synthesis of given circumstances and objective gave me the key I needed to work out what to do from moment to moment. Using these approaches now with a variety of Shakespeare's texts with students has resulted in some wonderfully fun results. Perhaps the value in synthesising Shakespeare and Stanislavsky is that it proves the "system" can be applied to any text as means of making specific physical choices in the pursuit of an objective.

ZURI ESHUN: James, one of your questions was, "Why is it that we choose something like Chekhov when there are other works that could serve as a vessel for this method?" It seems to me, as a participant, that it's easier to do given the logistics of setting up a term. After all, more students in the program fit that mould. So if you have a class of 12 students and one of them is Black, one of them is South Asian and everyone else in the class is white, it would not serve a great purpose to choose an August Wilson or Suzan-Lori Parks piece to work through. Most of your students lend themselves to Chekhov or align with Ibsen based on where the plays are set or who would be involved. It's not looking at things where the background, setting or time doesn't matter. All those things are essential to what the actor is pulling from the piece. So if I open this scene up and it's Russia at this time on this date, I know, "Okay, there's part of me I'm leaving behind to do this because I wasn't there." And especially with what was happening in the world at that time, a completely different experience was being had. It's almost as if the student has to leave a little bit of themselves behind if they are not in the majority. I think any pieces, whether they be Shakespeare or Chekhov, are chosen because they cover a majority of who is in the class. It may make sense from an educational standpoint. It's like, "Well, I have this many students. I'll get most of them, and then the other ones will just have to go along with it and assume that it is the standard," versus what I've been auditioning for right now. I'm not being brought in for Chekhov. I'm being brought in for world premieres by Black playwrights and Katori Hall pieces, and I wasn't trained in them. I had to go seek those things out myself.

So to answer that question, James, and to raise another, what do we do about the standard? Because, right now, the bar is overwhelmingly white. Any method we use toward that standard is going to complement it and, unfortunately, the standard hasn't been challenged in a while. You automatically know when you go into training, especially in the UK, you're going to cover Shakespeare. It's the first thing we did, and that told me, "Okay, for this program, Shakespeare is critical." I'm going through these units, and I know what's important based on what the university presents to me. Still, the university is not offering anything to me that is of my own background or narrative. That, in turn, tells me, Zuri, the Black actress from the US, "Your background is not necessarily our focus, or what's important to us is that you hit the standards we've set."

It's interesting to hear this conversation from someone who is a Head of Acting because our Head of Acting was also one of our professors. Those questions didn't get asked. I went to graduate school in 2014, and conversations around this had been happening among the students. It's only recently I've heard – at least in graduate or higher-level training – that it's something that's trying to be addressed from the other side.

But, to answer the original question, we choose the pieces to teach these methods based on who the majority of the classroom is.

SYLVAN BAKER: There's definitely something about a model, a business model and an ecology. I want to point out that your respective responses have been about questioning the standard. Can I ask both of you: whose responsibility is it to restore a balance or to find a balance? Or, if we go back to the beginning of our conversation, whose responsibility is it – within this conservatoire structure in which we find ourselves or which we have been through – to regain trust?

ZURI ESHUN: It is the responsibility of those who have deemed themselves the authority of theatre. For example, I'm coming in and paying $80,000 for my education. In that case, it is then that person's responsibility to make sure that I'm in an environment in which I'm acknowledged: that who I am, where I'm from and my lived experience will not be pushed aside. That I'm included in the work and I'm not trying to find my way into it. I feel that, especially in graduate training, it's like, "How do I fit into this?" And that is something that the professor takes on, because if I'm trying to figure out how I belong or where I belong, or if I can do this assignment or thinking "How do I get this?," or, "Oh, this thing is really awkward for me to do because I'm not of this," or, "I wasn't meant to be here," it is extra work for me.

I came here to act. I came here to gain training. I didn't come to solve this particular university's problems, which I fell into as a student. So on top of all my coursework and all the shows I had to do, I was also teaching. It's something I love to do and it's something that I took great pride in, but it was something that felt like if I hadn't done it, then the experience of the students on campus was going to be, "Okay, I've done this program. I have my training. But did I enjoy being there?" A little bit of the joy is lost when the responsibilities are placed on the students. So it is the institution's responsibility to do that work and to create an environment where no actor is left out of the learning process.

JAMES PALM: I think it's the responsibility of everyone who is employed by an institution. That's who is ultimately responsible – in whatever aspect of the work it is we're undertaking. We can't rely on the students to tell us – to tell *me* – about these issues or explain them to us. We shouldn't transmit our fragility about these intersecting issues and rely on students to carry us or our awkwardness or our lack of understanding.

These are really difficult conversations to have with oneself and to have with one's colleagues. We can't think of what we know and what we teach as divine or unimpeachable. I think this is really difficult for many people teaching acting to accept. I've always thought people teach a particular system or methodology because it embodies the way they interpret the world. We reach positions of authority due to our dedication to a certain lineage and the pursuit of expertise. It's really difficult to accept that these ideas might be alienating or irrelevant to our students.

We might have said a few years ago that a student challenging what we teach was evidence of them being difficult or even ignorant. This position is unthinkable now – and should have been then as well. If a student feels they are left out of the learning, then it's my job to facilitate their inclusion.

SYLVAN BAKER: It's interesting, because, often in those conversations, "everyone" – and I would count myself amongst them – is often characterised as being "the culture," and, therefore, "the culture" has to change. I wouldn't disagree, but I think it's interesting how it becomes an amorphous thing: "The culture has to change." But we are that culture.

I would also completely agree with you both that it's not the role of the student to take on this additional labour to ensure that their legibility is understood in the room. But what is their role? And where do we fit into this new, open and consensual practice that can be actor training? I recognise these are questions that we can't answer in the short time we have left, but I wonder what questions you might like to offer to those engaging with this conversation to reflect on or act upon as a result of this conversation?

ZURI ESHUN: This has been a conversation since I was in grad school and, I'm sure, since before that time. Two questions I would like everyone to ask themselves are: first, from an institutional or university standpoint, how do you ensure these conversations transition into action? And how do we make sure that action is implemented and sustained? And second, to the actors considering graduate school, what do you want from your training? What is the reason that you were drawn to acting? And how do you make sure that you don't let up? So when you're in a classroom, how do you keep pressure applied to ensure you're getting out of this experience what you need without taking on additional work or becoming your own professor in some ways? How do you ensure you keep enough pressure in the classroom to be acknowledged and that you are seen and accepted?

JAMES PALM: I think it's to go back to the fundamentals of what acting is, who actors are and the function of acting. Any system is a starting point or means of orientation. Classes and tutors are often branded by a particular methodology or system. Perhaps this is what we need to relinquish or at least question. We need to centre the individual and where they come from, what their experiences are, what their influences are, what their interests are and where they see themselves as contributors to society. I think that's where I sit. What am I doing and why am I doing it? When we're with a group of students, do we know what we're doing and why we're doing it, or are we all on a journey of finding out? How do we make sense of the world through imagining what training might be? The most exciting thing for me is when I see a student do or say something I could never have imagined. I trust that everyone I'll ever work with will reveal their genius.

SYLVAN BAKER: I think the questions I would pose would include: where can you add or bring consent into your practice? And is it not time to audit whether mastery is the place that you need to be to give and to receive training? What space is there for doubt or, I guess, ignorance? And how, as teachers, can we make ourselves open and available to the fact that there are going to be areas that we don't know?

I'm aware that we have barely scratched the surface on some of these thorny issues. But I hope what we've done is offer some scope for all of us to reflect on these issues of trust in approaches like Stanislavsky's "system" and to work out where we fit in this ecology of actor training and performance as artists, practitioners and teachers.

References

Carnicke, S. M. (2009) *Stanislavsky in Focus*, 2nd edn. London: Routledge.

Goffman, E. (1961) *Asylums: Essays on the Social Situation of Mental Patients and Other Inmates*. Garden City, NY: Anchor Books.

A REFLECTION ON RE/GAINING TRUST

Revelation and Responsibility

Joe Wilson, Jr

I come to this discussion holding three particular points of interest: as an artist, as a professor and as an advocate. I have been an actor for close to 30 years. I have worked on Broadway, Off Broadway and in theatres throughout the United States. I am currently in my eighteenth season as a member of the Resident Acting Company at Trinity Repertory Company in Providence, Rhode Island. I am also a member of the artistic staff at the Trinity and a professional theatre director. In addition, I am a Professor of the Practice of Theatre at Wheaton College in Norton, Massachusetts. In January 2023, I will be making a seismic shift in my career. I have accepted a position within the cabinet of the newly elected Mayor of my city; I will serve as the Director of Arts, Culture and Tourism for the City of Providence.

I give you this background because so much of what is explored in the robust discussion between Sylvan, Zuri and James speaks to me directly. I will in this response reflect upon and share points of personal connection to this topic, including my experience of attending a liberal arts college (namely, the University of Notre Dame) and receiving my graduate actor training at the University of Minnesota/Guthrie Theatre training program, where I was awarded my Master of Fine Arts degree in Acting. I will also respond in my roles as an educator of the practice and as a member of a long-standing acting company at one of this country's legacy institutions.

I would like to begin by responding to Zuri's statement:

> Trust, during my undergraduate training, was something earned by the teachers I had the pleasure of working with. It wasn't something that was assumed or something that was ever discussed. It was definitely something that was earned by whomever we were working with throughout the years. So when I transitioned into graduate training, trust was just

DOI: 10.4324/9781003330882-3

assumed in the room. We thought it would be a space we could play in, work in and learn in, and there wouldn't be any negativity or hostility. Just because of what it was. It was assumed that we were all on the same page. However, these assumptions turned out not to be true throughout my training.

So much of what Zuri offered resonated with me. My first exposure to the practice of making theatre, including using elements of Stanislavsky's "system", was in my second semester of college. I had a tangential relationship to the creative process through singing in church choirs, high school speech and debate teams, and seeing the very occasional live amateur or professional performance. But I was never in a play, took an "actor training course" or enrolled in arts classes. During the second semester of my junior year of college, I took an acting class so I wouldn't screw up my grade point average. I assumed it would be an easy A. I was heading to law school after graduation.

That class changed my life.

The people, the community, the openness and willingness to commit to "play" or "being a kid again" was revelatory. I also had an extraordinary professor, Dr Reginald Bain, and his requirement for the class was that each student had to audition for a play. I did, and that was just the beginning. Dr. Bain was kind but took the work seriously without ever being cruel or patronizing. He welcomed collaboration. He also allowed me to be me. He met me where "I was". He challenged me to speak with a loud, clear voice, but he also taught me the full breadth of what it meant to be a storyteller. My first production in the department was William Shakespeare's *King Lear*. I fell in love with the language and the sweeping scope of the story. I played Edmund, the bastard son. The part resonated with me deeply. It made sense in my mind and body as a young, Black, gay (I came out after college) man from New Orleans, Louisiana. Whether intentional or not, the director (who was also the professor of the class I was currently taking) taught me my first lesson about the necessity and power of intentionality in casting. Our canon of work over the next year and a half before my graduation included *King Lear, Julius Caesar, Our Town* by Thornton Wilder, and *Ah, Wilderness!* by Eugene O'Neill. I served as my professor's Assistant Director on *The Heidi Chronicles* by Wendy Wasserstein, and I directed a production of Eric Bogosian's *Talk Radio*. In that moment, he taught me that I had the capacity to do anything, to imagine myself in a multitude of capacities in the work. As a result of his nurturing hand, I also discovered my passion as an educator.

I did not attend law school as anticipated.

Graduate school became an opportunity not only to hone my craft, but also to soothe my parents' anxiety by my pursuit of a terminal degree. Like Zuri, my experience in graduate school proved to be very different from my undergraduate experience. We studied Stanislavsky and his "system", Uta

Hagen, Robert Cohen, Michael Shurtleff and Sanford Meisner, to name a few. The variety of approaches was very useful to me. I learned to pick and choose what worked for me and developed my own understanding of the process. We studied and performed some contemporary works, but the majority of the plays we explored were by Shakespeare, Molière, Henrik Ibsen, George Bernard Shaw, and Anton Chekhov. They were all white. And, like Zuri, I and my other classmates of color had to explore works by non-white writers on our own time, which was already very limited. In addition, I am from a very different generation as far as this industry is concerned. I'll best describe it by a message I give to my beginning acting students at the start of every semester: "I will not be responsible for 'too-ing' you into sub-mission: 'too short', 'too fat', 'too Black', 'too gay', 'too Southern'"; the list goes on. This was my reality in graduate school. Stripping an actor down to a place of "neutrality" was the desired outcome. The training made me hate parts of myself rather than teaching me to have a healthy relationship with all of who I was and have grown to become.

It was during this time that I first began to understand the concept of "colorblind casting", where an actor is cast without regard to race, gender or other aspects of their identity, as an absurd and destructive practice. Zuri mentions a particular aspect of her experience surrounding the extra labor that is placed upon the actor of color. I love playing the great roles in classic plays, but I would always ask myself, "How did my Black ass end up in this world?" My professors would not have the patience for such discussions because they were true believers in the notion of colorblind casting. To question would run the risk of being labeled as "difficult" or "resistant". This practice did not make space for my Blackness or queerness.

Furthering the dilemma for a student of color is the rejection by some theatre makers of color, specifically those in power. I had African American mentors who would decry my training because it "would make me ill equip-ped to succeed in the Black theatre world." I was literally told by a leader in the Black theatre community that, because of my training, "I would not be Black enough to do Black theatre." What is exposed is the conflict within any artist of color between training rooted in white Western European practices and struggling to hold on to cultural authenticity. (As a side note, I am grateful to artists such as the late Lorie Carlos, an inspiring actor, director and dancer/choreographer. She was the only experience I had at that time of an approach that was culturally specific to me. She worked with a "jazz aesthetic" developed during her time with the Urban Bush Women, founded in 1984. This New York-based non-profit dance company was the only professional African American women's dance company at that time. Unfortunately, this experience was an outlier.) As a result of my three years of training in my graduate program, I learned to speak in a loud, clear voice. I developed an awareness of my body and voice, and the full storytelling power it can possess. I learned how to scan texts. I became a better actor technically. But becoming a more confident person, aware of my unique place in this business and in this world, would have to wait.

I would also like to respond to another section of the conversation between the panelists that resonated deeply with me:

SYLVAN BAKER: There's definitely something about a model, a business model, and an ecology. I'm feeling a bit like Pandora at this moment. I feel like the box is open, and the butterflies are everywhere. I also feel a certain guilt because time is against us. But one of the things I want to pepper into the discussion, and your response, James, is that both of your conversations have been about what the standard is, and whose standard is it? In our final few minutes, can I ask both of you: whose responsibility is it to look into this to restore a balance, or find a balance? Or, if we go back to the beginning of our conversation, whose responsibility is it – within this conservatoire structure in which we find ourselves or which we have been through – to fix this, to regain trust, to rebuild bridges? Who should be doing it?

ZURI ESHUN: I feel it is the responsibility of those who have deemed themselves the authority of theatre.

JAMES PALM: I think it's the responsibility of everyone who is employed by an institution.

The question of who is responsible for changing the systems and culture within our theatre lies with *all of us*. Those in power carry the most burden. In order to provide some context around my response, I would like to give you a little bit of background. I had already been an Adjunct Professor at Wheaton College for two years before being offered a full-time position. I was offered the position in March 2020 at the beginning of the COVID explosion. Simultaneously, Trinity Rep, my theatre, was shut down. As I mourned the loss of live theatre I had to subsequently develop a curriculum that could be effective in the virtual/hybrid world. My professional theatre was also going through its own social justice reckoning led by members of the resident acting company who were part of the BIPOC community. Attempting to create a theatre that did not perpetuate harm forced me to confront my pedagogy in the same way. I did not want to make the same mistakes. I was committed to creating an environment in my classroom and in the rehearsal hall that did not continue to create undue harm. As a leader, that is my full responsibility.

Expanding the breadth of plays in rotation in my classes, giving students more agency in the kinds or material we tackle in class and providing space for all of my students to be seen was of paramount importance. These and other practices extended to the rehearsal hall. I have directed quite a few productions over the past two years, and artists are rightly demanding that the culture within those spaces change. Pronoun declaration and respect for gender identity, intimacy coaches and collectively creating community agreements are now part of our practice. These practices are embedded in the systems and facets of theatre making, included in leadership at most theatre's executive level positions, and devolved to EDIA/B (Equity, Diversity, Inclusion, Access, Belonging).

But some responsibility rests with all of us in this work. Creating a safe space cannot come at the expense of challenging ourselves and others. How can we desire effecting change within those who witness performance and not expect that we, too, can be changed or affected by the work? All of us want to create and experience theatre that is entertaining, provocative and dangerous. This cannot come at the expense of creating a safe work/learning environment. Each of us must begin the work of social justice and artmaking by taking responsibility for ourselves and the relationships we build with others. Just because we are makers, we cannot make the assumption that we are all on the same page as it relates to our understanding and acceptance of this social justice reckoning. The theatre community is not immune to racism, sexism, misogyny and all of the other "isms". Fragility is real. The face of theatre is changing. Room must be made for others, and, because of this, folks are feeling left out or pushed aside. There is resistance in our community to change. But it's not a matter of choice. It's about the viability and survival of our artform.

Lastly, I have had the unique privilege of working in an acting company. I have had a longtime personal relationship with most of its members. Because of our history of working together, we have the great luxury of being able to simply "dive into the work". Unfortunately, we can take a lot for granted as a result of being so familiar. We are in a moment that we must all re-commit to building trust. And our artistic practices must include moments where we can reflect on how the process is serving each of us and move forward as a collective. This part of the process cannot be taken for granted. Checking in with each other, clarifying boundaries and being clear about expectations is a critical part of our work. Humility and transparency can go a long way to creating positive systems that support our art and our health.

2

BLACK BRITISH PERSPECTIVES, PEDAGOGY AND POWER

Addressing the Canon through S.P.H.E.R.E.

Gemma Crooks and Erica Jeffrey

Modern Ideals and Traditional Attitudes

The recent and ongoing pandemic years have prompted a time for reflection, protests, accountability and justice in a world in which we must rely on each other to survive. Artists and practitioners are looking inward and examining traditions and practices within actor training institutions in search of inclusivity. In acknowledgement of the hegemonic system that has historically elevated middle-class, white male European academics, practitioners, and practices in higher educational institutions, we have chosen to address the gap between modern ideals and traditional attitudes. In this chapter we share our co-created reflexive framework S.P.H.E.R.E. as a model to reflect upon, reimagine and redesign training practices for contemporary actors. We also offer examples of how we have engaged with Stanislavsky's "system" using the S.P.H.E.R.E. framework when teaching students with intersecting identities and varied cultural backgrounds.

Collaboration

We are Black British women of Jamaican heritage and African descent in the UK who consider innovation, advancement and global thinking as priorities in developing new traditions of practice. Our sociocultural identity as grandchildren of the Windrush generation[1] influenced our desire to cultivate new practices to address inequities, hierarchy and exclusion. Our collaborative, practice-based research was initiated while we studied on the MA/MFA Actor Training and Coaching programme at The Royal Central School of Speech and Drama in London, UK.

ERICA: When we first met, we had multiple conversations about our individual presence within actor training conservatoires as students and teaching

DOI: 10.4324/9781003330882-4

artists. We reflected on our roles and responsibilities and shared candid observations on anti-blackness, patriarchal gate-keeping and racism within higher education.

GEMMA: *The conversations centred around our experiences training as actors, specifically when we shared that neither of us had been taught by a Black full-time or permanent faculty member. The impact of the lack of representation of Black practitioners was critical to our learning experience and sense of self-identity. Under these circumstances, as young students, we felt that cultural expression was minimised for the comfort of our white peers and teachers. The abstract forms of our identities were encouraged, including stereotypes, as a tool to access and emphasise cultural differences for theatre-making. These challenges were synonymous with students that we taught, who had also rarely or never encountered Black acting practitioners.*

ERICA: *It was particularly disheartening to share that collective experience, Gemma, especially given that you started your training in 1999 on the cusp of the millennium and I started training in 2012, the year of the Olympics in London, a period of time dedicated to celebrating the rich and diverse culture of our capital city. We both attended drama schools in two of the UK's largest multicultural cities. We were subsequently teaching artists reliving these events while acknowledging their continued existence for our students. I believe it was fate for us to have met online during the pandemic in 2020, following the resurgence of the Black Lives Matter movement and the subsequent chain of admissions, apologies and black squares on social media from individuals and institutions across social media noting systemic racism. I think we both had surreal experiences of being approached by peers who wanted to discuss anti-racism in their practice around this time.*

GEMMA: *Practitioners had been discussing "decolonising" the curriculum for many years before 2020, but I think the acknowledgement of racism in institutions across the globe highlighted a sense of urgency to address curriculum concerns and to action change. During training we both experienced a lack of consideration of our identities, which naturally prompted an anti-racist ethos. The idea of collaborative teaching with a shared ethos was refreshing for me. Working alongside a Black British practitioner – in a room – was an exciting way to expand our perspectives and create a pedagogy which will constantly be blooming. When we were looking at the fundamentals of conscious consideration in practice, we gently fell into rolese that supported our thinking and action in the room.*

ERICA: *I was specifically excited about the intergenerational nature of our collaboration. I think the roles we allow each other to take - and the ability to grow and develop as practitioners - has supported our work when we are in the room together and when we lead sessions separately.*

GEMMA: It does take trust and letting go in order to collaborate. The offer of collaboration is that perspectives will shift and alternate for a more holistic teaching practice. We asked a group of practitioners during one of our sessions about collaboration. I recall one practitioner expressed that the thought of them collaborating made them nervous and said it wasn't something that they felt they could accomplish.

INVITATION

We invite you to imagine how collaboration might serve you in your practice. Consider the work of another practitioner, perhaps a co-worker or an artist with whom you have worked. Imagine co-teaching.

Back to Business

Our curiosity and research began with simple questions to dissect the taut dynamics between our contemporary values and canonical (and mostly Eurocentric) practitioners. Stanislavsky proposes in his writings that "All peoples possess the same human nature" (1968, p. 170). Jonathan Pitches suggests Stanislavsky was indeed aligned with other European universalists of the 20th century and that his approach was consequently viable for global use (2017, p. 12). This led us to consider whether Stanislavsky had consciously considered the impact and application of his "system" on people of different racialised identities and cultural backgrounds.

When we mention the term "race" in this chapter, we want to clarify how we use this term. "Race" is not a biological fact, but a concept documented by Swedish botanist Carl Linnaeus in his *Systema Naturae* (1735) as a means of justification for colonialism, social and cultural dominance, and political power benefitting white Europeans economically. Philosopher Linda Martín Alcoff considers a "phenomenological account of racial identity" (2006, p. 179) and gives us a taxonomy of how we can consider the concepts of race, placing it in three categories:

- **normalism** – Race is not real [...] science has invalidated race as a biological category [...] racial concepts should be avoided [...] to further an anti-racist agenda
- **essentialism** – Race is always politically salient and always the most important element of identity. Members of racial groups share a set of characteristics [...] political interests, and a historical destiny. Current racial identities are stable across history
- **contextualism (objectivist and subjectivist)** – Race is socially constructed, historically malleable, culturally contextual, and produced through learned perceptual practice [...] (Ibid., p. 182)

We take a position of subjectivist contextualism when we consider the construct of race. We agree with Alcoff's contention that "one's designated race is a constitutive element of fundamental, everyday embodied existence and social interaction" (Ibid., p. 183). Our position consequently acknowledges the lived experiences of students, taking into account how those experiences affect their perceptions of self and others. Notably, the students that we teach are part of a generation for whom identity and accurate, self-defined labels play a role in their sense of freedom, individuality and place in society.

Kimberlé Crenshaw's work on intersectionality offers us an anti-discrimination doctrine that considers the individual as they present their identity in the present moment. In the seminal work, "Intersectionality: Mapping the Movement of a Theory", Crenshaw and her colleagues acknowledge that the work on intersectionality theory is never done but rather remains a work in progress (1991). We are aligned with the idea that new understandings and complexities are evolving. We hope our work not only advances that process as our world changes around us, but also reflects the nuances that students bring into our collective space. We do not aim to arrive at a one-size-fits-all practice or practitioner nor at a limited conclusion of self-identity.

Taking account of our own experiences of training as actors and our positions now as teaching artists, we give ourselves and each other permission to analyse our own pedagogical approaches and accountability within the classroom. bell hooks speaks of "the oppositional gaze" (1992, p. 116) that requires you to look beyond what has been shown to you and to look with consideration of your own agency. The fluidity of our pedagogy is influenced by a willingness to expand knowledge, awareness and understanding of ourselves and our students in relation to the industry and the world we are training them for. Heidi Safia Mirza discusses the fluidity of pedagogy and how it changes in relation to the times to support and embrace alternative ways of knowing. She suggests "real" diversity in democratic societies has to be a moral and legal imperative which fundamentally changes our pedagogy and moves us towards a decolonised practice that embraces "other ways of knowing" and being for all (Arday and Mirza, 2018, p. 176).

The ideology of "one right way" reflects a culture of paternalism to which Tema Okun refers in her characterisation of white supremacy culture. In 1999, Okun formulated (and reformulated in 2021) a list of characteristics specific to white supremacy culture as experienced across institutions and organisations: perfectionism, either/or and the binary, progress, worship of the written word, individualism, defensiveness and denial, the right to comfort and urgency (2021). We utilise Okun's work here as means to unpack harmful cultures that are embedded in systems. We foreground the aspects of her work that can be summarised as "those with power often don't think it is important or necessary to understand the viewpoint or experience of those for whom they are making decisions" (Ibid.) In the attempt to know other ways of working, we recognise our authority in spaces. Power is a key consideration within our work and how power is experienced. We regularly highlight structures that reinforce traditional hierarchies in form and execution and dismantle them for a more heuristic learning progress.

INVITATION

Consider other "ways of knowing", including imagination, as a means of expanding your practice. We invite you to examine both your own lived experiences and perceptions first, then consider the lived experiences and perceptions that you may not share with others.

S.P.H.E.R.E.

We share our methodology S.P.H.E.R.E. as a means of developing an inclusive learning environment to enable creativity with cultural specificity and awareness. S.P.H.E.R.E. requires conscious consideration to address how practitioners can design a plan and invite actors to explore practice-specific exercises both in training and rehearsal rooms. S.P.H.E.R.E. was established as a result of our findings from practice-based research with Black British actors at various stages of their professional careers. The specific elements of S.P.H.E.R.E. and their ongoing influences are represented in Figure 2.1 and listed here:

Self-Expression
Practical Engagement
Heuristic Approach
Expectation
Reflective Practice
Expansion

Our desire in this section is primarily for the reader to remain aware of the methodology. The exercises are a means by which you can engage with some of the ways we have implemented S.P.H.E.R.E. in our own practice. The invitations are practical contributions for the reader intended as points of inspiration only and can be modified to accommodate the requirements of your students. S.P.H.E.R.E. will work in many different ways, and can should challenge and shape your practice. S.P.H.E.R.E. can also be used to adjust and/or develop exercises that you might share with your students.

We will define each element of S.P.H.E.R.E. below and share how individual components can be useful in designing new exercises and adapting pre-used exercises. However, we should first state that the dimensions of this framework are underpinned by a practitioner's willingness to engage with the effects of time,

FIGURE 2.1 The elements of S.P.H.E.R.E. and their ongoing influences.

space and psychogeography for the students they teach - as they each influence the work on an ongoing basis.

Time – We place importance on the era and the ideas of the time in which we train actors, noting the relevance and specificities of working with students during the pandemic years. We remain alert to pressures that individuals set for themselves based on their own expectations of timescale as well as societal pressure in relation to the speed at which they achieve success. We acknowledge that time works in relation to productivity. Time is different for racialised bodies in how the world perceives us and how our stories are heard. We see past, present and future as external dimensions in a long process. We place the student at the forefront of their timescale, setting their individual pace for learning. We work across time zones.

Space – We refer to the The literal space that we work in, whether it is the room or the online platform that we log into in order to accommodate students who are studying from home. This consideration will shift our capabilities and may require some practice-based exercises to be reimagined.

Psychogeography – We train actors in different cities within the UK and are conscious of how the journeys of our students through these cities and their arrival to our sessions impact their sense of self and artistic contributions. Many of our students have attended government-funded schools before attending privately - run institutions. These spaces affect the emotions and behaviours of the individuals within them. Despite our own familiarity with these spaces, we consider this dimension key to remaining aware of the power that they hold for students consciously and unconsciously. The names attached to these buildings say something to the people inside. Psychogeography also considers how aspects of transport such as the underground, buses and trams can inform the individual student. The journey from "home" to school cannot be underestimated in a student's ability and willingness to practically engage and progress with the demands of actor training. An awareness of what it means to arrive at an institution is rarely a point of reflection within training, yet the unspoken feelings of awe and self-doubt can be brought into question. In utilising the S.P.H.E.R.E. methodology, we strongly believe that these dimensions are key to share with students to offer autonomy of their learning process and context to complex emotions and behaviours that may arise as a result of conflict in one of those areas.

We encourage you to consider how you could apply the S.P.H.E.R.E. model to the full range of practices that you teach and/or explore. Here we focus on Stanislavsky (we have continued to explore S.P.H.E.R.E. with the practices of Jacques Lecoq, Michael Chekhov, Rudolf Laban, and others). Through the course of our work, we have discovered that there is no requirement to apply the elements of S.P.H.E.R.E. in a linear way.

Self-expression

Self-expression is a necessary action for the survival of our values, beliefs and culture. Self-expression is a core element within our ethos as collaborative teaching artists. We actively offer multiple opportunities within our sessions for ourselves and our students to share elements of culture, identity and outward presence. This is a key way of building trust, setting the foundations of respect and celebrating our humanity. Philosopher Mitchell S. Green discusses the idiosyncrasy and conceptualization of self-expression as both culturally recognisable, assimilated and individual (2007). Theorist Stuart Hall asserts that cultural identity is more than being and an act of becoming and belonging (1994). Allowing Time in conjunction with self-expression, we encourage students to become more themselves. In conjunction with Crenshaw, Hall theorises that our identities go through shifts and transformations in our lifetimes and, as a result, we do not arrive stuck and silenced in our need to express our perspectives, but instead we learn and use them in making theatre and art.

How We Engage with Self-expression in Our Practice

Prior to designing workshops and exercises for students, we share with each other our knowledge, biases and experience with the specific practice that we are focusing on. Allowing ourselves the freedom to express different perspectives, challenges and delights of practice lay the foundation for accountability within the design of sessions, ensuring that we consider access for our students who will engage with this work at various stages in their formal training journey.

Exercise: The Name Game

There are many versions of the Name Game. We use a version introduced to us by Black British movement and drama therapist Christina Anderson, which invites Self-expression. We offer the game to foster community and break down hierarchical boundaries. It comes at the start of a session, particularly when working with new actors. This simple exercise reveals wonderful details in an individual's personal narrative. It also gives everyone the opportunity to learn names and pronunciations correctly. Firstly, we (Gemma and Erica) share our relationships to and tell the stories of our own names, then invite each student to share the origins of their name and/or what their name means to them. Students can share as much or little as they feel comfortable with.

INVITATION

There are quite a few versions of the Name Game. We invite you to use a game you feel will allow you to hear the voices of each of your students in a way that allows them to share as much of themselves as they wish.

Practical Engagement

Practical engagement can be defined as full, active participation in the work paired with the willingness to be present and perceptive. We prepare the students to engage in practice-based explorations, remaining cognizant of the individuals in the room and their requirements to consent to practical engagement. We adjust exercises to accommodate students' needs and to maintain an equitable environment. The willingness to be present and perceptive is a requirement for the practitioner *and* the student.

How We Engage with Practical Engagement in Our Practice

Developing a level of trust to encourage practical engagement, we focus on building trust by affirming students' contributions, celebrating their individuality and idiosyncrasies, and maintaining an awareness of the power dynamic. Students should feel they have permission to share honestly about their process.

Exercise: Speak Your Mind

Speak your Mind is an exercise that can offer a particularly enjoyable way to encourage spontaneity when exploring a practice. We initiate work with students by stating that together we will invite the renowned practices and practitioners ideas into our room. We centre the individuals in the room in order to reverse the expectation that students must meet century-old ideas or practices that do not centre them. By inviting renowned practices and practitioners into our collective space, we divert the power to the living, breathing humans creating the work today that will impact generations tomorrow. We also simultaneously acknowledge the innovators of the past and our own ongoing development. The exercise positions students as valuable contributors and provides an opportunity to connect to each other by sending and receiving information collaboratively while they build an image of the practitioner and practice as they move in the space. We sensitively guide the actors to welcome idiosyncrasies and initial perceptions through our quick-fire responsive game. We name specific practices and practitioners (like Stanislavsky or the "system") and encourage students to release whatever thoughts come to mind in relation to them.

- we establish an area in the space to be deemed "Point A"
- we invite the students to move in a circular pattern around Point A, (in effect, Point A is a spot on the circumference of the circle)
- once the students get to Point A they shout out their reflection on (or response to) the practice/practitioner
- students continue moving round the space arriving at Point A one after the other to share their reflections
- we acknowledge the student's immediate response and opinions in the moment. Ideally, the exercise naturally progresses from an initial focus on an individual practitioner to playful, responsive and critical engagement with peers. New revelations arise and preconceived notions are deconstructed

---

INVITATION

How does your environment encourage students to remain present and perceptive as active participants?

Heuristic (Process over Product)

A heuristic approach to actor training carves the necessary space for the artist to be a critical thinker. Self-discovery through the work ignites agency within the actor and a developed understanding of the self as a human and an artist. Self-discovery can unlock the freedom to continue exploring. We draw upon Brazilian educator Paulo Freire's ethos of students requiring freedom to question, understand and change their minds about the knowledge they obtain. Freire states, "Critical consciousness, they say, is anarchic. Others add that critical consciousness may lead to disorder. Some, however, confess: Why deny it? I was afraid of freedom. I am no longer afraid!" (1970, p. 35). The freedom to question in a more heuristic learning process can lead to acknowledging and dismantling structures that reinforce traditional hierarchies in their form and execution. For example, we argue it is not important for the student-actor to like the practices introduced solely because the practitioner's name is held in high regard across training spaces globally. It is, however, important for individuals to see themselves through the work.

bell hooks' work in *Teaching to Transgress* is also fundamental to our thinking of self-discovery in both an individual and communal sense. She suggests, "To begin, the professor must genuinely value everyone's presence. There must be an ongoing recognition that everyone influences the classroom dynamic, that everyone contributes" (1994, p. 20). We encourage knowledge and access to resources via research, group discussion and reflection.

How We Engage with Heuristic Process in Our Practice

We allow ourselves to practically engage with the exercises alongside the students. For example, we explore Stanislavsky's "circles of attention"[2] through an exercise that we established and named "Digital Gallery". Our exercise takes the actor through a triplicity of lenses. We see the first circle of attention as a focus on the relationship with the self (the actor); the second circle of attention as a focus on the relationship with others (character work); and the third circle of attention as a focus on the relationship to the world (wider circumstances/given circumstances). We use this exercise as a critical and practical device to address and revisit our relationship with the wider world as artists. We introduce technology as a "way in" for ease of access, contemporising the Stanislavskian concept and making it tangible. The Digital Gallery offers visual, kinaesthetic and auditory associations to address his – and our – circles of attention. The physical space is designed in a bespoke manner to accommodate freedom of movement through each circle for multiple students. This exercise ultimately provides an opportunity for students to be represented as part of a non-traditional art gallery. The space is intentionally built by students to offer ownership of their experience and artistic contribution.

Exercise: Digital Gallery

This exercise requires smartphones/tablets that can take a picture. All smartphones/tablets should be set to Airplane mode with lock screen enabled. (We recognise this exercise may not be suitable for your students, but we consciously chose to use digital technology in this exercise as it was readily available to us and our students.) Music is played at various stages throughout this exercise. The music offers another element to respond to.

- we invite the students to build an audio-visual narrative about themselves by asking them to take a selfie and add a complementary voice note; we encourage both present-moment awareness and self-focus since this narrative is about their relationship with themselves

- the students place chairs facing outward in a circle in the room with gaps between each chair (see Figure 2.2)

First Circle

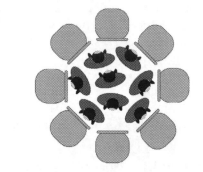

Second Circle

Third Circle

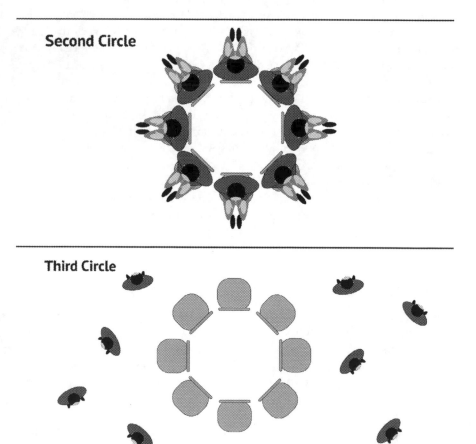

FIGURE 2.2 Circles of the Digital Gallery

- the students place their devices upright on their chairs, each phone facing away from the centre of the circle; the open area in the centre of the circle is now referred to as the "First Circle" (the actor)
- the space between the phone and seat edges represents the "Second Circle" (character work)
- the Digital Gallery is now formed with each of the chairs holding a device with sound and images to explore
- the "Third Circle" is the space beyond the chairs and bodies in the room (wider context)
- we invite the students to listen to the audio and gaze at the visual accompaniment within the Digital Gallery and select one audio-visual piece that they wish to explore
- once chosen, we invite the actors to consider this live art (the image and the voice note) and its human origin as they consider a day in the life of this person
- actors will create an étude and use their imagination to form a narrative, while considering the character and given circumstances
- gradually, we encourage the students to begin interacting with other students in the Third Circle
- significantly, the students are permitted to return to the First Circle at any point to rediscover self for grounding, to the Second Circle to revisit the character and to the Third Circle to shift to the character in the wider circumstances/given circumstances

---

INVITATION

We invite you to explore this exercise with your students and notice how they identify and position themselves, others/characters and the societal impact of the world around them.

Expectations

Oftentimes, when asked to share the expectations they have of themselves whilst in training, students share concerns and convictions that are exacerbated by their awareness of industry competition and the desire to succeed. Perfectionism and the urgent desire to understand embodied concepts prior to engaging with them practically is a common block for acting students. Abandoning expectations may require total trust in practice, practitioners and processes. However, we cannot expect to gain and sustain total trust from students within institutional spaces when the language and behaviour of white supremacist culture remain present. Despite recent institutional efforts to address and action anti-racist strategies within actor training in the UK, we still experience the effects of white supremacist language and behaviour in acting schools.

It is therefore imperative for us to consider the values and expectations we – and our students – hold in the work as institutions for actor training respond to the damaging realities of inequality.

How We Engage with Expectations in Our Practice

Our work delves into the personal and political realms of expectation that have been cultivated to meet the demands of productivity and capitalism. We focus on revealing to and reminding students of their power through the choices they make, as well as encouraging research of unconventional and alternative paths through the industry. Most importantly, we highlight the relevance of their individuality and contributions to the industry to alleviate concerns regarding competition. Collaboration with peers is valued above competition with others.

We value the intergenerationality of our collaboration which allows us to share anecdotes of our journey through the industry and speak to decades long experience, including our achievements related to development as opposed to singular moments of recognition, i.e., winning an award. We link success with ongoing development of craft and perspectives as well as using platforms to share experience of art-making. We demonstrate and encourage the actors we train to be playful, and remain in critical conversation with the practices, materials and exercises offered, allowing new findings that are not prescribed and cannot be predetermined. We ask our students to be present with current findings and embrace moments of discomfort along their journey, acknowledging their growth and overcoming perfectionism. Our chapter is a demonstration of how we have overcome perfectionism to share our current findings and navigate our way through systems and ideas productively.

Exercise: Before, Here, Future

We created and named this exercise to address expectations of self within the learning environment. This exercise is intentionally called "Before, Here, Future" while considering the character and given circumstances. We place any of these in a physical location to acknowledge legacies and contributions to the field of acting.

- we ask students to create a tableau that showcases their relationship with Stanislavsky's "system" – or another canonical practice/practitioner – prior to actually engaging in the practice; we phrase the prompt as, "How can you physicalise your relationship to the 'system' as a statue?" (the "Before")

- actors are invited to devise a new tableau or short piece with peers based on their relationship to the "system" now, with this tableau representing their current relationship (the "Here") to the "system"
- lastly, we ask the actors at the end of the session to create a series of tableaux imagining their relationship to Stanislavsky's "system" moving forward (the "Future")
- actors will then perform each tableaux: "Before", "Here" and "Future" are then combined to create a movement score from "Before" to "Here" to "Future"

INVITATION

We invite you to reflect on the expectations you have for yourself and your students in this new working environment. How might political shifts impact these expectations? How might shifts in expectations affect the work?

Reflexive Work

We invite students to continuously reflect on first thoughts, analysis, discovery and future engagement. In recognition of the multiple creative ways of reflecting, we avoid prioritising the written word in our pedagogical approach. Voice notes, drawing, colouring, peer-to-peer discussion, creating a physical score (as described in the previous exercise "Before, Here, Future") and journaling are some of the ways in which we invite students to take time to reflect on their engagement with a practice or practitioner (in this instance, Stanislavsky's "system").

How We Implement Reflexive Work in Our Practice

We foster reflexive work by asking ourselves and our students to take notes in any format, expressing and analysing their thoughts about the practice, and interrogating their personal process. Reflexive work can move the students away from the notion that the teacher/practitioner's words or expectations must be prioritised. Giving the actors time to engage in a reflexive mode is encouraged throughout the sessions.

Exercise: Notes Taking and/or Journaling

- we encourage our students to take notes throughout the sessions in any form they find useful, they might chose voice notes, drawing or writing
- we provide students with the space and time to reflect on the practice in their own words

> **INVITATION**
>
> You may want to offer specific moments for reflection or schedule short periods for actors to pause and make notes. We offer time in our sessions to take notes followed by a break for refreshments.

Expansion

Our creative outpouring becomes richer through individual and community learning, resulting in an expansion of knowledge and understanding. We encourage students to continue their collaborations in new spaces and build upon their learning, constantly revisiting how new and old information affects their creative process. Utilising research to seek new possibilities, new modes and uncharted territory beyond the canon sets the foundation for an expansion of knowledge. We invite students to be open-hearted in their exploration from different angles, engage with multiple perspectives and honour new understandings through revisiting practice-based exercises. As we expand our knowledge, we remember that our previous acting experiences and life experiences hold value, reinforcing the idea that there is no one "right" way of approaching the craft. We consider the artists that work with us as explorers, neither "emerging" nor a "final product" for industry consumption bell hooks suggests,

> To teach in varied communities not only our paradigms must shift but also the way we think, write, speak. The engaged voice must never be fixed and absolute, but always changing, always evolving in dialogue with a world beyond itself.
>
> *(1994, p. 11)*

How We Implement Expansion in Our Practice

Through engaging with materials outside of our lived experiences, we develop an awareness of our biases and understand the political and personal contextual limitations of engaging with a practice/narrative. There may be a level of discomfort and uncertainty or lack of knowledge and experience. We discuss the actor's responsibility to expand their own learning through practice and theory. Remaining open to discussion, discomfort and diversion from the source, we create a holistic and expansive training that allows the student and teaching artist to learn simultaneously.

Exercise: The Creative Artist – Text Narrative

This is not necessarily an exercise but a suggestion that teachers and coaches consider the texts they bring into the classroom. Students can share in the process of choosing texts and collaborate with teaching artists. We suggest you hold a critical discussion on authority and make space for further research to be conducted by acting students – rather than by the instructor/person deemed to be holding the knowledge. (NB: Practitioners may wish to share the course criteria or unit objectives with the students to guide the selection of the texts.) We ask ourselves the following questions: What purpose are we using the text for? Are we using this for an end-product or are we using it to understand human behaviours and view humanity through a new lens?

- we as practitioners join our students in researching and bringing in relevant texts from around the world, discuss these materials and welcome presentations on different cultures
- we find this collective research demonstrates the value of everyone's ongoing development of cultural awareness and the dismantling of unconscious bias
- we discuss perspectives on the text based on our individual cultural values and understandings
- we choose to discuss how the central themes, narrative structures, historical engagement with the central themes and the specific perspective of the playwright/screenwriter/poet/novelist might impact our processes
- this exercise allows students to begin to synthesise their new knowledge with lived experience in a collaborative environment

---

INVITATION

We invite you to consider how we can cultivate rooms in which young artists can expand their creative capacity and develop new understandings of approaching texts from multiple cultures. How do you meet practice, texts and collaborators?

Conclusion

Contributing to society through teaching and collaboratively designing practice for contemporary actor training serves as a reminder of the fragile, invaluable and temporal nature of both educating and art-making collectively. We argue that our responsibility as practitioners is to lead with a conscious consideration of the past, present and future journeys of our students. As our communities change and grow, so should our approaches to actor training. While tradition may guide us to regurgitate old ideas about practice and pedagogy, our power can be discovered in developing our own perspectives and guiding our students to do the same. We believe the call to the individual artist is far more important than adhering to external pressures.

The S.P.H.E.R.E. framework can be used in the planning and delivery of actor training by practitioners around the globe to reflect upon, reimagine and redesign training practices for contemporary actors as they consider the times, spaces and geographical impacts on the behaviours and attitudes of the students they teach. We offer a methodology as a call to practitioners who wish to continue offering such methods created by canonical practitioners and for those who work in spaces that maintain such methods as part of their curriculum. We also believe that S.P.H.E.R.E. is applicable to new practices that boldly experiment with technology or include other elements within actor training. The dimensions of S.P.H.E.R.E. welcome practitioners who are willing to expand their knowledge, awareness and understanding of their students' sense of self in relation to the industry and world for which we are training them.

Notes

1 The "Windrush generation" refers to the post-war immigration of Caribbean peoples to the UK in 1948, when the HMT *Empire Windrush* arrived in England from Jamaica. The rebuilding of Britain after World War II was dependent on migrants from the Commonwealth; with the prospects of work and a new start after experiencing limited job opportunities in Jamaica, many took the opportunity to start work in Britain. Though their presence was met with adversity, the people of the Caribbean sought to initiate ways in which they could thrive and build a positive impact for future generations. The Windrush has been widely associated with people from the Caribbean island, but also involves west African colonies, Nigeria and Ghana (Phillips and Phillips, 2009).
2 The concept of the "circles of attention" was developed by Stanislavsky and consists of three areas of focus. The circles of attention allow the actor to consider the areas in which they can focus their attention on self, relationship to others and/or the space around them.

References

Alcoff, L. M. (2006) "The Phenomenology of Racial Embodiment," in *Visible Identities: Race, Gender, and the Self*. New York: Oxford University Press, pp. 179–183.
Arday, J. and Mirza, H. S. (eds) (2018) *Dismantling Race in Higher Education: Racism, Whiteness and Decolonising the Academy*. Cham: Palgrave Macmillan.
Crenshaw, K. (1991) "Mapping the Margins: Intersectionality, Identity Politics, and Violence against Women of Color", *Stanford Law Review*, 43(6), pp. 1241–1299. doi:10.2307/1229039 (Accessed 23 February 2023).
Freire, P. (2017[1970]) *Pedagogy of the Oppressed*. Reprint. Harmondsworth: Penguin.
Green, M. S. (2007) "The Significance of Self-expression", in *Self-Expression*. doi:10.1093/acprof:oso/9780199283781.003.0001 (Accessed 23 March 2023).
Hall, S. (1994) "Cultural Identity and Diaspora", in P. Williams and L. Chrisman (eds), *Colonial Discourse and Post-colonial Theory*, London: Routledge, pp. 404–415.
hooks, b. (1992) *Black Looks: Race and Representation*. Boston: South End Press.
hooks, b. (1994) *Teaching to Transgress: Education as the Practice of Freedom*. New York: Routledge.

Linnaeus, C. (1735) *Systema Naturae*. Available at: https://www.linnean.org/learning/who-was-linnaeus/linnaeus-and-race#:~:text=Systema%20naturae%20provided%20a%20classification,%3A%20mineral%2C%20vegetable%20and%20animal.&text=Linnaeus%20was%20the%20first%20naturalist,%2C%20and%20the%20order%2C%20Anthropomorpha (Accessed: 3 March 2023).

Okun, T. (2021) "White Supremacy Culture". Available at: https://www.dismantlingracism.org/uploads/4/3/5/7/43579015/okun_-_white_sup_culture.pdf (Accessed: 4 March 2023).

Phillips, T. and Phillips, M. (2009) *Windrush: The Irresistible Rise of Multi-racial Britain*. London: HarperCollins Publishers.

Pitches, J. (2017) "A System for All Nations? Stanislavsky's Transmission in the World", in J. Pitches and S. Aquilina (eds), *Stanislavsky in the World*. London: Bloomsbury Methuen Drama, pp. 12–24.

Stanislavski, C. (1968) *Stanislavsky's Legacy*. Translated from the Russian and edited by E. Reynolds Hapgood. New York: Theatre Arts.

3

LOGUNEDÉ IN SALEM

Making Sense of Stanislavsky's Last Experiments in Contemporary Brazil

Diego Moschkovich

Identification as a Problem

When entering a new classroom or a new rehearsal room, I straightforwardly address the problem of identification. We should always take it for a fact, I say, that various degrees of disidentification wait for us in the first contact with the material we'll be working on.[1] This is inescapable regardless of the material, since the pile of words, images and actions that we call characters or figures were not created by us, but by someone other than us. But that's only the first degree in this instance. After acknowledging that, we should ask ourselves who wrote it, where, when and in which circumstances. Then, in the way we're about to take an anti-racist approach to our work, I continue, we should expect the distance between us and the material to become even wider.

Brazil, the country where I was born and continue to work, is heir to an almost five centuries-old tradition of racial segregation. To limit myself to the numbers related to theatre, cinema and entertainment alone, as of 2019, only 1.6% of all nominees for Best Original Script for one of Brazil's biggest cinema awards were Black or Brown men (women weren't even accounted for) (Afonso, 2019). As of 2022, only 7.98% of the actors in television identified as Black in a country where 56% of the general population identifies as being so (Marques, 2018). Racism is obvious and in every corner of everyday life. So much so that, to describe its wideness, Silvio Almeida, a renowned lawyer, sociologist and Black activist, has developed a theory of structural racism:

> a consequence of the social structure itself, of the *normal* way in which political, economic, juridical, and even family relations constitute. [...]

DOI: 10.4324/9781003330882-5

Racism is part of a social process that flows *by the back* of the individual and seems to them to be legated by tradition itself.

(Almeida, 2019, p. 50)

One of the most immediate reflexes of that assumption can be felt in an acting classroom, especially one that intends to mobilise such procedures as the so-called "classics" (European, in fact): William Shakespeare, Molière and Anton Chekhov, or, in the field of acting, the Stanislavsky "system" itself. But the white European hegemony in Brazilian playwriting is also astounding. Of all the characters in Brazilian playscripts from the 20th century, only a few are non-white. That said, of course, one of the most common complaints by the students in the beginning of the course would be, "I don't identify with this author", or, "We don't want to work with that, because it's too far away from our reality."

In one way, this shows that the dialectics of identification-disidentification between actor-character and collective-material remain mostly unsolved, despite being, by far, the focal point of theatre practice in the 20th century. Of course, we could trace it back to Shakespeare, at least, but it is at the end of the 19th century that it acquires the traces we have grown used to. Konstantin Stanislavsky, Vsevolod Meyerhold, Bertolt Brecht, Abdias do Nascimento, Augusto Boal, Jerzy Grotowski, José Celso Martinez Corrêa and Antunes Filho are just a few examples of theatre practitioners that developed important views on the matter when it comes to the actor's work. Stanislavsky's thought, even if usually attached to the general perception as akin to identification alone, can be read in two ways.[2]

The first – and most problematic to a diverse classroom – is the way of Western acting tradition. In the last century, Stanislavsky's "system" and its categories – the so-called *elements* – became Westernised, white-centred and one of the foundations of contemporary mainstream acting. Devoid of its original philosophic and revolutionary ethics, the "system" became a method for professional training in a market where the standards are usually set by a Western, white male-dominated industry.[3] This version of the "system" – the most well-known version throughout the world – is extremely violent. The main operation that makes it so is what I call the *reification*[4] of the character. By treating the characters in a play as existing beings (or existing *others*) that must be pursued by the actors by means of identification, this version of the methodology attaches *proposed circumstances* to *affective memory*, thus narrowing the field of bodies and experiences that might be suitable for a role. I will start with an example from my own practice.

Jackson, or the First Methodological Approach to Stanislavsky's Thought

Jackson França (he/him) is a 25-year-old Black queer actor who was accepted on my course at the Experimental Studio of SESI (ESS) in São Paulo in 2018.

The ESS was for 16 years – until the pandemic hit – a prestigious one-year specialisation course where recently graduated actors from universities and conservatoire training programs could spend a year training in different laboratories. I oversaw a three-month, practical intensive course on Action Analysis and the *étude* method,[5] and we chose to work on Arthur Miller's *The Crucible* through the course. The choice of the material had been guided by its apparent actuality: witch-hunt, paranoia, rape and religious fundamentalism all seemed relevant themes in 2018 in Brazil. Each of the 16 newly admitted students had read it, and the collective was excited to work on it.

The process of analysing a role or a play through action is a very delicate one. Much has been said and written on it, but nevertheless I find it important to outline the practice in the way I do it.[6] The first position is this one: Action Analysis is the analysis of action through action itself. Therefore, it is not work that is done around a table, but standing up, on the stage, almost right away after the first reading of the material. In this way, choosing the material is something of great importance. I try, of course, to actively influence the choice of the material we're going to work with so it has the required elements to work with Action Analysis: action, circumstances, events and so on. Nevertheless, any material must find at least a faint echo in the students' will, or else the process becomes dry – as Maria Knebel says – and dies out (1982, pp. 43–47). After choosing and briefly analysing a specific scene, the actors are invited right away onto the stage. They perform *études* on the chosen material to produce two things. First, they must find themselves performing those actions in the role. That is, they should *experience* the role's actions as their own.[7] Second, they are required to recompose the different fragments (Stanislavsky called them *bits*) of the role in a coherent physical line of actions, analogous to the one in the play, but with their self-experienced emotions. Then, in the end, I proceed to solidify the *mise-en-scène*.

But back to *The Crucible*.

After taking a few classes to prepare, the students had decided which scenes from the play were to be studied on the first day of *études*. Jackson had selected a very difficult scene from the end of the first act where Abigail, Tituba and Parris start to accuse the whole town of witchcraft. He would play Tituba.

In the scene, after being straightforwardly accused by Abigail, Tituba first denies involvement with the Devil and then slowly gives in to the pressure and confesses, calling out the names of townspeople suggested by Parris, which leads to the collective naming by all the girls as the act concludes. Miller's rendering of Tituba, despite playing a fundamental role in the unfolding of the play's events, is completely racist. In terms of language, Tituba speaks in an imitation of what would be English as spoken by enslaved people in 17th-century New England. In terms of character composition, if we follow Miller's proposed circumstances, we see an enslaved Black woman whose emotions dominate reason, a woman torn by the contradiction of feeling genuine love towards her enslavers and the need to do anything possible to survive. In other words, Tituba is presented in the text almost as an animal rather than a human being, and her dramatic arc confirms it by the pre-execution scene in the fourth act.

Jackson's first approach to the character was "classical", exactly the approach through Stanislavsky's "system" we previously described. First, he analysed Tituba's *proposed circumstances*, carefully picking those necessary to the selected scene. Among others, we can list here the conditions as her enslavement as a Black woman, the submissive relationship with the Parris family, the love offered by the Parris child (whom she probably nurtured from birth) and the fierce will to survive. After that, he started to look for corresponding *affective memories* that could justify and vivify these circumstances for himself – all prior to going onto the stage for the first *étude*.

And here's where the trouble started.

This was one of the few cases where the first *étude* was already full of emotion and *experiencing* despite the loose *physical line* of the actors. Jackson's Tituba moved from *bit* to *bit* (of course, in this stage of Action Analysis, lines are still improvised), enriched with his own emotions. The result of the *étude* was a growing atmosphere of tension and despair that led Jackson-Tituba to confess witchcraft and accuse Parris's enemies. The other students all concurred in evaluating the work as "very strong" and "touching". I complimented the students for the work done and moved on. After the end of the class, Jackson approached me and told me he hadn't been feeling right following the *étude*. We sat together to examine what had been going on.

Jackson, in a very open and frank conversation, told me by studying Tituba in that scene he had felt completely violated, that he couldn't understand what happened, but it was as if he were re-experiencing an analogous form of violence. I asked him to describe to me the process he underwent in exploring the character before going on stage, and he told me that to achieve the character he had sought to attach his own *affective memories* to the circumstances proposed by the author. For example, to explore the pseudo-familiar relationship with Tituba's enslavers, he had gone back to his own experiences escaping police brutality in Santos, his hometown. In contrast, to dig into the love Tituba developed for the Parris children, he had mobilised his own affections toward blond white boys as a teenager.

Now, I should say that Jackson was by this point in his training a somewhat experienced young performer, and that none of these procedures were brought to the *étude* in a *cliché* manner, where the actor re-lives their own memories in order to imitate this or that emotion. On the contrary, the work with *affective memory* and the *proposed circumstances* was done prior to going on stage, the *étude* had brilliant moments of *experiencing* and an interesting play was established between the actors. But Jackson, in his own words, was trying to achieve the character, dealing with a literary figure as if dealing with some actually existing *other*, transforming metaphors – that is, the aspects of the character – into things that had to be materialised. As if Tituba were a real person and he had to become her. The standard interpretation of Tituba – created both by Miller and by critical tradition related to *The Crucible* – took its toll. I had methodologically led Jackson to reinforce centuries of violence against Black people without even knowing it. Would it be possible, we started to ask ourselves, to explore the character in ways that broke with violence instead of reinforcing it?

This happened in 2018 as I was just home from a four-month research internship at the Moscow Art Theatre Museum Archives in Russia. Working on my dissertation, I was looking at Stanislavsky's classes at the Opera-Dramatic Studio. And this was when I began to see that there could be a second, more open way to approach Stanislavsky's thought.

The Opera-Dramatic Studio: Stanislavsky's Thought and the New Soviet *Habitus*

The Opera-Dramatic Studio was Stanislavsky's last studio and lasted from 1935 to his death in 1938. Even though it lasted only four years, its importance surpasses it by at least a decade beforehand and afterward. The story of its founding mixes with the story of Stanislavsky's struggle to keep his life's work alive throughout the fervent years of left-wing avant-gardism in the late 1920s and the dawn of Stalin's grip on culture throughout the 1930s. The initial project, focused on a giant Theatre Arts Academy that would keep the original Moscow Art Theatre research and methodologies alive by assembling new, ethically bound collectives, was accepted by the *Narkompros* (the People's Commissariat for Education) in 1934 as a small, experimental studio for opera and drama.

The new Studio, which started operating in 1935, had several differences from the previous studios that shaped the history of the "system" and its pedagogical development. The first difference is that it was allowed to function without a pedagogical programme in place. However, it was created with the goal of developing a programme that would function for higher-education institutions in the USSR.[8] The second difference was that Stanislavsky's main work consisted in overseeing and training young pedagogues, and he taught the students only now and then. The third difference was in the composition of its students.

Here, apart from the very young group of pedagogues that had been drilled in the "system" by Stanislavsky's sister Zinaida Sokolova during the 1920s (Novitskaia, 1984, p. 14), we have an even younger student body, aged 16 to 20 (Moschkovich, 2021, p. 63–64). A person that was 20 years old in 1935 was born in 1915. These are the first students that had been born and raised in the Soviet Union, the very first generation that had been fully educated in its schools and that shared its new *habitus*.[9] An editorial article from the *Dekada Teatra* [Theatre Decade] journal from 1935, for example, develops the idea that a new layer of fresh and unspoiled "Soviet *intelligentsia*" were entering higher education institutions that year, and celebrates the fact that out of the 30 students selected for taking part in Stanislavsky's Opera-Dramatic Studio, 19 were distinguished members of the *Komsomol*, the Communist Youth League (Ibid.). In other words, these were students that claimed a completely different identity from the *habitus* from which Stanislavsky's thought developed.

Stanislavsky's old age and illness had brought back the habit of having a stenographer present in all his classes at the Opera-Dramatic Studio. In this way, a good number of the interactions between him and the pupils have been transcribed in the set of 38 stenograms kept at the Moscow Art Theatre Museum Archives. It is possible, by a careful reading of these transcripts, to notice that a silent culture clash between Stanislavsky and his students emerges.

Down with the Circumstances: The Second Methodological Approach to Stanislavsky's Thought

An interesting case of this silent clash takes place in a class on 5 December 1935. Stanislavsky proposes, after a short break, an exercise on *mise-en-scène*. He says: "You have a room, four walls and chairs. You don't know where I am going to sit. What kind of *mise-en-scène* can you have with such a situation?" Here, Stanislavsky wants a simple improvisation: how can an actor internally justify a *mise-en-scène* given by the director? For that he asks the students to invent "whatever they want", e.g., talking trivially about their classes, playing cards and so on. But issues arise almost immediately. One of the students not only starts to develop circumstances to justify the given *mise-en-scéne*, but also attaches specific *affective memories* to them. The student says:

> I've come up with something, though I don't know whether it's going to be of use. […] I have a husband, we're both at a party cell [that is, a grassroots Communist-party organisation]. My husband ended up being a traitor and I am a fervent communist. I can't live with him anymore, but I love him with all my heart.
>
> *(KS 21147)*[10]

Stanislavsky immediately tries to convince the student to take something lighter, but she insists on the circumstances created: "Wait, I still must get to the main idea. I helped him to flee the country. I know that I did wrong, but I did it for love. So, I summoned my comrades over to tell them of what I did" (Ibid.)

Stanislavsky accepts the setup, but insists that "Anything will do, this is all fine, but I want to know where you are going to seat your comrades" (KS 21147), that is, how she can utilise the *mise-en-scène* for the situation.

Despite a series of attempts to bring the student's attention back to the main task of the *étude* (that is, justifying a given *mise-en-scène*) the *étude* ends up in "tragedy", according to Stanislavsky's own account. Firstly, we see that Stanislavsky lacks understanding of the situation itself, of the importance of the theme brought by that specific student. Secondly, unable to relate to the circumstances, he fails to prevent the attaching of these *proposed circumstances* to the *affective memories* of the student. The exercise is ultimately subverted.

Stanislavsky's tactical answer to this problem started to develop in 1936. Due to medical reasons, Stanislavsky spent most of that year in the Barvikha complex, a sanatorium for medical healing outside Moscow. There, we can read in his account of a strong discussion he had with actress Maria Lilina about the matter of *proposed circumstances*. Lilina was basically insisting that the circumstances presented in Aleksandr Griboyedov's *Woe from Wit* were so different from the conditions they were living in that it made the circumstances unperformable. Stanislavsky then writes in his notebook:

> To say and to explain [to Lilina] that it is possible to perform the physical action here, in this room, and acting for real. What does 'here' mean? It means that I always take myself and always take the conditions of the place I am in. Khlyostova arrives at the ball and wants to cause an impression, to manage her prestige, but right here, in our Barvikha apartment's living room. I think: couldn't Sofia live here? Why couldn't Khlyostova have come here, too? Why couldn't this place be filled with high society dames, as well? Let's suppose they are here. Then I'll ask: what would I do, if I were Khlyostova, to cause fear and respect to them, to keep my authority?
>
> *(Stanislavsky, 1957, p. 528)*

Surely, the play's circumstances continue to be present – there's no way around them – but what Stanislavsky is proposing here is that they are put in the background rather than concretely mobilised as a *sine-qua-non* element for action on the stage. We can see something similar taking place with the students in the Opera-Dramatic Studio later in 1937. In a class on 27 April 1937, Stanislavsky is rehearsing his student Elena Rubtsova in the part of Juliet's nurse in the first act of William Shakespeare's *Romeo and Juliet* where she's actively looking for Juliet with Mrs Capulet on the evening of the ball. Rubtsova performs the same *étude* a couple of times and, after repeatedly failing it, says that it is too hard to imagine the circumstances. Stanislavsky promptly answers:

> Where are you now? You are Juliet's nurse, but you are here, at Stanislavsky's house. You are here and the room is full of students. Maybe you'll speak things in a whisper, but you must go from what is given here. Today, here. Do you understand why I need you to use this room? I

don't need you to invent another world, that's too hard. Notice: I am now right here, in this room. Fantasy (imagination) should be flexible (resilient) [...] Explain what could happen if you were here, today, and were looking for Katia Zakhoda [the student playing Juliet]. Imagine that you both live here. It is completely possible, if you were looking for Zakhoda, to find yourself in the middle of a class.

(KS 21162)

Rubtsova-Nurse then starts looking for Zakhoda-Juliet in the space using the concrete surroundings of the classroom as the leading impulse to action. She approaches the other students, asking whether they have seen Juliet and directly addressing them as participants of the scene. In the end, she accidentally finds Zakhoda-Juliet in a faraway corner of the room. Stanislavsky celebrates the *étude* as a success. In both cases – with Lilina in 1936 and with Rubtsova in 1937 – Stanislavsky shifts the actress's focus toward the concrete relationship with their partner and prevents them from attaching themselves to *affective memories* of any kind. Instead, the materiality of *today, here, now* is what justifies action in the character's dramatic arc.

Organic Action: Action without Circumstances

Today, here, now wasn't only a tactical approach in Stanislavsky's late practice. It was part of a broader theoretical elaboration of his thought on *organic action*. The theory of *organic action* started to be developed in 1936 while Stanislavsky was away in Barvikha and accepted only a handful of students at a time to work on different materials. In the meantime, he dictated to his secretary what would become the last part of *The Actor's Work on a Role*, focusing on a fictional rehearsal process for Nikolai Gogol's *The General Inspector*. In this manuscript, we read how the fictional director Arkadi Tortsov comes up with a new procedure for rehearsing. The novelty, he says, is that any role can be played right away, without previous work on the *proposed circumstances* or *affective memories*. He then rehearses the student Kostia Nazvanov in the role of Khlestakov by developing a series of actions that create organic relations with both the scheme of actions in the scene and the concrete circumstances of the rehearsal room (Stanislavsky, 1957, pp. 352–363). It's in the practical work in the Studio, however, that Stanislavsky defines the process of *organic action*.

In the class of 27 April 1937 – the same class that was dedicated to working on *Romeo and Juliet* – we see that Stanislavsky is dealing with the students' complaints about not having the text and therefore not being able to work with its *proposed circumstances* and *affective memories*. After spending the previous year away, Stanislavsky had collected, in one of his assistant's words, a whole set of new positions that had to be put to practice (Novitskaia, 1986, p. 119). The first of these innovations was giving the students only the rough scheme of actions connected to the role and nothing more. Everything would be built from that scheme of actions. When the students complain about not having enough *proposed circumstances* to work with, he answers:

> I don't need any of this, now. When you perform actions without objects [...] for instance: when you take off your jacket, you must first unbutton it and then slide your arms through the sleeves. These actions are mandatory, no matter what the proposed circumstances are. In other words, there are physical actions that are organic, regardless of the proposed circumstances. What we need now is the line of organic action.
>
> *(KS 21162)*

The idea here is that each action works as an *organism*, a closed system with its own inner finality. If we investigate one of these *organisms*, let's say, the action of taking a jacket off, each necessary small action – to unbutton the jacket, to slide your arms back through the sleeves – must be considered an indissociable part of it, and will therefore remain the same no matter the *proposed circumstances*. For Stanislavsky, this is true both for small physical actions and for the bigger, more dramatic actions in a play. In the latter, of course, the constituent parts of the *organism* will be of a different kind. Stanislavsky goes on:

> There is no Romeo, no Juliet. The only thing is you have to do whatever it takes to establish communication among yourselves. We always seem to forget the most elementary on the stage. [...] And what do we need to establish the communication? It is necessary to get into the partner's soul with your eye's tentacles, and they should do the same to you: that's called irradiation. And for that, the first thing you'll need is a partner. [...] You step onto the stage before a multitudinous audience. You see your partner very clearly. You touch them with the eyes of your soul and establish communication with them. Here you have it, a moment of truth, and that is already a lot. I am talking to you about the most elementary psychological line. You all should know this line. Now, we are following onto this organic line without breaking it.
>
> *(Ibid.)*

In other words, the materialisation of dramatic action on stage is itself an *organism* constituted of smaller parts that function interdependently. If, in the first example, these were small physical actions, here in the performance space the smaller parts of the organism are the performer, the dramatic material, the stage, the scene partners and, of course, the audience. The condition for these parts to be organically linked for Stanislavsky is to leave the play's *proposed circumstances* out. No Romeo, no Juliet. Students are taken out of the fiction – or *proposed circumstances* – and asked to establish relationships analogous to those in the play, but as themselves, with their own words, with their own stories, with their own corporeality.

It is interesting to note that the material used in these classes was by Shakespeare. Despite the Eurocentric tradition that elevates him as a "universal" playwright, there was nothing further from post-revolutionary 1930s Moscow than 17th-century Elizabethan England (or its imagined Verona, if we please). In fact, Stanislavsky's students had no cultural contact or shared *habitus* whatsoever with anything that could remotely resemble the circumstances described in Shakespeare's tragedy. Could that then be analogous to a collective of 21st-century Brazilian students working on the 20th-century United States (or its imagined Salem, if we please)?

Back to Jackson. Questions Instead of a Conclusion

The question we had asked with Jackson, just before entering this digression into post-revolutionary Russia, was whether it was possible to explore a character in the dramatic, psychological and situational structure, and also break with racist systems of oppression instead of reinforcing them. Stanislavsky's experience had little to do with consciously oppressive, let alone racist, structures of society and drama. On the contrary, it was aimed directly at mediating an apparent contradiction between different *habituses* and applying possible solutions in a way that the play (whether *Woe from Wit* or *Romeo and Juliet*) would be performable. Nevertheless, the process seemed to operate in an interesting way as we tackled our own contradictions.

I sat with Jackson and his partners to look at the material and prepare for the second *étude*. My first proposition, after briefly summing up the discussion with the group, was to get rid of the characters and their circumstances in the first place. We would need to shrink the text up to a point where only the rough structure of actions would remain. We gave up on Puritan New England, on Tituba's kidnapping from Barbados, on her language, on Abigail's interest in Proctor, and so on. What was left of the scene was one big *organic action* that spanned between two events: the flagrancy of the dancing in the woods – the event that sets the scene in motion – and the admission of witchcraft – first Tituba's, then Abigail's, then everyone else's – the fundamental, main event of the scene. That was their goal, as interpreters of the *étude*. First, regardless of words, *bits* and *tasks*, they should embrace *today, here, now* from the first to the last event.

The practice of an *étude* generally starts with an *exposition*. The *exposition* in the *étude* performs like the exposition in dramaturgy: it sets up all the conditions necessary for events to occur. It is a moment of free improvisation, where the actors can use whatever resources they have to accomplish two tasks: first, establish communication, and second, spark the *departure event* that will allow the action to develop and be studied.[11]

Jackson then stood up first and, after quickly contacting his two partners, began to address everyone in the audience. He started very calmly to tell us about his belonging to his mother's religion, Candomblé, and being consecrated as a child of Logunedé. Logunedé is an *orixá*, or deity, from the Brazilian tradition of Candomblé, considered to be a master sorcerer who gives divination and spelling powers to those in his service. More than that, he is the only *aboró* – male *orixá* – to have a connection with the ancestral mothers, the *Iami*.

After this brief introduction, Jackson then started to share aspects of his own life, describing to us several moments when he resorted to Logunedé's knowledge to solve different kinds of problems. The description – fully improvised – was so vivid that we all had the impression that Jackson could dominate us right away. Amid the narration, he also demonstrated part of the traditional singing of his *orixá*. Then he told a dramatic story about a friend from a conservative Pentecostal family approaching him for a love spell. After some months, their friend's family had discovered the exchange and caused a scandal, threatening both Jackson and his friend. Here, the *étude* properly began, or, as we say, the first *bit* of the scene opened.

The other actors, playing the parts of Abigail Williams and Reverend Parris, took the opportunity and immediately began accusing Jackson-Tituba of witchcraft. At first, he wholeheartedly denied it by defending the right to his religious beliefs. Then, when Jackson-Tituba saw such a defence was useless, he changed before our eyes. The initial story helped Jackson move away from the stereotypical representation of Tituba and toward the creation of a powerful sorceress. Then, the almost instinctive love toward the Parris family (that seems to be the main contradiction in Miller's character) gave way to a sharp political understanding of the situation. The admission of witchcraft was completely framed inside a strategy to implicate Abigail and the other girls, and to gain power within Salem's high circle. The end of the first act, where we usually see the beginning of "mass hysteria", became instead a true triumph for Jackson-Tituba, who stood calmly watching as the other five girls fell into despair.

The collective and I watched the *étude* with astonishment. The line of action remained the same, but what we saw were two completely different and mutually exclusive ways of playing Tituba. If the first *étude*, even though touching, operated in the realm of pre-conceived images informed by Miller's *habitus* and racist stereotypes, then the second approach had something original. After the *étude* ended, we all sat down to talk, and I rushed to ask Jackson of his impressions. He said he felt good, that the experience was, in fact, empowering.

Of course, this is only one successful example among several non-successful ones in my own practice and in the practice of my fellow actor trainers. Nevertheless, it is an experience that, in my opinion, bears sharing with others as we all navigate anti-racist practices and pedagogies. The question remains: how deep can we dig into Western dramaturgy without surrendering to the racist *habituses* that generated it? Even in this case with Jackson, we weren't supposed to stage *The Crucible*, so the *études* remained a random cluster of exercises. But were we to stage the play, how would we have approached Tituba's cruel end in Miller's play?

Such questions remain open, but I would argue that some of the conditions and historical forces that created the systems derived from Stanislavsky's thought – if cautiously studied and decolonised – offer a different approach to theatre altogether. By breaking with the direct need of representing something still or given, an unchangeable figure or character, an *other*, we can appropriate and re-signify images, develop the power to allow marginalised bodies and experiences to go on stage, and build an experimental space of resistance within the performance space.

Notes

1 Disidentification is a category proposed by queer performance theorist José Esteban Muñoz in his 1999 book *Disidentifications: Queers of Color and the Performance of Politics*. For Muñoz, white mainstream and cis-heteronormative performance is deeply rooted in the *identification* between the performer and what is performed. In the book, he analyses various contemporary pieces of queer-of-colour performances looking for its opposite, *disidentification,* as a typically queer methodology of building relations between the performer and what is performed. I find it interesting to start by placing the binary of *identification/disidentification* as a major problem to be explored in practice throughout my courses as some forms of this problem have been central to 20th-century theatre and continue to be.

2 In fact, Stanislavsky's thought can be read in three ways. The third way would be the traditional Soviet way of dealing with it. Even though methodologically closer to Stanislavsky's last experiments in the Opera-Dramatic Studio, this version of the "system" has settled on the specifics of Soviet theatre production. For a critique of this approach, see Sergei Tcherkasski, *Stanislavsky and Yoga* (2016) and Diego Moschkovich, *O último Stanislávski em ação: ensaios para um novo método de trabalho.* [The Late Stanislavski in Action: Experimenting on a New Method] (2021).

3 To a recovering of the non-Western roots of Stanislavsky's thought, see Maria Shevtsova's *Rediscovering Stanislavsky* (2020).

4 *Reification* is a term coined by the Hungarian critic philosopher Gyorgy Lukacs and is presented mainly in this work *The Ontology of Social Being* (1978). From a very specific reading of Marx's concept of *fetishisation*, Lukacs develops the term to denote the process by which subjects become objects and then are alienated from their own. Kevin Floyd gives a more contemporary rendering of the term in his book *Reification of Desire: Toward a Queer Marxism* (2009).

5 Even though there have been several discussions on how to name the different methodologies derived from Stanislavsky's late period, in this chapter we're following Maria Knebel's definition of the *étude* method as a part of the broader Action Analysis methodology. Here, the *étude* is an improvised experiment performed by two actors on a given scene from the play, after a brief analysis of the main structural elements of the dramaturgy.

6 There are mainly two Russian schools that claim the centrality of Action Analysis as a valid method for staging. The Leningrad school, developed at the State Institute for Theatre, Music and Cinema (LGITMiK) by Gueorgi Tovstonogov, and the Moscow school, whose main theorist was Maria Knebel herself. The main difference between them is the role of the *études* in the process. While in the Leningrad school *études* are but a helping device, often done around surrounding themes to

the play, in the Moscow school *études* are the central procedure of the rehearsal, always done with the dramatic material itself.

7 *Experiencing* here and throughout the article follows Jean Benedetti's translation of the Russian *perezhivanie* in Stanislavsky's *An Actor's Work* (2008).

8 On 4 June 1938 Stanislavsky says the following when preparing his group of assistant-pedagogues: "Now I don't have any programme. The *Narkompros* has entrusted us to start to work without a programme, and put an immense responsibility in our hands. We are to create a programme" (KS21138).

9 Professor Maria Shevtsova was the first to use the Bourdieusian category of *habitus* to explain the cauldron of cultural, poetic, religious and daily practices shared by the late 19th-century Russian intelligentsia, and it played an important role in the development of Stanislavsky's thought. According to Loïc Wacquant, the *habitus* for Bourdieu is "the way society becomes deposited in persons in the form of lasting dispositions, or trained capacities and structured propensities to think, feel, and act in determinate ways, which then guide them in their creative responses to the constraints and solicitations of their extant milieu." ("Habitus", p. 318). To Professor Shevtsova's use of *habitus* and Stanislavsky's thought, see her book *Rediscovering Stanislavsky*.

10 All the citations from archival material are given in the following manner: the two first letters of the collection in which the document is, followed by its number. Here, KS (from Konstantin Stanislavsky) and the number 21147.

11 In the practical terms of Action Analysis, the play's *event* is generally split into two *events*, to create the necessary and all-encompassing tension required for dramatic action. The first is the *departure event*, the event from which all dramatic action departs. The second, the *fundamental* or *main event*, is the event at the end of the play, the event that ceases all the contradictions sparked by the *departure event*.

References

Afonso, N. (2019) *Dia da consciência negra: números expõem desigualdade racial no Brasil*. Available at: https://lupa.uol.com.br/jornalismo/2019/11/20/consciencia-negra-numeros-brasil/

Almeida, S. (2019) *Racismo estrutural* [Structural Racism]. São Paulo: Pólen.

Floyd, K. (2009) *Reification of Desire: Toward a Queer Marxism*. Minneapolis: University of Minnesota Press.

Knebel, M. (1982) *O deistvennom analize piesy i roli* [On the Active Analysis of the Play and the Role]. Moscow: Iskusstvo.

Lukacs, G. (1978) *The Ontology of Social Being*. London: Merlin Press.

Marques, G. (2018) *Globo, Record e SBT têm, em média, apenas 8% de atores negros em novelas*. Available at: https://tvefamosos.uol.com.br/noticias/redacao/2018/05/16/globo-record-e-sbt-tem-em-media-apenas-8-de-atores-negros-em-novelas.htm

Moschkovich, D. (2021) *O último Stanislávski em ação: Ensaios para um novo método de trabalho* [The Late Stanislavski in Action: Experimenting on a New Method]. São Paulo: Perspectiva.

Muñoz, J. E. (1999) *Disidentifications: Queers of Color and the Performance of Politics*. Minneapolis: University of Minnesota Press.

Novitskaia, L. (1984) *Uroki vdokhnoveniya* [Lessons of Inspiration]. Moscow: VTO.

Shevtsova, M. (2020) *Rediscovering Stanislavsky*, 1st edn. London: Cambridge University Press.

Stanislavsky, K. (1935–1938) *Class Stenograms from the Opera-Dramatic Studio (1935–1938)*. (The Konstantin Stanislavsky Fund). Moscow Art Theatre Museum Archives.

Stanislavsky, K. (1957) *Sobranie Sochinenii v 8mi tomakh. Tom 4. Rabota nad roliu.* [Collected Works in 8 Volumes. Volume 4. The Work on the Role]. Moscow: Iskusstvo.

Stanislavsky, K. (2008) *An Actor's Work.* London: Routledge.

Tcherkasski, S. (2016) *Stanislavsky and Yoga.* London: Routledge.

Wacquant, L. (2005). "Habitus", in *International Encyclopedia of Economic Sociology.* London: Routledge.

4

EMOTION MEMORY VERSUS PHYSICAL ACTION

Towards Anti-racist Pedagogies that Make Way for Critical Praxis

Evi Stamatiou

Introduction

The resurgence of social movements such as Me Too and Black Lives Matter has prompted scholars and practitioners to investigate social inequalities in actor training and develop decolonising and decentering pedagogies. Anti-racist pedagogies address how what Konstantin Stanislavsky calls "the art of representation" (2008, p. 22) works with and against social representations that are implied in texts used for actor training, manifested by actors during the process of training and facilitated by actor trainers in the studio. The manifestations can be categorised as problems with underrepresentation, sometimes even absence, of the Global Majority in scripts and studios, but also problems with misrepresentation when actors, through their art, reproduce historical stereotypes and narratives.

Stanislavsky training problematises representations because it assumes that "human nature is universal and that the essence of acting is to uncover the human spirit, to bring out the universal in the specifics of human life" (Thompson, 2003, p. 128). Debbie Thompson continues:

> The way the actor's emotions and identities are experienced, then, will (in a post-structuralist model) be very much embedded in the ideological situations of the actors, but will be presented as 'impulsive,' 'instinctive,' 'natural,' 'the truth of human nature.' Naturalism, in other words, naturalises ideology.
>
> *(Ibid., p. 129)*

In light of this quote, the ethics and effectiveness of post-Stanislavsky approaches for anti-racist pedagogies become a matter of how and to what

DOI: 10.4324/9781003330882-6

extent actors (and writers and trainers) have internalised white supremacy as "natural", and whether methods of representation invite them to acknowledge and address this.

Writers, actors and trainers affect representations, often unintentionally. Pierre Bourdieu's concept of the *habitus* illuminates how individuals might unconsciously perpetuate dominant ideologies during their interactions, including acting. Most commonly understood as "the internalisation of externality and the externalisation of internality" concerning how individuals embody biases (Bourdieu in Wacquant, 1989, p. 26), an individual's *habitus* is "a system of structured, structuring dispositions" that "is constituted in practice and is always oriented towards practical functions" (Bourdieu, 2008, p. 52). All actions are a result of the *habitus*, which derives from an individual's family and schooling (Ibid., p. 50), which is also true for acting and actor training. In the context of theorising the logic of human actions and practices, Bourdieu writes that biases "generate and organise practices and representations that can be objectively adapted to their outcomes without presupposing a conscious aiming at ends" (Ibid., p. 53). This suggests that the reproduction of stereotypical representations in training and performance results from the unconscious dispositions that writers embody and manifest in the narratives and characters of their scripts, that actors embody and manifest in their characterisation choices, and that trainers or directors embody and manifest in their practices and interventions.

In bringing Bourdieu's concept to performance studies thinking, Harvey Young writes that "racial assumptions" are embodied by Black people as "acts of violence" which, among other things, shape "social behaviour or everyday social experiences (black *habitus*)" (2010, p. 5). Black *habitus* "allows the black body to be singular (black) and variable at the same time", and "allows us to read the black body as socially constructed and continually constructing its own self" (Ibid., p. 20). In his later writing, Young more explicitly links Bourdieu's concept to racial identity as a combination of biases "as well as the choices that a person makes concerning how he self-identifies and how he treats others" (2013, p. 14). Young is optimistic in stressing that "although it can be difficult to not embrace or, more strongly, to reject the beliefs, practices, and expectations of the group [that has raised an individual], resistance is possible" (Ibid.). This suggests that actors can resist the reproduction of racial stereotypes through a process similar to what Young describes as "critical consideration of the experiences of racial interpellation, socialisation, and habitus" (Ibid., p. 67), and ultimately create progressive representations.

To understand how such critical consideration is possible in the studio and can result in progressive racial representations, it is useful to consider bell hooks' drawing on Paulo Freire to discuss Black resistance against racial assumptions as a self-liberating learning process that is two-faceted: it is triggered at an "historical moment when one begins to think critically about the self and identity in relation to one's political circumstance", and is completed with "verifying in praxis what we know in consciousness" (1994, p. 47). This suggests that anti-racist pedagogies for Stanislavsky training should facilitate a journey that invites the student-actor's critical awareness of racial assumptions within the studio, and manifest such awareness in making character choices that represent social justice.

The first part of this chapter uses the *habitus* to critically analyse how two often oppositional devices – emotion memory and physical actions – problematise anti-racist pedagogies. The second part of the essay uses the *habitus* to reflect on exploring emotion memory in a training studio influenced by Yevgeny Vakhtangov, Stanislavsky's colleague at the Moscow Art Theatre and proponent of "fantastic realism". Throughout, the essay illuminates post-Stanislavsky thinking concerning how the studio can bring the unconscious dispositions of the actor to consciousness and help the actor to create progressive social representations.

I should preface the body of this chapter by stating that I am a white, middle-class, cisgender, straight, abled female. I was born and raised in Greece as a second-generation refugee before migrating to the UK. I am grateful as a practitioner-researcher to be given space in this volume. We know Global Majority authors are underrepresented in academia, and I hope the field offers increased opportunities moving forward. I also hope the representation of Global Majority authors in this book shows progress since hooks stated, almost 30 years ago, that critical pedagogies have been primarily the concern of white people (Ibid., p. 9). I recognise that my positionality as a white woman might be seen as problematic, so I invite the reader to engage with my work in critical friendship, as hooks suggests when referring to Freire (Ibid., pp. 49–50), a white pedagogue committed to decolonisation. Since 2010, I have been training actors in the UK, within diverse groups with multiple and intersecting identities, dominant and dominated, protected and unprotected, and visible and invisible. Such complex environments frame, inform and develop my allyship and complicity (Clemens, 2017) with the Global Majority.

Tackling White Supremacy: Emotion Memory versus Physical Action

Because the various training processes of emotion memory and physical action involve actors, writers and trainers in different ways, the use of the *habitus* to unpick them can illuminate how the two approaches problematise race differently and help relevant interventions develop. A big debate among Stanislavsky teachers of the Western world is whether acting processes that prioritise emotion memory, such as those from earlier Stanislavsky, Vakhtangov, Richard Boleslavsky and Maria Ouspenskaya, and Lee Strasberg, are less effective and ethical compared to approaches that build on physical action, such as those from later Stanislavsky, Maria Knebel, Sonia Moore, Sharon Marie Carnicke, Bella Merlin and Nick Moseley.

The essence of the difference between the two approaches is described in Stella Adler's quote in favour of physical action:

> To go back to a feeling or emotion of one's own experience I believe to be unhealthy. It tends to separate you from the play, from the action of the play, from the circumstances of the play, and from the author's intention.
>
> *(Soloviova et al., 1964, p. 143)*

Adler comments on the actor's well-being, but she also identifies that acting processes that utilise emotion memory draw on the actor's own experience, which, according to Bourdieu, results in predisposed decisions concerning character behaviours and reactions. Predisposed and individualised, the actor's social representations might be different or even conflictual with the play's world, actions and circumstances, which ultimately reflect what the author intended or how they imagined social representations on stage. According to Bourdieu, the author's intentions and suggested social representations are affected by their social dispositions. So Adler's quote implies that the author's social dispositions should be prioritised over the actor's social dispositions, which is better achieved using Stanislavsky's Method of Physical Actions. Ultimately, the merging of the dispositions of the writer and actor is expressed through the imagination, the voice and the body of the actor with the purpose of what has been described as helping "[s]pectators learn about the characters on stage" (Moore, 1984, p. 33). Therefore, with emotion memory processes, the audience's learning is more affected by the actor's social dispositions, rather than the writer's, whereas with physical actions it is the opposite.

The key elements of the Method of Physical Actions can be understood from Stanislavsky's rehearsal room, where "[a]ctors analysed the events and investigated the psycho-physical behavior of the characters on stage, in action" (Ibid., p. 47). By psycho-physical, Moore means that "[i]nstead of forcing an emotion before going on stage, the actor fulfils a simple, concrete, purposeful physical action which stirs the psychological side of the psycho-physical act, thus achieving psycho-physical involvement" (Ibid, p. 19). To achieve this, "before and after physical action, the student must use gestures of the body in order to project mental processes, such as thoughts, feelings, decisions, evaluations, attitudes" (Ibid., p. 22). The main difference between the two approaches is whether the actor has consciously tried in their imagination to associate their experience to the role prior to engaging in études, by which I mean improvisations on the given circumstances and beats of a play not for the purposes of performance but as a rehearsal process "purely for the actors to understand something for themselves" (Stephenson in Dunne, 2015, p. 185). So if we are looking at the racial representations that the audience sees, the difference is whether they have been created through études initiated by the actor's personal affinity to the role and scene (inside out) or by what is suggested by the author in the script, to which the actor responds emotionally (outside in). This suggests that there is a more conscious inclusion of the actor's social experience and dispositions, or *habitus*, in emotion memory approaches, which decenters the rehearsal process from the play and the writer's dispositions.

Often scripts internalise white supremacy in complex ways, and various representation tests have been developed to tackle the reproduction of stereotypes (Wide Angle Media, 2020). If the texts are the main problem, then the actors should be encouraged to scrutinise and resist "the action" and "the circumstances" of a text, as well as "the author's intention", all of which might reproduce the author's racial biases. So a first assessment using the *habitus* suggests that approaches that draw on emotion memory are less problematic for anti-racist pedagogies than approaches that draw on physical actions because the actor can resist the unconscious biases of the writer.

The *habitus* of the trainer or director is also less central in emotion memory approaches. For Stanislavsky, emotion memory invites the actor to use their experience, or *habitus*, creatively to bring "a logical, truthful [...] genuine [...] physically embodied" (Stanislavsky, 2008, p. 196) approach to a dramatic character. This quote implies an appreciation of acting decisions that draw on the real experience of the actor, with little room for questioning whether such decisions are truthful because they have been experienced before. When at the later stages of his work he describes the Method of Physical Actions, Stanislavsky implies a stronger intervention from the director's or trainer's *habitus*:

> a new approach to the role that involves reading the play today, and tomorrow rehearsing it on stage [...] Everyone can act this, guided by their own life experience. So, let them act. And so, we break the whole play, episode by episode, into physical actions. When this is done exactly, correctly, that it feels true and it inspires our belief in what is happening on stage, then we can say that the line of the life of the human body has been created [...]
>
> *(Stanislavsky in Carnicke, 2009, p. 194)*

The invitation to the actor to embody their "own life experience" is scrutinised by the director's assessment concerning whether "it feels true and it inspires our belief in what is happening on stage" (Ibid.). Once more, emotion memory approaches feel more ethical concerning race because the individual actor is less dominated by the writer's representations and also the director's assessment of what is "exact" and "correct" in acting choices.

This indicates that emotion memory-inspired pedagogies are more decentered, and therefore liberating because they are less likely to impose the writer's and director/trainer's potentially problematic dispositions. However, the *habitus*, or the unconscious dispositions, of the actors can also problematise race. So anti-racist pedagogies need to develop ways to address the dispositions of all participants. Therefore, to decolonise actor training studios, individual actors need to process their racial assumptions during the processes of shaping characterisation decisions, alongside critically addressing the racial assumptions embedded in the texts and in the training methodologies.

The decentering of the classroom and the bringing of unconscious dispositions to consciousness were pioneered by Freire's *Pedagogy of the Oppressed* (1996), which considers that critical consciousness in adult education and active engagement with their political, social and economic frustrations can help individuals take action to improve their reality. The potential of emotion memory to bring oppressive structures to consciousness can be extracted from Sanford Meisner's criticism of Strasberg's work that "all artists are introverted because they live on what's going on in their instincts, and to attempt to make that conscious is to confuse the actor" (1987, p. 59). Meisner implies that when unconscious experience and the behaviours related to it – the two of which comprise the *habitus* – are brought to consciousness the actor will lose the focus on the script and rehearsal room and turn their attention to their own experience, which might be unproductive for the aims of a director or a specific production.

As part of a holistic training process that combines critical consciousness with well-being (hooks, 1994, p. 17), if what is brought to consciousness relates to the student actor's frustrations concerning oppressive experiences and behaviours then such processing can be productive towards taking the kind of action that improves social representations on stage. Freire decentered the classroom by reframing the teacher as a facilitator of "student *conscientizacao*", which "refers to learning to perceive social, political, and economic contradictions, and to take action against the oppressive elements of reality" (1999, p. 3). Depending on techniques employed, actor trainers can consider how their studios invite actors to acknowledge how their *habitus* shapes acting decisions and invite them to engage in processes to develop acting decisions that mobilise biases towards decolonisation. And because the *habitus* is fluid, by which I mean it changes through life experience, actor training can develop actors to embody improved representations of marginalised communities throughout their acting careers.

To explore in the studio how emotion memory invites acknowledgement of the *habitus* and prepares the ground for manifesting such new awareness, the next section narrows the focus to one emotion memory approach and one physical actions approach and reflects on my embodied experience in specific training contexts. The following part of the essay exploits my reflections on acting practice and therefore involves a phenomenological approach. It is a preliminary investigation that will benefit from further practice research explorations to corroborate and enrich its findings. My narrative and reflection invite post-Stanislavsky trainers to associate my insights with their own practices and utilise them towards anti-racist pedagogies.

Emotion Memory and Critical Consciousness

Strasberg's Method is well-known for prioritising emotion memory in the approach that he developed at the Actors Studio in New York City. The words "emotion" and "memory" have been associated primarily with psychology. My use of a sociological lens to reflect on the actor's feelings as a result of previous dispositions and social interactions highlights an alternative approach to studying and developing that part of Stanislavsky's "system". My experience of training in the Method with Andreas Manolikakis from the Actors Studio and consequent application of such embodied knowledge in an étude within a different context indicates an opportunity for the actor to acknowledge inherited dispositions and develop progressive representations.

Because my experiences reflect my positionality as a white woman, this part of the essay can be seen as inherently flawed, similar to what hooks describes as "unclean water" concerning Freire's work (1994, p. 50). I offer my experience of gender in this instance as one way to apply the work I propose. I do not intend to conflate a gender experience with a racial experience. There are intersections but there is no equivalence, and space should be left for the lived experiences of Global Majority actors. If the reader chooses to dismiss the rest of the essay, I invite you to draw on your own resources to investigate the possibility of the Method prompting an acting process that facilitates critical consciousness and critical action against oppressive social structures. I believe studios should proactively offer protection to prevent Global Majority students from experiencing re-traumatisation in relation to racial oppression. In this context, it is, of course, dependent on the experiences and desires of the Global Majority actor to engage with or avoid memories associated with identity, family and racial injustice. Ideally, such an investigation should be enriched with processes that facilitate reflexivity that sustains the well-being of trainees, which was not a priority in the studio of Manolikakis that I discuss here.

The bringing to consciousness of embodied oppressive structures resonates with Stanislavsky's main goal "to cultivate in students, abilities and qualities which help them to free their creative individuality – an individuality imprisoned by prejudices and clichés" (Zakhava in Malaev-Babel, 2011, p. 23). Stanislavsky neglected the investigation of his system's potential to develop actors in the studio in favour of facilitating characterisation during the direction of plays in rehearsal rooms and on stages. Nikolai Demidov observes: "If [Stanislavsky] did practice pedagogy, he only did so in the course of rehearsals, in passing: it was done to help the actor bring to life a particular moment of the role ... He never taught School – there was no time ..." (in Malaev-Babel, 2011, p. 8). The potential of the "system" to liberate the students from their embodied dispositions has been left in the hands of post-Stanislavsky tutors.

Among other complexities of isolating and studying parts of the "system", is that the several variations of practices have been also tacitly informed by the previous training of post-Stanislavsky tutors and from associated historical moments. Demidov observes:

> As for the teacher's work, sometimes it brought good results sometimes bad ... Why? ... in the case of the teacher's failure, no one ever asked the question: perhaps, the imperfection of the method is to blame? And in the case of success ... perhaps the teacher, except for using the established methods, also used some other methods of their own, sometimes without noticing it?
>
> *(Ibid., p. 8)*

My use of the *habitus* retrospectively to reflect on practice investigates how the specific professional development studio of Manolikakis facilitated my critical consciousness as an actor. Throughout the training, Manolikakis repeated Stanislavsky's quote that "Vakhtangov teaches the 'system' better than me" and Strasberg's advice to his students that "Vakhtangov is there, in his books waiting to answer your questions" (Manolikakis, 1996, p. 13). So my training in 2008 both enacted and invited a critical engagement with Vakhtangov's writings. For my retrospective reflection, I reviewed old notebooks and I corroborated my memories from the training with fellow actors-participants through phone and social media conversations.

The Actors Studio developed from the acting processes of Stanislavsky's "best student", Vakhtangov, and prides itself to be a studio instead of a rehearsal room or stage, where "actors are free to develop privately without the glare of commercial pressures", in a "safe environment to stretch and grow their talents" (The Actors Studio, n.d.). The main criticisms against the Method concern how it invites the actor to work with their imagination in ways that draw on personal experience and use those associated behaviours in characterisation. My training with Manolikakis in the summer of 2008 in Athens focused solely on how the actor can draw on emotion memory for characterisation, without any movement or voice training. The four-week workshop was addressed to professional actors. The classes were delivered in the empty auditorium of the theatre of Moraitis School and involved a weekly showing of work-in-progress on the proscenium stage. The actor was invited to graft their personal experience onto the text of a duologue that they had been assigned. The training day was broken down into two parts: emotion memory exercises and scene study during which the emotion memory exercises were enacted in études.

The first part of the session involved recurring concentration and relaxation exercises. The actor sat on a chair with their eyes closed and used their imagination to release any tension from their bodies until they reached a fully relaxed state. Manolikakis instructed tasks such as "release your left foot" but the process gradually became individualised and independent. When the actors were fully relaxed, Manolikakis invited the visualisation of imaginary scenarios. He always narrated a miserable scenario, which the actors would gradually personalise in their imagination to move themselves to tears.

For example, a scenario invited me to remember the last big holiday in my family home in detail from smells, sounds, objects and a particular focus on "the person who loves me most in the world", and then returned me to the home during a future holiday when something was eerie and the person "who loves me most" was crying. Towards the end of the narration, it was revealed that I had died and they were mourning me, and I was invited to articulate the last words that I would tell the "person who loves me most". After the end of the narration, we were given time to explore the sense memories in our imagination again, observe what moved us most and try to reproduce the emotional distress.

During our independent time, we were expected to invent scenarios that would be productive for our duologue. Vakhtangov describes how such exploration of past experiences could trigger the activation of the character with a push of a button:

> An actor seeks within himself the feelings that he needs to experience in order to bring to life the character. He discovers in his soul the buttons he can push to evoke these feelings. Each actor's buttons are individual … Everyone knows for himself what combination of factors he must proceed from in order to experience certain feelings at a given moment, and what button, known to him alone, he needs to push for that. As an actor digs deeper into his role, the number of these buttons gradually diminishes, until the artist can finally control his feelings through one combined button. In one push, he can evoke the entire range of his character's feelings and live his character's life.
>
> *(in Malaev-Babel, 2011, p. 105)*

During our weekly showing of an étude, we would assess in the studio whether this button had been discovered or not. In the early improvisations, we used our own words after studying the scene at home but without learning the lines. We would get feedback from Manolikakis about what was working and then gradually substitute our text with the text of the playwright. We were encouraged to use a personal object in the scene that would provoke an emotional response. This process would help with grafting our personal experience onto the text.

During these four weeks, I visualised myself in various tragic narratives. The process of my imagination involved substituting the characters from Manolikakis's scenario with people from my own life experience to explore what might be a sense memory that triggers emotional distress. Manolikakis's scenarios were not the same every day, which helped me recognise the types of narratives that moved me more. Because of the emotional intensity required, I mainly visualised close family members and recalled relevant interactions. I gradually developed an ability to activate sense memories, such as images and sounds that concerned the interactions. I was surprised to discover that I couldn't always predict what moved me and I was relieved that these explorations were never discussed or shared in the studio.

As the days moved on, I observed a subtle pressure from such narratives to cry at the thought of a family member dying. But my relationships with my family were much more complex and what made them vivid were the conflicts, the disappointments, the manipulations and the oppressions. The grief that I manifested during the exercises seemed to derive from a combination of self-pity for the unfair behaviours that I tolerated in these relationships and, most importantly, of mourning the close relationships that I wished I had experienced instead. Towards the end of the four weeks, I noticed a pattern in my explorations: most conflicts and disappointments derived from expectations concerning my role as the daughter of the family. Aggressive and microaggressive behaviours were shaping me according to patriarchal narratives. This realisation of my positionality as a woman in the family, school and broader social network brought my *habitus* to consciousness.

Returning to hooks' suggestion that a self-liberating learning process starts with a "historical moment when one begins to think critically about the self and identity in relation to one's political circumstance" (1994, p. 47), the Global Majority actor's renewed awareness could be a result of browsing through their memories in search for the most appropriate experience that could be grafted onto a duologue. The focus on the actor's task can create a critical distance. Such distance would have been difficult to achieve in Strasberg's studio because of vocabularies such as "Freudian sense" and "therapeutic value in art" (Cohen, 2010, p. 28) that guided actors towards a psychoanalytical processing of past experiences rather than a sociological one. For example, during an emotion memory exercise, Strasberg observes that a female actor "seemed to be in conflict or in contradiction with what she was trying to will herself to do", and interprets her frustration as a result of her father's wordings that "women actors are 'all tramps' and that she should '[…] at least sit ladylike'" (1987, pp. 99–100). From a sociological perspective, this actor is frustrated because her father enacted unconscious biases against women and against actors. The "conflict" and "contradiction" that Strasberg observed is a result of confronting oppressive systems in the relationship and body of a "loved one". The personal relationship is exposed as a relationship of power, which confuses the actor but at the same time reveals their *habitus* to them.

This confusion can be understood through Bourdieu's suggestion that "when the *habitus* encounters a social world of which it is the product, it finds itself 'as a fish in water', it does not feel the weight of water and takes the world about itself for granted" (in Wacquant, 1989, p. 43). When the actor fails to cry during a Method exercise that invites them to imagine that a family member is dead, and even if they cry as a result of feelings more complex than grief, they find themselves as fish out of water. This experience can activate the historical moment of the Global Majority actor reflecting on embodied racial assumptions, and the struggle against what hooks describes as "the colonising process and the colonising mind-set" (Ibid., p. 46). The acknowledgement of constructing their identities "in resistance" (Ibid.) invites actors to consider how their progressive characterisation choices become what hooks describes as "my right as a subject in resistance to define my reality" (Ibid., p. 53). Progressive social representations on stage can contribute to an anti-racist reality.

I recognise that the awareness of identity in resistance to white supremacy and the burden of decolonising scripts and stages can be taxing for the student-actor and should be only part of a holistic pedagogy that prioritises well-being. hooks writes:

> [m]any of the issues that we continue to confront as black people – low self-esteem, intensified nihilism and despair, repressed rage and violence that destroys our physical and psychological well-being – cannot be addressed by survival strategies that have worked in the past.
>
> *(1994, p. 67)*

Such issues become even more complex if we consider intersectional identities, as extensively accounted for in hooks' work. Because actors from the Global Majority might encounter traumatising issues during emotion memory training, anti-racist pedagogies need to be developed to facilitate the two-faceted learning process of critical consciousness and critical praxis as part of a learning trajectory that supports individualised physical, psychological and spiritual well-being.

Anti-racist pedagogies that focus on emotion memory are invited to resist Strasberg's often patronising and exposing tactics and exploit Vakhtangov's writings that encourage a sociological assessment of the human experience. Vakhtangov aimed to "strip away the mask people wear in everyday life and to break through to the true, secret human" (Malaev-Babel, 2011, p. 38). This implies a studio that invited social processing to liberate the actor from oppressive systems. Vakhtangov's acknowledgement of "social masks" (in Ibid., p. 40) implies an understanding of social power. His observation that "a social moral that comes with the mask protects [people] from any doubts and inner struggles" (in Ibid.) resonates with the feeling of a "fish in water" when the *habitus* is validated. In Vakhtangov's characterisation,

> only a character who has the courage to shed his or her protective social mask exposes their heart to the ultimate struggle between Good and Evil. By doing so they remain *morally* above the rest of the characters in the play and near the kingdom of ultimate life.
>
> *(in Ibid.)*

This quote implies choice, which resonates with Young's suggestion concerning the black *habitus* that "individuals choose whether to accept and adopt the beliefs and perspectives that surround them" (2013, p. 14). To facilitate such courageous choices in the studio, Vakhtangov "continually designed situations that caused his characters, and subsequently the actors, to shed their skin and bare their nerves. At such moments, both characters and actors were forced to lose their masks and live their hidden, 'essential' life" (Malaev-Babel, 2011, p. 38). This process invites the actor to recognise what is meaningful for them, through the exploration of "what button, known to him alone, he needs to push" for the purposes of characterisation (in Ibid., p. 105), leading to a transformation "by the power of their inner impulse" (in Ibid., p. 211). This resonates with what hooks describes as "engaged pedagogy" that facilitates meaningful learning (1994, p. 19). In actor training, this can mean connecting characterisation processes with the Global Majority actor's life in meaningful ways, including their racial experience. Even though not fully realised, Vakhtangov's characterisation processes could facilitate explorations of racial assumptions and aim at bringing these to consciousness to achieve meaningful – and progressive – representations.

Even though Vakhtangov was not aware of the family's role in shaping the actor's unconscious dispositions in a Bourdieusian sense, the private exploration of family memories invites actors to draw such links. The effort to recall memories should be led by an investigation of "the 'what for' behind [each exercise]. [The tutor] cannot give an answer to this question, as everyone, in time, should discover his own answer" (in Malaev-Babel, 2011, p. 88). In this manner, the actor independently develops their "knowledge of self", which Vakhtangov considers as "[t]he important result of the 'system'" (in Ibid., p. 102). The actor discovers what is meaningful and inspiring to them and links such values to specific experiences and visual stimuli to a level of detail that can be exploited to provide subtext and support internal monologues.

The processing of memories as manifestations of social power within interactions can transform the perspective and attitude of the actor towards oppressive behaviours, which then leads to critical praxis concerning characterisation. Such an opportunity has been observed in Vakhtangov's studio as he "brought an actor's point of view on his or her character into the foreground, foreshadowing the Brechtian principle of 'alienation'" (Ibid., p. 4). The processing of dispositions – or *habitus* – inherited by the family as social masks to be shed invites actors to enact critical praxis in the studio by creating appropriate behaviours for characterisation instead of reproducing oppressive behaviours. An emotion memory studio that "teaches to transgress" oppressive systems in hooks' sense offers room to process how dominant ideologies have shaped the actor through their family and schooling. An inspiring and highly acclaimed actor who interrogates her unconscious dispositions in characterisation and makes critical choices is Viola Davis, who invites young actors to develop the associated "courage" required that is eventually rewarded with life fulfilment (BUILD, 2018, 02:17–3:13). In the context of a holistic process that prioritises the actor's well-being such a studio could inspire resistance to racial assumptions and materialise anti-racist choices in Global Majority characters.

Emotion Memory and Progressive Social Representations

According to hooks, critical consciousness only initiates the self-liberatory process that is complete by individuals "verifying in praxis what we know in consciousness" (1994, p. 47). In the case of the Global Majority actor, this means creating progressive social representations instead of racial stereotypes. Even though the studio of Manolikakis offered me space to explore my *habitus*, I did not find any associations between my experience and the role of Amanda from Tennessee Williams's *The Glass Menagerie* that I was cast in. Vakhtangov explains that "I can make an author's circumstances my own when they are true to me" (in Malaev-Babel, 2011, p. 90) and that "an actor must live with his own passion and 'fall in love with the character'" (Ibid., p. 103). But when a week later I explored the role of Irina from Anton Chekhov's *Three Sisters* during an étude in a different training studio, I observed that the social knowledge of self that was triggered by the emotion memory exercises in the studio of Manolikakis transformed my approach to characterisation.

I will reflect on improvisation around the scene in which Soleni confesses his love to Irina and she rejects him. This exploration happened in the context of a weekly professional development seminar on Stanislavsky's Method of Physical Actions, run by Greek director Stathis Livathinos, a distinguished graduate of the Russian Institute of Theatre Arts (GITIS). Livathinos spends a week reading the play with the cast in the rehearsal room before they move to études. The actors study the play independently to save most of the time for études during the training.

I had studied *Three Sisters* before this particular seminar. Returning to it after the Method training, I noticed an affinity between myself and Irina as a woman who tolerated the aggressive and micro-aggressive behaviours around her during a rite of passage between family life and independent life. According to Vakhtangov, "[i]n art – comprehending is experiencing" (Ibid., p. 96), by which he meant that a character is created from the first reading when the actor connects with a role that "pushes their buttons". Because I recognised myself in Irina, I was "inspired by the material offered by the author" and found the "essence" of Irina in my own inner world, in the sense of understanding the character's tasks in the play "as my own" (Ibid, p. 100). I was assigned a love confession scene between Irina and Soleni, which opens with Irina alone after the mummers have been sent away. The scene pushed another button because, like Irina, I was raised in Orthodox Christianity, which encourages rejoicing on particular calendar occasions such as name days, Sundays and the carnival, and implies that the purpose of a woman is marriage. So I associated Irina with my personal experience in a way influenced by my training on the Method.

During my independent process, I recalled how the carnival affected my interactions with people around me and observed in my memory that the anonymity behind costumes and masks altered the behaviours of people in liberating ways. I visualised putting on a mask to liberate myself from inhibitions, which evolved into a fantasy of calling out the aggressive and micro-aggressive behaviours of the people around me, with a surprising focus on people, especially women, who did not stand up for me or with me. I associated the memory with Irina's circumstances, deprived of the opportunity to express herself without social inhibitions during the carnival, and navigating the disrespectful or unsupportive relationships with the people around her. During another visualisation, I recalled that in my teenage years I was expressing such thoughts and feelings in a diary. When I later realised that my parents were reading it without my consent, I used it deliberately to call them out in ways that I would not have dared face to face. The diary mediated the shedding of my social masks. By containing my anger, it liberated me. To graft the diary experience into an object from Irina's world, I crafted a domino mask which covered only my eyes and the space between them. I imagined that Irina was eager to use the mask during her interactions with the mummers and now was left with it in hand, a contradictory object associated with both joy and disappointment. The first étude was silent, without text. Alone on stage, I put the mask on and looked at the audience of my peers as if in an imaginary mirror. In my imagination, I was substituting all the characters from Irina's world with people from my life looking for associations that would allow the grafting of my personal relationships onto Irina's. I observed which associations established clear and impactful relationships with the characters in Irina's world. I constructed the broad strokes of Irina's internal monologue and fantasised about calling out each one of the people around me/her. When Soleni entered the stage, he interrupted a fantasy of triumph over Irina's oppressors. I confronted and challenged sexist behaviours while I had the mask on, but when I took the mask off I contained my anger as a well-mannered woman. During the scene with Soleni, I followed a trajectory of avoiding, tolerating and eventually rejecting him. The étude got encouraging feedback, especially for the use of the mask before the scene.

I had two days to process my experience and prepare for the presentation of the étude with improvised words. According to Vakhtangov, the creative process itself takes place "in the intervals between rehearsals" when the "subconscious processes the acquired material" (Ibid., p. 111). While working with my associations with my close social environment, I noticed that I was raised to refrain from calling people out, which resulted in repressed anger and self-pity. But the reproduction of such feelings on stage, or experiences of oppression, contradicted Vakhtangov's feeling of joy in an actor/improviser performing a character "with 'an energetic desire' to express, or rather, to create" (Ibid., 109). I realised that my attitude to avoid confrontation was an inherited bias against women that perpetuates patriarchy, which I decided to tackle in my work with Irina. I was excited to transgress the patriarchy with my acting, and experienced pleasure in hooks' sense (1994, p. 7), namely as a liberatory practice. So during the presentation of the spoken étude, I verified my critical consciousness and enacted my new *habitus*: after putting the mask on, I addressed people in the audience as the characters from Irina's world and called them out for how they oppressed me directly or indirectly in making the best decisions for my house, my leisure time, my work and my well-being. When Soleni came in, I did not avoid his presence in my private space or tolerate his romantic advances, as was my first instinct. Instead of the polite attitude that is expected from a well-mannered woman, expressed with my initial sequence of avoidance, toleration and rejection, my attitude changed to a trajectory of dismissing, commanding and humiliating. My personal experience raised the scene's stakes to life and death because the prospect of becoming Soleni's trophy wife dehumanised Irina. The feelings evoked from this attitude combined anger and rejoicing for both the actor and the character. Irina's anger was self-protective from oppressive behaviours and her joy was in commanding people in her house. The actor was joyful in representing women who hold their oppressive environments accountable instead of harming themselves through tolerance and self-pity.

My experience illustrates how emotion memory can support the actor in developing progressive representations independently, privately and quickly. Vakhtangov suggests that "an actor must be an improviser. This is what we call talent" (in Malaev-Babel, 2011, p. 119). My reflection on practice indicates that social self-knowledge through the exploration of the *habitus* could help Global Majority actors develop as improvisers in Vakhtangov's sense. In their imagination and in their own time, actors can develop unique perspectives on a play and character and create anti-racist representations that resist racist experiences and narratives.

Vakhtangov decentered the studio by prioritising the experience of the actor over the author and director, which was clear in his saying that "[w]e don't need characters, characterisations. Everything you have makes up your characterisation; you have individuality – this is your character" (Ibid., p. 21). The liberating potential of an independent acting process is also time-saving: as if a button were pushed, a single étude was sufficient to develop clear and nuanced attitudes against all the characters of Irina's world, which further developed into an anti-patriarchal through-action score that informed both her subtext and inner monologue during the staging of the work.

Most importantly, the grafting of the Global Majority actor's personal experience and anti-racist desire onto a text can hold the writer accountable for the social representations indicated and develops such representations in anti-racist equivalents. Vakhtangov valued the actor in the room, the real human, more than the fictional character in a play, which is implied in his words: "as far as an actor can preserve his own individuality, he must preserve it ... A character must consist of the material that you possess" (Ibid, p. 103). The personally-grafted études of Global Majority actors can juxtapose individualised and localised racist manifestations. The merging of layers of the world of the text and the world of the actor into one character has been described by Vakhtangov as a "method of creative existence" and living "truthfully in a fantastic reality" (Ibid, p. 80). This indicates that the use of emotion memory in improvisations makes way for actors to resist their contemporary realities and enact such resistance in characterisation choices.

Because experiences of social oppression are linked to emotional distress, the invitation to explore the actor's "buttons" is an invitation to social self-analysis which can be exploited to develop progressive racial representations within holistic anti-racist pedagogies that invite critical consciousness and praxis while prioritising well-being. If we reconsider as the core of emotion memory training the development of the actor's meaningful creativity as valuing "the richness of an actor's soul and his ability to reveal this richness" for an audience (Ibid, p. 88), practices can seek to leave space for actors to tackle the stereotypical representations in scripts through grafting their experiences of resistance onto texts.

Conclusion: Making Space for Anti-racist Praxis

This essay has employed Bourdieu's concept of *habitus* to assess the liberatory potential of emotion memory and invites the development of anti-racist pedagogies. It has identified potential in reimagining and reframing Vakhtangov's use of emotion memory in the studio from a sociological, rather than a psychological, perspective to make way for progressive social representations through the development of actors who can independently graft their personal experience onto texts privately and quickly.

The comparative analysis of emotion memory versus physical action-based approaches through the *habitus* demonstrated that both practices problematise race because the writers, actors and trainers involved internalise white supremacy in unconscious ways, which, in turn, affect their contributions to the actor training process. In emotion memory approaches, the starting point for acting decisions is the actor's prior experience, rather than the social representations that are suggested in the script, which reflect the writer's prior experience, or the interventions of a director/trainer. Such a studio is more decentered as it invites the actor to lead in creating social representations through characterisation.

The socially-inclined process implied in Vakhtangov's writing and work resonates with hooks' writings in *Teaching to Transgress* (1994). Vakhtangov's studio leaves room for actors to explore how they embody racial assumptions. Such exploration can bring to critical consciousness how multiple and intersecting identities affect the actor's experience and opens the way for realising how such experience affects characterisation. Drawing on the writings of hooks and Young, this essay indicates Vakhtangov's desire that the actor "ultimately must be a good human being [...] inwardly pure" (in Malaev-Babel, 2011, p. 101) can be fulfilled by supporting the Global Majority actor to acknowledge that their body, voice and imagination have been developed in relation to white supremacy, among other oppressive systems, and verify such awareness in their acting choices. The processing of memories as social experiences reveals the actor as a social agent who can instigate social progress through progressive social representations.

To create socially-inclined characterisation practices, contemporary Stanislavsky-based studios can consider how to develop the actor as a social agent who is offered the time and space to develop both self-knowledge and self-assessment mechanisms that can be used toward meaningful and progressive characterisation. Interventions should invite the actor to resist assumptions and push against the boundaries to challenge racism, sexism, classism and other forms of oppression that they have experienced. My reflection on practice has shown that an affinity with a character can maximise the possibility for a characterisation of resistance and has the potential to contribute to the decolonisation of performances of problematic scripts. More investigation is required into this as part of a holistic approach that protects Global Majority actors from being re-traumatised. Having said that, the use of the *habitus* as a critical lens to reflect on practice and understand how the dispositions of actors, writers and trainers affect the Stanislavsky-based studio can generate awareness and understanding that could be used toward the development of anti-racist pedagogies.

References

Bourdieu, P. (2008) *The Logic of Practice*. Translated from the French by R. Nice. Stanford, CA: Stanford University Press.

BUILD Series (2018) "Viola Davis Urges Young Actors To Ask 'Why?'", 12 November. Available at: https://www.youtube.com/watch?v=JpOtJ7W4boE (Accessed 19 February 2023).

Carnicke, S. M. (2009) *Stanislavsky in Focus: An Acting Master for the Twenty-First Century*, 2nd edn. New York:Routledge.

Clemens, C. (2017) "Ally or Accomplice? The Language of Activism". Available at: https://www.learningforjustice.org/magazine/ally-or-accomplice-the-language-of-activism (Accessed 19 February 2023).

Cohen, L. (ed.) (2010) *The Lee Strasberg Notes*. London: Routledge. doi:10.4324/9780203863138.

Dunne, J. (2015) "Stanislavski on Stage: The Benedetti Legacy", *Stanislavski Studies* 3 (2): pp. 171–201. doi:10.1080/20567790.2015.1079046.

Freire, P. (1996) *Pedagogy of the Oppressed*, rev. edn. Translated from the Portuguese by M. Bergman Ramos. Harmondsworth: Penguin.

Freire, P. (1999) "The Banking Concept of Education", in D. Bartholomae and A. Petrosky (eds), *Ways of Reading*, 9th edn, pp. 1–8. New York, NY: Bedford/St.

Martin's. Available at: https://www.everettsd.org/cms/lib07/WA01920133/Cen tricity/Domain/947/BANKING%20CONCEPT%20OF%20ED.2.pdf. (Accessed 19 February 2023).

hooks, b. (1994) *Teaching to Transgress: Education as the Practice of Freedom*. New York: Routledge.

Manolikakis, A. (1996). "Σημείωμα του μεταφραστή (Translator's Note)", in *Βαχτάνγκοφ: μαθήματα σκηνοθεσίας και υποκριτικής* [The Art of Stage: For the Director and Actor] by N. Gorchakov. Athens: Medousa, pp. 11–15.

Malaev-Babel, A. (ed.) (2011) *The Vakhtangov Sourcebook*. London and New York: Routledge.

Meisner, S. and Longwell, D. (1987) *Sanford Meisner on Acting*. New York: Vintage Books.

Moore, S. (1984) *The Stanislavski System: The Professional Training of an Actor*. London: Penguin.

Soloviova, V., Adler, S., Meisner, S. and Gray, P. (1964) "The Reality of Doing", *Tulane Drama Review* 9(1), pp. 136–155. doi:0.2307/1124785.

Stanislavski, K. (2008) *An Actor's Work*. Translated from the Russian and edited by J. Benedetti. London: Routledge.

Strasberg, L. (1987) *A Dream of Passion: The Development of the Method*. Boston: Little, Brown.

The Actors Studio (n.d.) "Our History". *The Official Site of The Actors Studio*. Available at: https://theactorsstudio.org/who-we-are/our-history/ (Accessed 19 February 2023).

Thompson, D. (2003) "'Is Race a Trope?': Anna Deavere Smith and the Question of Racial Performativity", *African American Review* 37(1): pp. 127–138. doi:10.2307/1512365.

Wide Angle Media (2020) *Media Tests for Diversity and Representation*. Available at: https://www.wideanglemedia.org/blog/media-tests. (Accessed 19 February 2023).

Wacquant, L. J. D. (1989) "Towards a Reflexive Sociology: A Workshop with Pierre Bourdieu", *Sociological Theory* 7(1): pp. 26–38. doi:0.2307/202061.

Young, H. (2010) *Embodying Black Experience: Stillness, Critical Memory, and the Black Body*. Ann Arbor, MI: University of Michigan Press. doi:10.3998/mpub.235634.

Young, H. (2013) *Theatre & Race*. London: Red Globe Press.

5

BREAKING AWAY

Latinidad and Moving Beyond the "System"

Marissa Chibás, Michelle Jasso and Tlaloc Rivas with Siiri Scott

In a candid conversation moderated by co-editor Siiri Scott, Global Majority artists Marissa Chibás, Michelle Jasso and Tlaloc Rivas discuss their experiences in both Latine and intercultural performance spaces, and their individual relationships with Stanislavsky and the "system". The following is an edited transcript of their wide-ranging discussion.

SIIRI SCOTT: Thank you all for your willingness to take part in this conversation. Each of you brings wonderfully unique perspectives as performers, directors and teachers to the discussion. Your viewpoints will be invaluable to us as we interrogate a "system" within a system, both of which have long neglected the needs of BIPOC artists. I am not Latine; I was a cisgendered, female, biracial conservatory student in the United States in the 1980s and 1990s, and I recognize that my experiences were unique to my background and environment. Would you each describe your individual relationships to the "system"? I'm specifically curious about whether multicultural rooms, specifically Latine rooms, are more or less inclined to work within the "system"?

MICHELLE JASSO: This is such a loaded question for me. I will tell you that, in my early days as a performer, I was definitely code-switching before even realizing what that was. Because I am a fair-skinned Latina, I played many white roles throughout my training and through most of my early performance career. It was very difficult for me to break out of that and to find my place – and my voice – as a performer. This is an ongoing struggle, to be honest, but I spent a lot of my training and much of my early career simply not talking about my *Latinidad* at all. So my early relationship with Stanislavsky – and the Method and Sanford Meisner and all these spin-offs of the "system" – is that it was the be-all and end-all.

DOI: 10.4324/9781003330882-7

That's what you did in order to learn your craft as an actor. That was the foundation of what you were doing as an actor. You learn this method and you study your Shakespeare, your Ibsen and your Chekhov. I didn't quite clock at that time – or fully understand – how Eurocentric it all was. I was too young and naive to understand how that was affecting my path as an artist, and it took a very long time for me to sort that out. So my original relationship with Stanislavsky was that it's just what you do. You just adhere to it. It was never questioned. Teachers and directors and producers are going to reference it all the time. And that's the way it is if you want to be an actor.

SIIRI SCOTT: Did you feel as if there was a mandate – either spoken or unspoken – that discouraged you from talking about your ethnicity and culture, in part because your identity did not align with the majority in a Eurocentric classroom?

MICHELLE JASSO: Oh, absolutely. And that was evident in the literature that we were doing, what we were studying, what we were rehearsing, the stories that we were telling. They were not Latine stories. Or if they were, they were Latine stories that were written by white men. We had our *West Side Story* and our *Man of La Mancha*, but we weren't talking about María Irene Fornés or Estela Portillo-Trambley or Nilo Cruz. There was definitely a filter – a viewpoint – that wasn't necessarily true or from lived experience. So, to answer your question, I do believe that there was an unspoken directive. It was understood and supported.

SIIRI SCOTT: Do you remember the story you told yourself in order to reconcile that erasure with your training to be an artist?

MICHELLE JASSO: Yeah.

(Pause).

SIIRI SCOTT: I remember wanting to be cast – and that's all I cared about. However, to be cast you needed to perfect a kind of racial ambiguity, the "white" version of racial ambiguity.

MICHELLE JASSO: Yes.

SIIRI SCOTT: My skin was darker than my classmates, and there was no doubt that I was an "other", so I tried to become the ideal version of the ethnically ambiguous.

MICHELLE JASSO: Yes. And that racial ambiguity gave me value to agents and directors early on in my career. I was "ethnically ambiguous". I told myself that I was lucky to be there and that I needed to just fit in.

SIIRI SCOTT: I think students and actors are still telling themselves that.

MICHELLE JASSO: Oh, yes. I mean, we're taught as actors – we have it drilled into us very early on – how replaceable we are. So, it makes it very, very, very difficult when we even think of having these conversations, especially as a young actor. There is a deep sense that we are replaceable and, therefore, have very little value.

MARISSA CHIBÁS: This is very loaded.

MICHELLE JASSO: It's heavy stuff.

MARISSA CHIBÁS: It *is* heavy stuff. All these emotions started bubbling up as you were both talking about memories. I remember vividly the first time I saw a Latino story, basically seeing myself reflected in a film, when I was 19 years old. I hadn't seen anything other than children's television shows like *The Electric Company* and *Sesame Street* in the US that featured young people of color. Anyway, it was a film called *El Super* by Leon Ichaso and it was huge. I remember just being so emotional, feeling like, "Oh, my God, there's actually a place where I can be in the story." A young Elizabeth Peña played the young girl in that role. (Rest in power, Elizabeth.) But seeing her and seeing this story being told, I was like, "Wow," because I also had the *West Side Story* experience, and that was very different from what this film was. There is no question that there have been advances. There have been so many - in terms of curriculum, in terms of opportunities, in terms of these high-definition cameras that democratized filmmaking in a certain way for new kinds of content to be able to emerge, and in terms of streaming services. I also think normalizing subtitles and multilingual content has opened up a lot in regard to whose stories get to be told and who gets to tell them.

I went to my conservatory training at the State University of New York (SUNY) at Purchase in 1978. My mentor George Morrison taught there at the time, and back then you had the same acting teacher for four years. I was introduced to Stanislavsky and Stanislavsky's books through him. We were taught that if you wanted to be an actor, this was the road to use. I remember, in particular, Stanislavsky's *Building a Character* (2013 [1949]) just opened everything up for me. And this idea of interiority being accessed through external means was amazing. I really responded to the idea that if I put on a coat, it could be a portal to the whole character, the character's world, the character's inner life. However, I did have many times where my experience of human behavior did not fit into what was considered "real". I mean, two people in a room talking was seen as "real" in class, but you could come and visit my Cuban family and you'd see two people in a room right next to each other and *shouting*. It was just the way it was in my experience.

I remember our junior year. We did a Gertrude Stein play. Everybody hated working on this play and I loved it because I felt free. There was something about her work that told me I didn't have to worry about being "real" or whatever somebody's idea of "real" was. I found I was being released from the "system"'s sense of realism and I was able to be fully expressive in a nonlinear way. Gertrude's words opened me up and I found her to be the opposite of what people said. They said, "Oh, she's so intellectual." And I thought, "No, she's hysterically funny." I found her so alive. As a teacher, I've used that material a lot, and I've had students say, "I've never felt more vulnerable on stage. I've never felt more honest."

There's something to this idea of discovering "real". It's a little bit like reality TV – and there's nothing more surreal than reality TV – because the more we try and find reality, the further we get away from reality. I've seen so many actors completely tense themselves up and get so self-conscious by trying to be *real*, rather than actually just experiencing the scene. As a teacher, I'm very aware of bringing all kinds of pathways into the room. Ways of engaging with material and with the imagination, ways that don't limit us to a singular idea of reality.

TLALOC RIVAS: My introduction to Stanislavsky came later than most students or practitioners (midway through college). Reading Anton Chekhov's work led me to his influential collaboration with Stanislavsky and their relationship with the Moscow Art Theatre (MAT), and how their acting methodology came out of it. Once I transitioned from acting to directing, I discovered how there were general "interpretations" of their precepts: a misunderstanding of their work by American artists who visited MAT at the time. What was brought back could be interpreted as "lost in translation" or unscrupulous teachers wanting to stand out from the crowd from what they coined the "system", which really became variants of what we now call the "American Method".

These fundamental building blocks were introduced to me by a number of very sensitive instructors who were acolytes of Sanford Meisner, Stella Adler and the like, and many of them had been through the wringer as actors in New York. So while my acting instructors were introducing me to those methods of building a character, making active choices, understanding dramatic action and so on, they were extraordinarily patient and treated students with care, unlike the kind of abuse they were legendarily subjected to. My teachers also reminded me that this was all about a process and not about finding the right answer. And, although my experience differs from what we often hear about abusive schools, programs, instructors (and the like), it doesn't mean it didn't happen to others – even within my own classes. I'm sure it had a lot to do with the fact that I had privileges as a man, with a majority of these incidents occurring under a power dynamic between male instructors and female students.

Because I was so new to the theatre, I was likely naive to what was happening around me due to the fact that I remember being singularly focused on learning technique. I felt like I was "catching up" all the time because in my mind I was late to all of it. As I entered graduate studies, many of my classmates had been involved in theatre since they were children. I was made to feel like an outsider for asking for so many clarifications of things I supposedly "should have known" already. I had little choice other than to focus on myself – my own interior life and work.

There was a great deal of trial-and-error to hone in on the things that worked for me as an actor and director.

In terms of race and ethnicity, we have to approach the "system" as a series of notes rather than a prescribed "Right Way of Acting". I cannot tell you the number of syllabi I have collected that contained sexist or racially offensive terms. Is it possible to decolonize the "system"? Sure, but it's going to take a really deep dive into what, where and how Stanislavsky got his ideas, which may have been appropriated from other cultures and civilizations where theatre and ceremony were part of an artistic and civic life.

In my heart, I knew there was more to acting than just the "system", Meisner and Shakespeare. In the middle of college, I began an apprenticeship with El Teatro Campesino, which was founded in 1965 by Luis Valdez, and was introduced to their training called Theatre of the Sphere. It had a very clear, cultural connection to ancient Mayan philosophy along with a physical training that had some connection with commedia dell'arte. It was so freeing to be able to explore all of it, and it was an experience that unlocked how performance can be created from the neck down.

It also made me think about why American acting is so fixated on the psychological in the "system" as opposed to unlocking some of the other things that are underutilized in terms of gesture or physicality. When I went to the University of Washington, they had successfully integrated Tadashi Suzuki's training[1] and Stanislavsky, which seems like it would be at odds with one another. But it finally started to connect for me then. I needed that grounding in order to embrace Stanislavsky. Three years of that completely changed how I directed my classmates and professional actors. It also unlocked how I approached modern classics like Chekhov, Henrik Ibsen, Tennessee Williams, August Strindberg and others, but it also helped me unlock plays that would allow for me to experiment with non-Western approaches to my projects.

SIIRI SCOTT: Marissa, both you and Tlaloc have talked about bringing in multiple modalities for students. My sense is that if we don't offer options, we limit the students to one way of working. We *implicitly* suggest there is only one path. However, if we suggest there are multiple paths to the work, a metaphorical corridor with multiple doors, and tell students, "Hey look at all these doors! There is more than one way into the material," then the work becomes more accessible for individual students. I'm wondering if any of you can speak to experiences you've had – or have seen – when you've watched an actor try to work within the "system" with little or moderate success, but blossom when offered an alternative modality?

MARISSA CHIBÁS: Oh, yes. I tell this story a lot to my students, but there was an actress I was working with who was doing a production of Bertolt

Brecht's *The Good Person of Sichuan*, and she came to me as her mentor. She said, "You know, I'm having such trouble in rehearsal. I have this thing that I'm using that is so painful. I'm offstage, I'm crying about it. It's a really tough thing in my life. And as soon as I get on stage, it all stops." And I said to her, "Well, I guess your body's really telling you something. Your body is saying, 'Don't use this'." And we worked together on finding a method that worked for her.

You know, I really believe in the power of the imagination, and I really believe in empathy, and I really believe in imagining stepping into somebody else's shoes. But I have found, personally, as an actor witnessing certain things in acting classrooms, and then later as a teacher, how harmful this idea of "anything about me is up for grabs" as a performer is. It's not healthy, it's not sustainable and it's ultimately not going to get us the best performance because our experiences as performers are going to be limited.

I really believe our art form is all about expanding. Of course, we cannot help but bring ourselves and our personal experiences, but it's also about making a leap outside of what we know into imagining other people, other worlds, and other circumstances. Once we allow that, it's an incredible pathway to take – the pathway of empathy – of putting myself in this person's circumstances. Then, emotionally, there's so much more that can come in, so much more of the emotions, right? It's because we're relying on something our bones know, of all of these stories within us. We retell the same stories in each generation. It's all in our bones, and we know this in a deep sense. If we can access that collective memory, we can really deepen that imagination in connection to our work.

I use archetype work a great deal. The archetype is the opposite of a stereotype. Archetypes are age old personas that live in our bones, and they have no ethnicity, age, culture, ability, or gender. You can be any of those things I just listed and be the hero, right? Any age, any gender, any ability and any *thing*. And there's something about accessing how those archetypes can open up for us and give us permission for those things that we and our personal history may not know about.

TLALOC RIVAS: From the get-go, I was already reading works by Latinx playwrights and other writers of color during my educational training, and it was clear that the "system" wasn't going to be enough to engage in work that was non-realistic in terms of language and theatricality. For example, engaging in a work like María Irene Fornés' *Mud* or *Conduct of Life* requires you to go beyond what Stanislavsky's "system" can provide. Most directors, particularly Anglo ones, approach her work by going naturalistic or dialing up the "hyper-realism", which is a terrible and unimaginative choice prone to abusive demands upon the actor. Yes, her work is deeper and darker than most of her contemporaries. (Fornés had many imitators but no equals.) To approach Fornés, you have to explore archetypes (which are ancient) and you also have to accept her identity as a Cuban immigrant, a lesbian and a generally elusive artist (except when she was teaching playwriting). In *Mud*, many make the mistake of truly avoiding the psychological games they are all playing with one another. Add to that the presence of violence, the sexual depravity, the incomprehensible poverty, and you have a play where literacy is both currency and a threat to the status quo. You must be able to understand all of that before you can even begin to scratch the surface of her work – and that's before you get into how to conceptualize this world.

Encountering the "system" and tying it to work by Latinx playwrights was always a struggle in my classes and in productions – putting those together was always uneasy. My white directors and instructors could only take me so far, which always left me wanting. I know we all feel like we could've done more, but this was different; I wanted to be culturally and spiritually enriched by the experience. And it was disappointing for it all not coming together the way it could have.

What is particularly troubling – and the reason systemic racism still exists – is the idea that only White people are deemed the most qualified to teach across many disciplines in the American theatre. The "system", Viewpoints and even Suzuki are held tightly by acolytes and disciples of particularly notable instructors, and those disciplines are taught by those people, and unfortunately a kind of nepotism exists whereby they exclude those who don't share their Eurocentric cultural background. Unfortunately, some predominately White institutions say, "Our students really need a 'White woman' to teach our predominantly White curriculum and to take on the emotional labor of caring for students' needs."

We're currently losing thousands of instructors around the country – many of them BIPOC or from underrepresented communities – and when you don't give us the resources to succeed, it becomes a vicious circle of students only getting a Western, myopic perspective of what theatre can be. Acting programs must have diversity and inclusion in its ranks, majors, curricula, and programming.

SIIRI SCOTT: While you were talking, Tlaloc, I was thinking about the corridor metaphor I offered earlier. Now I see 50 doors instead of just one. When we include imagination, the corridor expands into a really long hallway with doors everywhere, giving us endless options, yes?

MICHELLE JASSO: Absolutely. And, Marissa, what you said about availability, and this idea that anything that is available emotionally to the actor is considered acceptable, I was thinking about how unsafe that is. It allows for abuse in the room. It allows for abuse from directors and from teachers. The idea that you have to be willing to go anywhere, do anything, bring up any trauma, any pain, if you want to be an actor, or, if you want to actually be a really good actor, you have to be willing to basically bleed on the stage. Nothing is off limits, and that promotes the types of scenarios that, unfortunately, we see happening again and again. Even though we have come so far, and we have had these discussions, and we have had some great change occur, it's still happening. It's still happening because this idea gets fostered in these rooms. It's allowed because of this idea that if you're gonna do this, you have to be willing to go anywhere and do anything.

MARISSA CHIBÁS: Yes, that abuse is real. I've witnessed it and I've experienced it. People will say, "Well, you know, we're playing lovers, so we ought to behave like that offstage." Excuse me. We're pretending. It's called pretend. Any kid in a playground knows the difference. And that's the problem, right?

SIIRI SCOTT: Do you have a sense of whether the abuse is inherent in the "system"? Or if these abuses grew out of the "system"? Is it the hierarchical nature of how it is taught? Or do you have a sense that the problems don't necessarily lie with the "system" itself, but that it's the person teaching the "system" who is, metaphorically, "holding the bomb"?

TLALOC RIVERA: I mean, I was fully aware of how gendered the "system" was. I had a dynamic Meisner teacher, Marcia Taylor, who taught at the University of California, Santa Cruz. In hindsight, she filtered all that toxicity out of the training. She made it her own, which is, I think, what most of us do anyway when you start teaching a particular methodology. You bring what worked for you – or what might work with a particular group in terms of learning objectives – and do it.

This might sound strange, but I had been taught Meisner before encountering Stanislavsky. And it took me a bit to rewire that in my body and my head. That's why fundamentals in the "system" are so important. It's accessible for anyone, but it has to be gradual. Scaffolded. But back to Meisner for a sec: it was bold and exciting, but, inevitably, not right for me at such an early age or limited level of experience. I really leaned into physical and psychological gestures while acting, not only for myself, but also looking for them from my partners. I really needed to "get" in order to "give". And here is where it gets complicated in terms of gender: women's roles (at least through the mid-90s) were generally in service to male protagonists. So women were working doubly hard to "give" based on the material they were getting. And I haven't even begun to touch upon the racial dynamics in plays. Black, Latinx and Asian writers were just starting to turn a corner in terms of recognition and having their work produced.

In terms of my experience as instructor, if my young White actors didn't get praise or accolades from me, instead of taking the note or accepting the challenge of my saying, "Here's what you need to do in order for the work to be better," they would resist or give up and look for validation from their White instructors. It happened a lot when I taught in the Midwest. There were even times when students, who thought they knew more than I did, would run to my senior colleagues and leverage their privilege to get what they wanted. And don't get me started on racially biased student evaluations.

But even with the harm I experienced, I continued to insist that my students' attitude and behavior (subconscious as it was) wasn't going to fly in my classroom and would only hinder their progress. I emphasized that those with a kind, generous and open work ethic would succeed, and that resistance to the work is a road that only leads to frustration and despair.

MICHELLE JASSO: I feel that there are things about the "system" that are great. And I do feel that, in my personal experience, the worst offenses have been in its interpretation. Much like the US Constitution. The Constitution, similarly, was written without the inclusion of certain people in the room.

SIIRI SCOTT: As was the "system", and it was never intended to be used by BIPOC actors.

MICHELLE JASSO: So if those voices weren't present, then how can we possibly be served?

MARISSA CHIBÁS: That's right.

SIIRI SCOTT: Michelle, you've said there are some things about the system that you think are great. Are there some specifics that you can share with us? For example, are there techniques that you return to time and again? If you feel comfortable sharing, I think it might be helpful for practitioners to identify what has been useful to actors.

MICHELLE JASSO: Well, what's coming to mind right now is that I always go back to the truth of living in a moment and finding the lived experience of the moment by pretending to be in the character's shoes. It's what Stanislavsky called the "Magic If". I also look for clues about characters by combing through the text, which is Stanislavsky's "given circumstances". However, it's always *my* interpretation of these ideas, as the text is often not about moments or circumstances created for me or relatable to me as a Latine person. So imagining myself in a Eurocentric character's shoes may be an extra stretch for me, and, depending on the playwright, the given circumstances may not be relatable to me. And "emotional memory" can be extraordinarily difficult. I had to do something else to make it work for me.

SIIRI SCOTT: What did you do?

MICHELLE JASSO: I made it work by putting a similar lived experience into it, which didn't necessarily have anything to do with what I was "supposed" to be doing in that moment.

SIIRI SCOTT: I think it's important that we articulate the reality of your experience in this chapter. There are teachers and practitioners who don't know that BIPOC actors have to do this additional labor, so thank you for bringing it to our attention.

MICHELLE JASSO: Absolutely.

TLALOC RIVAS: For me, specifically, Michael Chekhov's psychological gesture opened up worlds for me – that my body can speak just as loud as my voice. And it didn't have to be huge. It could be the way I slide a piece of paper across a table or a tilt of my head or pulling away from someone: anything that connects to psychic expression of the moment. Personally, it's always been hard for me to facially hide what I'm really thinking. Even when I'm directing, I'm very conscious of exuding the slightest sigh lest the actor thinks I dislike what they're doing in the rehearsal room or on stage.

I was recently watching *Get Back*, the 2021 Peter Jackson documentary about The Beatles, and it was fascinating to watch it as a theatre practitioner. It was all about their very specific process, which was at a crossroads, the evolution of their personalities and how it was beginning to strain them collectively. But they still tried and tried, musically, to find a new harmony or a rhythm or a set of lyrics despite all the outside distractions and growing egos in the room. I'm fascinated by process and how something might work on one project but be entirely terrible for the next. In terms of acting training, we're dealing with a generation of students where metaphor is becoming a difficult concept for them to grasp. It's "real" or it's nothing. And losing that imaginative spark that is required to succeed as an actor will have consequences for the art form. The "system" allows for the hypothetical and abstract to be explored.

MARISSA CHIBÁS: I mentioned earlier that I was excited by Stanislavsky's *Building a Character*, and I described the situation with the actress looking for a way into the work that was healthy. I think the solitary process of finding something external that creates the internal life for you is really useful, and I've taken that idea and let it evolve into different kinds of exercises for students. There's something very universal about, for example, an object that can open up a whole world for someone emotionally, trigger the right memory and all of that.

SIIRI SCOTT: Michelle, when you direct and want to create a rehearsal room or a space for performance, are there any activities or ideas from your own background or culture or family of origin that you bring in and try to incorporate into the space because they were absent from the rooms in which you worked? Rooms, which, as we said, were not intended for you?

MICHELLE JASSO: What a great question! Yes, certainly. I really value true collaboration, not just spoken collaboration. I can't tell you how many times I've been in rooms with directors who have talked about how they want it to be a truly collaborative space and that everyone should have a voice. But they didn't *really* mean that everyone actually has a voice. They meant the voices that were in agreement with the director were welcomed.

SIIRI SCOTT: Those contributors are considered the "good" collaborative voices?

MICHELLE JASSO: Yes, they meant *those* are the collaborative voices they wanted. They did not mean that truly *everybody* should have a say. And when the conversation becomes difficult – and it does because there are, of course, different personality types in the room – and by the simple nature of who you're working with, one person's voice might be stronger than another. It might make someone else in the room feel as though their voice isn't as worthy. So I'm intentional about creating a collaborative environment. I try to meet regularly with everybody individually to make sure everyone knows I value their contribution. We meet one-on-one again and again and again. That way they know I'm going to come back to them multiple times, and they know that we can always have a dialogue. I have found that to be very helpful. I have also found that I get so much more from each individual person by setting up these one-on-one meetings than what I get in the group setting. In addition, I find that, as the process goes on, everybody's voice has become stronger because we've checked in so regularly. In my experience, anytime a director pulled me aside, it was usually negative: I was in trouble, I was doing something that wasn't working for them, it was a problem, and they didn't want to call me out in front of the group. So I actively try to change that dynamic. I have had plenty of experiences where, early on in the process, I have pulled an actor aside and they have that disheartened look on their face, like, "What did I do?" I decided that having one-on-one time can be a positive, reaffirming and supportive act. It doesn't have to be any kind of reprimand.

MARISSA CHIBÁS: I think I do a lot of things that are coming right from my culture. I love to speak in Spanish a lot in class. I'm like, "You're going to know who I am. You're going to learn a little Spanish because you'll be spending some time with me, you know?" We do one thing our first week together to fall in love with the room. I tell them to find different things in the room. Each person can find something that can be the most insignificant thing, like a smudge on the wall or something else, that they fall in love with. And we each go to the thing, our love, and we talk about our love to everybody else. And we open up to each other. I then have them do monologues from that place. And it's very interesting because the monologues come out completely differently than the way they originally practiced them. The students don't feel put on the spot, like, "Now, I'm going to do a monologue for you all." Instead, we do mission/manifesto-building together.

Also, I play music. I play a lot of music from different places. And I talk about ancestors a lot. That's a big part of our work. I feel like a very important part of our work as artists and as people is knowing they (the ancestors) have our back, and that listening to them, following the guidance of the ancestors and listening to those inner voices is necessary. I was recently messaging with a Cuban artist who is actually in Cuba right now. She had taken photographs of these different dressing tables for different shows throughout her career. I've been wanting to make a book about our dressing tables for a long time now because they are *altars*. You learn so much about each performer based on their altar, their dressing table. I don't think I've ever done a show or a film that didn't have an altar in it somewhere. My father was a revolutionary, so, to him, religion was the opiate of the masses. However, later in life, spirituality became more and more important to me, and I now have faith – without an organized religion. So altars are really important to me. Those kinds of practices are important to me.

I think about my very first time in a rehearsal room with all Latino actors and a Latino playwright. It was such a moving experience. It was Eduardo Machado's *The Floating Island Plays* at the Mark Taper Forum in Los Angeles. Everybody was talking, music was playing and we were drinking *cafecitos*, a Cuban coffee drink. It was unlike any other rehearsal room I've ever been in. And I loved it. I loved it. So I try to bring those beautiful elements that I've experienced in these great communal Latinx spaces to my own spaces. Oh, and the Latinx Theatre Conference that recently convened in Boston had an essential central spirituality bringing us all together that was not apologized for. There was no apology for that. Instead, the vibe was "we" are here, the ancestors are with us and we're doing something together. We're not going to apologize for who we are or for what our practices look and sound like. And that was very empowering. I have a sense that has grown since then through decades of doing this that we have a lot of solid ground to stand on from our traditions.

SIIRI SCOTT: I'm hearing you say that these were the rooms that allowed you to bring your *whole* self to this work. These spaces were created for you and welcomed your authentic self. And once you have the experience of being fully yourself in a creative space and find that others value and accept you fully – you are then more your whole self everywhere else. Would you say that you seek out these rooms to find your whole self? I feel like there's a sacred sort of transformation that happens when we can be authentic, feel seen and be accepted. The space nurtures you, fills you up and allows you to ground your work in your truth.

MARISSA CHIBÁS: That's why it's so important. That's why our actors, artists and students have to have those experiences, because it's unlike anything else when they can be in their own truth that way. From then on they know who they are. There's a whole new sacred space that gets created.

TLALOC RIVAS: Civil rights activist John Lewis said, "Make good trouble." And that's what I do. I don't hesitate in terms of what I think will work best with any particular group of students. I'm already unabashedly Chicano. I can't hide who I am. I don't hold anything back in my classroom. I don't sugarcoat that some of the students have advantages over others and that they need to be mindful of that. "And what will you do with that privilege?" I ask. You can replicate the same systems of oppression and keep others down or you can be the one that says, "It ends with me."

While I'm teaching at two different predominantly White institutions in Connecticut, we're not totally invisible. The Northeast is filled with many Latinx immigrants and their descendants, and many of the universities and colleges here have some of the most diverse campuses in the country. I think that's why I appreciate being here – where I am wanted and needed and have access to great theatre in the Northeast region of the US.

On a personal note, as a descendant of Mexican immigrants, you are saddled with the idea to never be indebted to anyone. And that is really hard to shake off, and it keeps many of us from pursuing the arts. And family is a HUGE tether to which the arts isn't necessarily amicable to supporting. Many Latinx students I encounter feel like they have to give up a part of their identity in order to pursue acting – and that's not true at all. Often, the industry says otherwise.

SIIRI SCOTT: You each bring so much to your classrooms and rehearsal spaces. I see your presence in the classroom as a form of activism and is – in itself – a methodology for mitigating harm. As representatives of the Global Majority, trained in the *lingua franca* of the "system", I'm wondering if you were able to reconcile Stanislavsky's "system" with your own positionality or if you had to break away from it?

MARISSA CHIBÁS: In my artistic practices as an actor, writer, filmmaker and teacher, I had to break away. I had to break away and it was very liberating. And that's why I love Fornés and the avant-garde, because I don't have to worry about someone's idea of realism. I can bring all parts of myself unapologetically to the practice.

I have a feature film I'm writing right now that is part of the Sundance Institute feature film development track. It's a narrative. It has its moments of wild imaginings, which I think is absolutely part of Latinx culture and Latin American culture and Spanish culture. I love Federico García Lorca's essays on the *Duende*. Those writings have been really important and influential. In these essays he talks about the importance of claiming our North African heritage, talks about the Spanish claiming different influences, which are very different from northern Europeans. It's a *very* different thing. So, yes, I feel I had to break away from Stanislavsky's "system". And even to this day, as I'm getting notes, and as soon as things are in a straightforward, linear trajectory of storytelling, there's a part of me that goes, "Now I have to put a little wind in here. I need to add a little ordinary wonder," which is what our world is. I don't like the term "magic realism". I feel like saying, "What do you mean, it's *all* magical!" The magical is not just in Latin American countries. It's always present. Just look out the window. It's wondrous, right? Real life is stranger than anything we can imagine. I mean, look at the world we're in. Who could have imagined this?

SIIRI SCOTT: As you were speaking, I started to wonder if we always have to break away from the original "system" in order to become who we're supposed to be?

MICHELLE JASSO: That loops back to what we said before, because the "system" wasn't designed for us, right? So *of course* we must break away. Of course we do.

SIIRI SCOTT: I wonder if it becomes incumbent upon us to start to develop safety mechanisms early in actor training so students still know the "system", the *lingua franca*? I feel like I wouldn't be setting them up for success if they weren't able to communicate with that language, but to make it very clear from the beginning that there are multiple ways to enter the work.

MARISSA CHIBÁS: Yeah, I like that. I do the same thing: "I'm going to talk to you about actions and objectives. We're going to talk about the 'system'. You're going to know that language because there will be people out there who use that language and you need to know it. We're going to talk about operative words. We're going to talk about those things that you're going to hear. But there's the deeper work we're going to do as well." I guess I don't want to throw anything away, you know? What works for me can be very different from what may work for an actor I'm directing or a student I'm guiding, right? It's intuiting what's going to be the best portal for that person. It's just that we need so many more of these doors, like you said, than what I had in my training, which was one door.

SIIRI SCOTT: Michelle, is there anything else you want to add? Was there a point where you felt you either had to continue to bring more Stanislavsky into the room or that you needed to break away from it? Or do you feel like you've allowed it to evolve and/or found an amalgam that is useful for you?

MICHELLE JASSO: In theory, the ideas aren't bad, but I don't think the "system" meant the same thing to Stanislavsky and his peers that it does to us today. And we know it's not about *us*. What it meant to him and what it means to us is different. We can ask the same questions, perhaps, but, in reality, we don't have the same lived experience.

TLALOC RIVAS: It really comes down to this, and Jay-Z said it best: "Let me be great" (2013). I always say that it isn't the training that's the problem, it's who is teaching the training: the naysayers and the gatekeepers that say that acting or Stanislavsky can only be taught "their way". To that I say, "Take your retirement package and leave. You're only upholding systemic discrimination." The art form can only evolve if BIPOC artists and instructors can work and thrive and inspire the next generation of actors and theatre makers without burdening BIPOC instructors with the emotional labor that you so woefully swept into the corner for us to deal with.

There are genres and plays that require you to go beyond realism, and while Stanislavsky emerged from realism, it also provides a template to explore how to perform other genres and experimental work. The thing I'm always after, and this is what the "system" taught me, was to always keep learning, keep reading new texts, search for new ideas, like in Marissa's book *Mythic Imagination and the Actor* (2021), to help find another tool, another key to unlock the actor's imagination. Today's writers are experimenting and creating dynamically challenging work, non-linear work, with characters playing mastiffs and plants, and they're also coming from BIPOC experiences.

It is a fireable offense to have an actor of color complete an undergraduate theatre degree and not have experienced Lorraine Hansberry or David Henry Hwang or Josefina López in their coursework. I hope this chapter starts a conversation (ugh, I hate that overused phrase) that we hold extraordinary power in the development of actors and theatre-makers. It is never frivolous, and we must be deliberate with every step of their training. Today's students want to get it right *the very first time*. So we absolutely must hold firm to the idea of process and to equip them with the tools to turn the switch on when it needs to be and off when the work is done. If actors don't find that switch for themselves, they're gonna find themselves in a very deep, dark place where they're always trying to manufacture something for a result – which can cause harm to the body and spirit.

SIIRI SCOTT: I agree, Tlaloc. We need to bring this particular conversation to a close, but I'm sure it will spark exciting conversations among other artists, teachers and students moving forward. I also want to thank each of you for your generosity. I hope your nuanced examination of the "system" within your own training and careers will serve as models for our readers.

Note

1 Tadashi Suzuki's method of actor training is rigorous physical and vocal discipline drawn from such diverse influences as ballet, martial arts, and traditional Japanese and Greek theatre. It draws attention to the lower body and a vocabulary of footwork, or a "grammar of the feet", which ultimately sharpens the actor's breath control and concentration.

References

Chibás, M. (2021) Mythic Imagination and the Actor. New York: Routledge.
Jay-Z (2013) *F.U.T.W.* [CD] New York: Roc-A-Fella Records.
Stanislavski, C. (2013[1949]) *Building a Character*. Translated and edited by E. Reynolds Hapgood. London: Bloomsbury.

A REFLECTION ON BREAKING AWAY

Looking through All Kinds of Windows

Sandra Marquez

I think it's important to introduce myself prior to sharing my response to the panel. I'm a middle-aged woman, I use she/her pronouns and I'm cisgendered. I grew up in the United States in California, where I called myself Mexican-American and sometimes Chicana. And then I moved to the Midwest, where I discovered that I was really Latina. I've moved through all those words and phrases, and I feel that I continually reposition myself to what they mean inside me at any given time and what they mean in the world. Chicana, in Central California at that time, felt like a political statement and a badge of honor.

To be honest, in some ways, I very much relate to the experiences described by the panel, but in other ways, my experiences differ. For example, like Tlaloc, I had really great teachers. I had some terrific undergraduate professors at California State University, Fresno. They really led me through a way that worked for my brain, for the way I think – my need for clarity and specificity – and the "system"-based technique made sense to me in that way. It gave me something to latch on to. When I went on to graduate school, I had some more terrific teachers who built on that foundation.

It was at that time that I remember thinking, "I need to know what my people are doing … Are there others out there?!" I mean, coming from Central California, I definitely knew about Luis Valdez, but that was pretty much it, and I never had the opportunity to study his work in depth. So I went to the theatre history professor, Dr. Robert Graves, and I asked him if we could do an independent study. I wanted to read as many plays by what I would have probably called Hispanic playwrights at that time and learn more. I just felt incredibly ignorant in this area and that seemed, I don't know, sad to me. He was enthusiastic and he did his best. It was wonderful because I read plays by all kinds of folks, but in retrospect, I think he didn't know a lot

DOI: 10.4324/9781003330882-8

about younger playwrights. My guess would be he was kind of scrambling to see what he could find for me. I point that out because there wasn't a structure in place then to expose students to a plurality of stories. It wasn't part of the zeitgeist. I mean, *at all.*

When I think about training in a Stanislavsky-based "system", I think about the actual training itself: objectives, super objectives, "Magic If" and so on. I loved it and I loved digging into it. However, in the practical usage of it, I think I found its limits. I was like an entity within a container. I was sealed off, and I could only work on what was being introduced in the class. And those weren't Latine stories, which meant leaving a WHOLE part of the reality of me aside.

When I moved to Chicago and did my first show with Teatro Vista, a company founded in the late 1980s to address the lack of opportunities for Latine artists, I met people who looked like me and, suddenly, it felt like home. Sometimes, as artists, we don't feel completely a part of our own families because we might be the only artist. It's a thing for artists of all stripes. And even though I'm very close to my family, I do feel quite alone in that way. Meanwhile, in the theatre I met other artists, but nobody looked like me or came from a similar background – this was true throughout my education and the early part of my teaching and acting careers. I had checked the cultural part of myself. When I met the people at Teatro Vista, it was the first time I met people where art and my culture intersected, and I didn't even know that could happen. (I mean, I hoped it could happen.) And so when I did that first show in Chicago, *Santos and Santos* by Octavio Solis, I didn't sleep that first week! I was so excited, and immediately fell in love with these people: John Carlos Seda, Eddie Torres, Cecilia Suarez, Andrew Carrillo – and there was so much to talk about! A shared culture, a shared sense of humor. Latine sarcasm and banter. Such good times. Plus, the food at rehearsals and the dancing at parties (of which there were many). I didn't know until I met them how deeply lonely I had been for all of that.

I joined the company soon afterward. Eddie Torres had just become the artistic director, and I believe because I was vocal at meetings and eager to share ideas, he very soon after asked me to be Associate Artistic Director. I found that my work was changing – *deepening* – because I was bringing more aspects of myself to it. That had to do with the material we were producing, of course. We were reading Octavio Solis, Edwin Sanchez, Migdalia Cruz, Nilo Cruz, all these amazing playwrights who were new to me. It was a very exciting time. So after working within that environment, I was able to bring more of myself to these pieces. It was liberating! And my work with this company and these playwrights informed my work in other genres and in other venues as well. Later on, when I did the ancient Greek playwrights or anything else, I was able to tap into more of my deepest core. I was bringing a fuller sense of myself because I didn't feel like I had to check any parts of myself at the door.

When I think about Stanislavsky-based techniques, I think about how it must have been for that original group of people who were developing something new for themselves. They had a desire for something different – to evolve from what had been. We are at a point now when we are taking the necessary opportunity to evolve further. It's overdue. Underrepresented communities are working so hard to bring our histories, cultures, playwrights and multiple modalities to the fore. We want to get to a point in this educational system where we can allow people to say "Yes" to the "system", but also "Yes" to other entry points that might be even more helpful at this particular time in history.

I've been at Teatro Vista since 1997, and, over the years, there have been many iterations of the company. I feel like an elder now. The types of training people bring to the table now are very different from what it was early on, and, just by virtue of that, there are more techniques that are in conversation with each other. In the past, it was about the folks who had training – like the "system" – and the folks who didn't, and we had to figure out how to build a language together. It wasn't ever a matter of talent. It was about who was coming in and what their practice looked like. We had to find a common language as an ensemble and build it together. I find that, as a director, I work to develop and facilitate a common language in a rehearsal room rather than assuming that we all have the same one. How do we build a language together based on who each of us is, what each of us has to offer, and what this piece is asking us to do?

I truly believe in lifelong learning, and I take classes whenever I can. Some of the best classes I've taken are with Paola Coletto. She was in Chicago for several years and now she's back home in Padua, Italy. She is from the clown world, what we would call "physical theatre" here in the United States. Her response to that is, "All theatre is physical!", which makes complete sense to me. I took a red nose clown and a couple of mask classes from her. I marveled how different the work was from my own training. I learned so much. It was like a different set of muscles.

Later, when I started using some of these techniques in class, my students were so skeptical. It was their knee jerk response because it wasn't the "system" or something like it. I said, "Look, imagine we have been looking into a house from one set of windows. All we are doing now is walking around the house and looking in from a different set of windows. Same house, different perspective." Getting to the core of your art and your expressive ability is getting to the core of yourself.

I'm really interested in using various skills that I've learned along the way – from all kinds of teachers – and learning new ones, too. Why wouldn't any artist be interested in that? It's incumbent upon us to give our students a space that introduces different modalities so they can get to the core of themselves from whatever way makes the most sense for them. Once an actor has been exposed to more options, maybe beyond Stanislavsky's "system", they will have more tools at their disposal. It's a "Yes and" proposition.

In the end, I'm grateful for the foundation of Stanislavsky's "system", but sometimes it feels so limited, you know? I want us to think of this work more broadly. What worked in my own graduate training might not work now, so what else can we use? How can we find more compassion in the work? I want our work to effectively address and nurture our diverse cohorts and serve different learning styles. I'm honestly grateful that we're at a point – and it took a long time to get here – when we can pass on so much more to our students. We're at a time when we can say "Yes" to multiple modalities, "Yes" to using Stanislavsky with something else, or, as the panel suggests, "Yes" to breaking away from Stanislavsky, "Yes" to looking through all kinds of windows. In fact, I think that's the best thing we can pass on to our students: "Say 'Yes, and' even more!"

6

A JEWISH JOURNEY

Stanislavsky's "System" to the American Method

Conrad Cohen

Who Are the Jewish People?

Like many innovations from around the world at the turn of the 20th century, Stanislavsky's "system" of how to train actors migrated to America. However, this process was less of a direct import and more a development of human adaptation as Stanislavsky's teachings evolved into what has now become generally known as "the American Method" for actor training. This evolution was also less natural selection and more intelligent design as the "system" was deliberately filtered through several practitioners throughout the last hundred years. A significant number of these practitioners were Jewish, and in this chapter I will explore the context of the "Jewishness" of a selection of the progenitors of the American Method, specifically: Stella Adler, Lee Strasberg, Sanford Meisner and Harold Clurman. Why these four? Adler and Strasberg due to their clear positions "as the most important teachers of acting in America in the twentieth century" (Butler, 2022, p. 129). Meisner due to his considerable influence on American actor training and the increasing prevalence of his technique in Europe even several decades after his death (Strandberg-Long, 2018, pp. 11–19), and even longer since the publication of Dennis Longwell's records of his teaching methods (Meisner and Longwell, 1987). And Clurman as the ideological figurehead of the Group Theatre,[1] "the most important theatrical experiment in American theatre" (Chinoy, 2013, p. 9) which established Stanislavsky's "system" as canon in the English-speaking world of actor training. By asking whether the Method is simply the "system" through a Jewish lens, I will explore the influence of these practitioners' ethno-religious identities as Jewish-Americans on their praxes as some of the most influential actor trainers of all time.

I first wish to address a key axiom to the thread of this chapter: defining Jewish identity as a race. Jewish identity is multifaceted and extremely

DOI: 10.4324/9781003330882-9

complex, all at once able to encompass a race, religion, ethnicity, nation, heritage, culture and many more things to many people. Rabbi Lord Jonathan Sacks[2] even uses words like "destiny" and "vocation" to describe what it means to be Jewish (The Rabbi Sacks Legacy, 2018). Being Jewish has consequently become difficult to classify under contemporary definitions of identity. When it comes to official categorisation, such as by governmental bodies like the Office for National Statistics in the United Kingdom, the question of "Jewishness" has often been relegated to simply a religion. The consequences of this are that Jewish experience and identity have often not been accurately accounted for. The non-Jewish world inaccurately defining to Jews what they are is a common theme throughout Jewish history and is one reason amongst many for the prevalence of antisemitic discourse and violence through the ages. Jewish author, educator and research fellow at the Institute for the Study of Global Antisemitism and Policy Ben M. Freeman explores how antisemitism is founded on non-Jewish "fantastical perceptions of the Jew" (2020, p. 72).[3] This resulted in the *othering* of the Jewish people throughout their histories in Europe, the Middle East and North Africa.[4] I will argue that such influences played a role in the lived experiences of the many influential Jewish Method teachers and consequently how they interpreted and passed on Stanislavsky's practices and philosophies.

To further compound the problem of defining Jewish identity, various Jewish communities often disagree on how to categorise themselves. Freeman (2021, p. 15) defines Jewish people as an ethno-religious group and explores how specific characterisations by non-Jewish individuals and institutions misrepresent Jewish people as only a religion or only a race, rather than encompassing the full complexity that comes with being Jewish. Freeman suggests that Jewish identity specifically in the United States regressed from a complicated peoplehood at the beginning of the 20th century to a mostly apathetic[5] religious denomination by the next century. Jewish immigrants to America fleeing racial persecution, mostly in the Tsarist Russia that Stanislavsky grew up in, arrived in a nation whose first amendment to its constitution guaranteed religious freedom. (The US Constitution to this day does not similarly protect its citizens based on their racial identity.) The result was that the majority of America's new immigrant Jewish communities identified more easily with a religious identity, thus gaining some legal protection from antisemitic persecution in ways that they had not experienced even in Enlightenment Europe. This greatly shifted Jewish identity within a country that post-Shoah has maintained the largest Jewish population of any nation (Jewish Virtual Library, 2022). Ultimately, American Jewish identity regressed in complexity, largely becoming only a religious denomination. This tension also exists within British Jewish identity and is exemplified by British comedian and author David Baddiel, who comments on his Jewish identity as consciously not a religious one.[6] Baddiel's Jewishness, though, still fulfils a significant role in his, and more pointedly, other Jews' cultural and ethnic positionalities. Such a position is common for secular Jewish artists and writers, and is certainly a reasonable proposition for how some of the Jewish Method teachers may have identified. Adler, for example, proudly referred to herself as "a Jewish broad from Odessa" (Stella Adler Studio of Acting, 2014) despite being born in New York. I will therefore operate with the axiom that, amongst other things, the Jewish people constitute a race. Whilst such an assertion is potentially problematic, as it accepts what many racist ideologies perpetuate about Jews and Jewishness, I still feel it necessary to do so here at the very least for ontological purposes. Also, almost every construction of the concept of "race" can be made to fit a description of the Jewish people, which is significant enough for my purposes here of investigating to what extent Jewish identity influenced Stanislavsky's "system" in 20th-century America. Some acting teachers and their approaches, including the four Method progenitors under discussion here, have been categorised as white, culturally and racially homogeneous, and have thus contributed to ideologies and rhetoric that at their most extreme contribute to the institutionalisation of white nationalism. Given their Jewish identities, this is, at best, an inaccurate and, at worst, harmful assumption when made of Jewish acting teachers and their methods. This ignores Jewish individuals' lived experiences in theatre industries, making it difficult to combat anti-Jewish prejudice which, as with many other racisms, remains a systemic problem. Senior Fellow at the Southern Poverty Law Centre Eric K. Ward (2017, p. 14) argues that combating anti-semitism is key to dismantling wider prejudices prevalent in society, and I would add that the same is true within actor training institutions and practices. If one of the goals of re-evaluating the work of Stanislavsky in this volume is to address systemic prejudice, then Jews and Jewishness must be acknowledged, included and celebrated.

Emma Green (2016a; 2016b) explores the precarious place of Jews in American society today as a group who experience bigoted hatred from both ends of the political spectrum. She asserts that understanding Jewish identity in the context of race is complicated: "Race is not just a matter of skin pigmentation or ethnic background. It is determined by both individuals and their observers, and the boundaries of who's in or out of one group or another change constantly" (2016a).

The mercurial concept of race also played a part in the lives of the Method teachers. They would have grown up under conditions where they were outsiders, part of the Yiddish-speaking immigrant culture who were, at least, excluded from organisations and, at worst, targets of racialised violence. And yet, throughout all their lifetimes, they will have seen Jews become undeniably, although not indefinitely, safer within American society. Does that necessarily mean that Jews became part of white America in the 20th century? Not really. Freeman (2021, pp. 137–142) expands on the danger of categorising Jews as white without nuance as even light-skinned, white-passing Jews have not experienced the safeties that come with being "white", never mind the lived experiences of Jews who cannot pass as white. Freeman analyses Jewish experience from a contemporary viewpoint, taking into account the 21st century's understandings of race and identity. During the first half of the 20th century, when the Method teachers grew up and began to teach, Jewish people experienced life categorically differently than their white, non-Jewish contemporaries. As an illustrative example, writer Paul Gallico describes Jewish athletes with distinctly racialised prejudice (1938, p. 349). Whatever contemporary predispositions exist categorising Jewish people as a race, including in popular culture, they were undoubtedly considered as a different race to the hegemony of "white" at the time Stanislavsky and his colleagues brought the "system" to America.

As noted, the recognition of Jewish as a "race" is complicated. It was complicated for the Method teachers in the first few decades of the 20th century and remains complicated now in the first few decades of the 21st century. Were the Jewish people considered a race in the early 20th century? Yes. Can they still be considered a race today, separate from white, hegemonic America which has so strongly influenced systemic racism? Probably, and certainly enough for this discussion to have significance in terms of how Stanislavsky and the practices of his successors are used within institutions of actor training today. It is also worth acknowledging that whilst I will operate with the axiom that the Jewish people do constitute a race, I will be dealing with the full complexity of Jewish identity, including religion, culture and the many other aspects that come with being Jewish throughout the rest of this chapter.

So Just How Jewish Were the American Method Teachers?

By 1930, almost a third of New York City identified as Jewish (Lunfield, 1929). Jewish people have existed in the US since its inception, but these mostly consisted of Sephardi Jewish communities who fled antisemitic pogroms in Spain, Italy and Portugal. The later pogroms in Russia in the late 19th century saw an influx of millions of Ashkenazi Jewish immigrants to America. It is then no wonder that the burgeoning theatre industry of America, focused on Broadway, had such a Jewish feeling to it. David Cesarani highlights the important relationship between working class Jewish immigrants to America around the turn of the 20th century and the development of left wing politics, including the influence of a member of the U.S. House of Representatives, Meyer London, who "played up his Jewish immigrant roots and unashamedly addressed a range of Jewish immigrant concerns" (2021, p. 47), becoming one of only two socialists in the United States Congress. So New York was, and to some extent still is, very Jewish. But there is a difficulty with these numbers, and, as with most statistics, they do not tell the full story since, as previously suggested, statistics from censuses have historically omitted the nuances of Jewish identity. Therefore, I will explore some of the specific experiences of the four architects of the American Method I am focusing on, i.e., Adler, Strasberg, Meisner and Clurman.

Each of these teachers, in their own way, followed in Stanislavsky's footsteps by developing his "system" into the Method in 20th-century America, beginning with the emergence of their practices whilst working within the Group Theatre. The fact that all four of these individuals were Jewish is well established, but I will highlight a few key points here. They all grew up in a New York steeped in Yiddish theatre. Theatre in early 20th-century New York was heavily influenced by Yiddish theatre troupes and practitioners, so much so that American premieres of acclaimed international plays such as Anton Chekhov's *Uncle Vanya* (*Dyadya Vanya* in 1914) and August Strindberg's *The Father* (*Fadren* in 1899) were performed in Yiddish (Peck, 2017).

Adler's parents were both stars of Yiddish theatre and she made her start as an actor performing in Yiddish with Maurice Schwartz's Yiddish Art Theatre (Chinoy, 2013, p. 22). New York's Yiddish theatre scene, having been generated by tours from theatre troupes from the Yiddish-speaking parts of Europe such as the Vilna Troupe, had a profound influence on Adler and consequently on the development of the Method. Howard Kissel, who compiled and edited Adler's seminal book *The Art of Acting*, notices a distinct Jewishness in the Group Theatre, suggesting that its Jewish members were drawn to this work by "messianic aspirations" (Kissel, 2000, p. 275) they gained from their Jewish backgrounds. He acknowledges that these practitioners' Jewishness heavily impacted upon their lives and praxes, even though they were more religiously secular than previous generations.

Both Strasberg and Clurman grew up speaking Yiddish in their homes (Caplan, 2018, p. 211). Clurman and Meisner were both the children of Jewish immigrants, and Strasberg himself was an immigrant having been born in what is now Ukraine (but was at the time part of the Austro-Hungarian Empire). Clurman remained fascinated with Yiddish theatre for the rest of his life, and there are even suggestions that Clurman's and Adler's love for Yiddish theatre is what brought them together to form the Group Theatre (Chinoy, 2013, p. 205) and possibly even influenced their subsequent marriage. Additionally, Strasberg, Clurman and Meisner all met whilst working for the American Theatre Guild in the 1920s. Here were three young Jewish men amongst an intimidating and hegemonically white Christian-American organisation who grew fond of arguing together about what made good theatre with astonishing heat and pedagogic finesse (Clurman, 1946, p. 11). Whether consciously or unconsciously, these three Jews, these three *outsiders*, found a commonality with each other that, at least in part, later led to the formation of the Group Theatre. At least eleven of the Group's members were "first generation American Jews" (Caplan, 2018, p. 211) who would have grown up attending Yiddish theatre.[7] By the time of the Group's formation in 1931, the popularity of Yiddish-language theatre had waned, and so this next generation of Jewish theatre-makers sought to create something new but not necessarily any less Jewish.

The Group's egalitarian nature in allowing all its members, large and small, experienced and novice, to contribute to the interpretation of text seemed similar in structure to a *yeshiva* (an institute of Jewish learning). The debate and experimentation by which consensus was reached in the company echoed Jewish approaches. Henry Bial even identifies the empowerment of performers as active critics, where they interpret the text of a play to make choices pertaining to objectives, as being Jewish in origin: "We might even see the twentieth-century actor's emphasis on textual exegesis combined with extratextual collaboration as similar to the Jewish distinction between written law (*Torah*) and oral law (*halacha*)" (2005, pp. 55–56).

Jewish approaches to textual exegesis involve ascertaining meaning from both the writings in the *Torah* (Hebrew Bible) as well as writings from subsequent scholars and sages. Extratextual collaboration, then, is the synthesis of these writings with the rest of life and practice, aiding *mitzvot* (commandments) to become part of everyday custom. American Method actor training fits this model well. There is a fixed written text from which all knowledge and practice originates, i.e., Stanislavsky's "system", and there are the oral interpretations of the various fixed written records of the "system" passed down in acting classrooms through generations from master teacher to neophyte student. Isaac Butler references how Strasberg and the Group would gather and digest the writings of Stanislavsky and his students:

> Strasberg brought Russian-language articles and books on theatre with him […] The company sat rapt with attention as, night after night, [Mark] Schmidt read aloud about the First Studio, and Meyerhold, and Vakhtangov. Clurman would later compare their attention to that of the sultan listening to Scheherazade.
>
> *(2022, p. 156)*

Such a scene conjures the imagery of a revered Jewish sage sharing stories from the *Mishnah* (Oral Torah) with their community or of a Jewish parent sitting around a table leading the *Pesach Seder* (Passover festive meal) for their family. Schmidt translating from Russian operates like a *chazzan* (prayer leader), orating the material so that Strasberg, as a *rosh yeshiva* (a wise, revered leader of Jewish educational institutions), can elucidate meaning from these texts for their *kollel* (gathering of scholars). Even Clurman's reference to Scheherazade distinguishes the scene as distinct from America or Europe, relocating it to something more familiar to Jewish culture and custom.

What Are Jewish Methods?

In order to establish how these practitioners' Jewishness influenced their methods, I have focused on Jewish approaches to text, not only because the realms of theatre and acting largely revolve around text, but also because approaches to text are one of the few consistencies across the full range of Jewish experience. The Jewish Method teachers would hence have had specific attitudes towards text that would have been influenced by these Jewish approaches that they (perhaps inadvertently) brought with them to their own work.

Adler, Strasberg, and Clurman were each first exposed to Stanislavsky's teachings whilst studying at the American Laboratory Theatre, where two former Moscow Art Theatre practitioners, Richard Boleslavsky and Maria Ouspenskaya, led sessions teaching Stanislavsky's new approach to actor training (Caplan, 2018, p. 219). Adler later clarified the "system" by learning directly from Stanislavsky in Paris for several weeks in 1934 (Butler, 2022, pp. 168–173). Meisner was introduced to the "system" by these three fellow Group Theatre founders, and was also influenced by Michael Chekhov, one of Stanislavsky's most successful students and credited with bringing large swathes of Stanislavsky's "system" to America (Malague, 2021, p. 6).[8] They also were all undoubtedly influenced by the Moscow Art Theatre's 1923/24 season in New York City where they were able to see first-hand the work of these theatrical practitioners (L. Cohen, 2019, "Concise Introduction"). Ultimately, the most important sources for most of these practitioners' subsequent adaptations of the "system" came from Stanislavsky's writings.[9] So what influenced these practitioners' approaches to interpreting text?

In Jewish life, text is central to everything. For the last two and a half millennia, the texts of the *Tanach*[10] are what defined not just what being Jewish was, but also how to live it in everyday life. Text has been so central to Jewishness that most Jewish religious texts have not changed for thousands of years, and the oldest surviving complete copy of the *Tanach* is almost letter for letter the same as any Hebrew version that can be bought in bookstores today.[11] Moshe Halbertal describes text as a "central operative concept" (1997, p. 2) to Jewish tradition, and explains that whilst even the concept of G-d[12] differs in different branches of Judaism, its canonical texts remain consistent. There is a clear analogy between this and the Method teachers' approaches as whilst their main ideas came from a set of core texts, their interpretations of said texts and resultant practices as teachers differed substantially.

Jewish life and practice is, to a great extent, about interpreting texts. In their treatise on Jewish culture's relationship to text, *Jews and Words*, Amos Oz and Fania Oz-Salzberger detail the history of this relationship to texts from an oral tradition to a written one. They assert that the "formative stamp of a library" (2012, p. 29) is part of a Jewish inheritance where books act as literal, physical anchors to culture. The parables to the Method teachers are quite direct in that not only did they take the "system" and interpret it for themselves, but they also went beyond and centred theatrical texts (plays, screenplays and the like) as objects to be interpreted. The Method teachers developed distinct relationships with text that established them as semi-sacred objects to be interpreted, and the way that they subsequently interrogated these objects and ascertained their meaning was inherently Jewish. "We are in a field where words are important. In everything that you and I will be dealing with, we will share the importance of text" (Adler, 1999, p. 32).

From an early age, Adler understood the importance of text and ideas for the actor. She encouraged her students to combine text with their own imaginations and passions to bring it to life. Many Jewish texts relate to living the ideas within them, and so I argue that Adler's particular methods around text had clearly Jewish influences.

Also central to Jewish interpretation and learning is the relationship between teacher and student. In Jewish custom this relationship differs from the Greco-Christian models that most Western education is based on. In Jewish culture this relationship, and, therefore, the whole process of teaching and learning, is much more dialogical: "Jewish tradition allows and encourages pupil to rise against teacher, disagree with him, and prove him wrong, up to a point" (Oz and Oz-Salzberger, 2012, p. 15).

From a gentile perspective, this seemingly disagreeable dynamic may present as disrespectful or even disruptive to a learning environment. However, in the Jewish classroom such manifestations of argumentative dialogue serve to strengthen students in their convictions, teach them to recognise gaps in their knowledge and encourage them to proactively engage with knowledge bases to truly learn and grow. Whether due to my own Jewish background or not, this is a model that always appealed to me as a learner, and some of my most effective teachers (both Jewish and non-Jewish) were those I was able to engage with in productive, if sometimes volatile, dialogue. My most influential and formative acting teachers were those who engaged with me and my learning as collaborative partners and gave me the space to argue, to be brave and (perhaps most importantly) to fail, but who were also there to pick me back up again. Whilst I could not acknowledge it at the time, my most effective teachers were those who modelled the Jewish structures of Adler's, Strasberg's, Meisner's and Clurman's classrooms whilst tearing down (consciously or not) the problematical "guru-like" authoritarianism that has become synonymous with teaching the Method. In the discourse of Jewish learning then: "Disagreement, within reason, is the name of the game. A fine student is one who judiciously critiques his teacher, offering a fresh and better interpretation" (Ibid., p. 9).

There is also an embedded tension between the innovative and the sacrosanct in Jewish learning. Exegetical examples come from the likes of *The Book of Job* where Job is lauded for his fervent challenges to G-d at the unjust treatment he received, thereby validating protestation as a legitimate form of dialogue between divinity and humanity and, by extension, validating this within the teacher-student relationship as well. Rabbis call this *chutzpah kelapei shemaya* (audacity towards heaven) and Rabbi Lord Sacks (Sacks, 2000; Sacks, 2021) identifies this as a distinctly Jewish attitude contrasting with dominant culture and theology. Jewish approaches are to question and argue to gain deeper understanding. Uninformed obedience is valued less than conscientious disagreement for the sake of bettering the world (Laytner, 2004,). For the Method teachers, they argued with and questioned each other, often vehemently, to improve the world. Dialogical approaches were passed down through generations of Jewish thinkers to become an integral part of Jewish learning where questioning authority figures was an inherent part of education. It comes as no surprise, then, that the Jewish Method teachers and their students gained a reputation for interrogating their authority figures[13] and even each other. It is possible they were genuinely standing up to what they saw as ineffective systems, but it could also simply be the way they discoursed as young Americans brought up in a heavily Jewish immigrant community. Again, Kissel's use of "messianic" to describe the Method teachers highlights how strongly their Jewish concepts of learning influenced their teaching. Helen Chinoy (2013, p. 14) also uses this word to describe Clurman's oratory style in the early days of running the Group Theatre. It can thus be argued that the forge of the Method, i.e., the Group Theatre, was a distinctly Jewish phenomenon characterising approaches to interpreting Stanislavsky which are similar to those used by rabbinical sages through the ages:

> The fierce disputes they had with each other over the interpretation of Stanislavsky's teaching, the techniques they had developed for interpreting dramatic texts can easily be seen as a secular outgrowth of thousands of years of wrangling over knotty questions in the Bible and the Talmud.
> *(Kissel, 2000, p. 275)*

Throughout history, such wrangling was central to being Jewish, both religiously and culturally (Sacks, 2021). From the earliest Judaic traditions Jews are encouraged to wrestle with G-d, and, by proxy, their teachers. It is, therefore, reasonable to suggest that the Method teachers wrestling with Stanislavsky was an inherently Jewish process. The Group Theatre, consciously or unconsciously, adopted this methodology of wrangling with how they interpreted Stanislavsky's "system", with how they taught their actors to interpret dramatic texts, and with how they challenged each other's approaches as the best way to progress.

How Does the "System" Synthesise with Jewishness to Create the Method?

Having established the Method teachers' Jewish approaches, including a Jewish textual exegesis and a methodology of wrangling, there emerge other aspects of their practices which have been influenced by their individual and collective Jewishness. This includes the fact that the Group Theatre excited the zeitgeist at a time of horrific economic and social depression to such an extent that it led Waldo Frank to assert that he joined because of its innovative social vision towards "a new humanity in the moral and spiritual as well as in the economic sense" (quoted in Clurman, 1946, p. 78). This undercurrent of seeking to create a better world fulfils the Jewish concept of *tikun olam* (repair of the world), and by establishing a socially conscious theatre movement at the height of the Great Depression, Clurman and his compatriots may have been inadvertently fulfilling a very Jewish ambition. Charity or social consciousness are not exclusively Jewish, of course, and the Group consisted of non-Jewish members, too. However, for its Jewish members, especially the four under discussion here, it seems to have provided them with a means to channel their Jewish understanding of these concepts in artistic ways that enabled influence from their secularised Jewish identities (Kissel, 2000). Rabbi Lord Sacks (2000, pp. 49–58) describes a metaphorical allegory wherein the biblical patriarch Abraham sees a palace in flames and wonders who its owner is to leave such a magnificent building on fire. In the story, the palace's owner pops their head out of a window and says, apparently unconcerned for the blaze around them, "I am the owner!" Rabbi Lord Sacks interprets the palace as the physical world and the flames as a representation of injustice, positing that it is humanity's duty to put out the flames. For the Method teachers, the palace in flames was the destitute American society of the Depression era, and I argue that their attempts to improve their society through their work in the theatre was their Jewish attempt to put the fire out.

There is also the recurring theme of "truth" first established by Stanislavsky: "Each and every moment must be saturated with a belief in the truthfulness of the emotion felt, and in the action carried out, by the actor" (Stanislavski, 1938, p. 142), and then expanded upon vigorously by the Method teachers, such as Meisner who states: "The best way to act well is to live truthfully, and don't create a phony situation" (Meisner and Longwell, 1987, p. 123). Truth (and by extension the search for truth) is a core tenant of Jewish life and *Torah* study, as the Tzemach Tzedek[14] said, "Love Aristotle, love Socrates, love Plato. But love the truth more than all of them" (Mendel quoted in Jacobson, 2016).

And, of course, there is Adler's passionate pedagogical style, including asserting that actors must become fierce warriors (Adler, 2000, pp. 226–234), possibly inspired by the dozens of fierce Jewish women featured in Hebrew legend. Adler's teaching style had an "Old Testament quality", and the way she adapted elements of the "system" modelled "a secular version of the interpretive battles in which Jews have been engaged for millennia" (Kissel, 2000, p. 277). Kissel attributes Adler's methods, both theoretical and practical, to a heritage and an attitude to disagreement that is inherently Jewish.

Another Jewish aspect of the Method, so stark it deserves extended analysis, is the significant Jewish relationship between emotion and memory. As with many immigrant ethnicities to the United States, the outwardly emotional, foreign-language speaking, "loud" Jews arriving in New York at the turn of the 20th century conflicted with the considerably less emotional white population at the time. This correlates to José Esteban Muñoz's analysis of white America's emotive stamina as "minimalist to the point of emotional impoverishment" (2000, p. 70). I contend the correlation between the quest for emotive performance both within Stanislavsky's work at this point in its development and that of the subsequent Method teachers speaks to a reaction against their societies' acceleration away from heterogeneity; Stalin's "Sovietisation" of the many Russian ethnic groups and America's "melting pot" mentality leading to homogeneity in these two specific countries. Henry Bial extrapolates the emotiveness of Method acting was due to "its ethnically Other context" (2005, p. 57) where diverse emotional responses, and especially Jewish ones, were validated. Whilst Bial acknowledges that emotional acting is not necessarily "Jewish", he does establish that the Jewishness of the original Method teachers enabled them to access a relationship with emotion in performance they otherwise may not have done had they not been Jewish. The Method teachers' Jewishness, through necessitating an emotional connection with the material, allowed them to experiment with emotion in their acting classrooms in ways that had not been seen before in American theatre. I would further suggest their emotional persuasions went beyond the approaches they sought to impart to their students as they were also crucial to their personal pedagogies. Strasberg, in particular, became infamous during his time leading the Group Theatre for the way he dealt with his own emotions. Sometimes he attempted to conceal his emotions by hiding behind newspapers, but would also frequently lose his temper at actors, becoming animated and furious in a way that would have likely shocked most puritan predispositions, leading Clurman to describe his demeanour as "driving and fierce" (Butler, 2022, p. 151). Adler commented on cultural homogenisation in America and how a disconnection from background, especially emotionally vibrant persuasions like her own Jewish ethnicity, is a problem for the training of actors: "The American actor has pushed his feelings down to such a level that it is almost impossible for him to arouse himself to the force and the dynamic that you have to use as an actor" (Stella Adler Studio of Acting, 2014).

Whilst, rather famously, Strasberg and Adler went on to disagree on the engagement with emotion in actor training, it remains a core aspect of the Method to this day. My own actor training, which took place in an institution in New York heavily influenced by these practitioners, was laden with explorations of emotion and how to act with truthful emotion on the stage. This included the teachings of Stanislavsky, Strasberg, Adler and the other Method teachers, but any Jewish contexts were omitted. Such contexts, I argue, were key influences on how Strasberg framed emotion through memory: "I believe emotional memory is the key to unlocking the secret of creativity that is behind every artist's work, not just the actor's" (Strasberg quoted in L. Cohen, 2010, p. 28).

Strasberg's version of the Method relied on engaging with personal, meaningful memories in order to be able to access emotions when acting. One of the possible reasons why he may have been so strongly drawn towards Stanislavsky's emotion memory is the way that they interact in Jewish tradition. Another explanation, theorised by Clifford Odets in his diaries, could be the lack of affection Strasberg had received in his childhood (Butler, 2022, p. 157), but this may simply have exacerbated his desire to understand emotion as it constituted a major missing piece of his otherwise very Jewish childhood. So what does Jewish tradition say about emotion? The Baal Shem Tov[15] was frequently outwardly emotional, laughing and crying, dancing and singing as the need took him. He taught that we should be joyous and not shy away from expressing this openly, especially in the service of G-d (Buxbaum, 2006, pp. 150–152). More recently, Rabbi Lord Sacks describes a key attribute to Jewish prayer being that it encompasses the full range of human emotions "from despair to jubilation" (2021, p. 117), and that we shouldn't be afraid of engaging with our emotions as they can lead to *simcha* (joy).

And what about Jewish approaches to memory? Recently, a cousin of mine passed away. Upon reflecting on this cousin's life with my grandmother, she highlighted the importance of memory to Jewish people like us. The Jewish memorial prayer, *Yizkor* (literally "remember" in Hebrew), which is recited four times a year during specific festivals, asks G-d to remember the departed. In Judaism, even the Almighty is called upon to engage with memory. Entire Jewish festivals are dedicated to remembering specific events from Jewish history and the *Torah*: Chanukah is about remembering the Maccabees' rebellion against the Seleucid Empire; Purim is about remembering the avoidance of genocide whilst in exile in the Persian Empire; and Passover is about remembering the exodus from slavery in Egypt. Beyond specific concepts of memorial through Jewish festivals, the commandment of *zikaron* (memory) occurs throughout Jewish liturgical literature. One pertinent example is Psalm 137 which details the experience of a diasporic people and urges remembrance of both the Temple in Jerusalem and its destruction. The Jewish people, through our thousands of years of exile and our almost continuous status as refugees (or close descendants of them), have developed intergenerational coping mechanisms through engagement with our collective memory: "It has been remarked that a scattered people which remembers its past and connects it with the present will undoubtedly have a future as a people, and perhaps even a more glorious life than the one in the past" (Birnbaum, 1988, p. 194).

I argue then, that for a Jewish immigrant like Strasberg, memory and emotion were inextricably linked and by receiving validation of this link whilst learning Stanislavsky's "system", Strasberg was then able to construct his Method. Strasberg's Method, of course, was only one variation and the fact that there are others from other actor trainers like Adler, a woman, and Meisner, a (closeted) bisexual man, speaks to the great diversity of Jewish interpretation.

Where Did It All Go Wrong?

I have established that the Method teachers' Jewish cultural identities played a key role in the formation of their practice and art. However, the Method did not subsequently become a shining example of an approach to actor training that engaged directly with the problematic aspects of Stanislavsky's "system", specifically in regard to race and prejudice. As I will point out, some even allude to the opposite. So how can this be? How can four practitioners clearly distinct from the cultural and racial hegemony of their time (and ours) not have addressed racialised intolerance embedded in the acting industries? In other words, where did it all go wrong?

One avenue that may begin to answer this question is arguing that the Method teachers were conscious of, at least, bias and, at most, overt prejudice in 20th-century American society, and perhaps covertly sought to dismantle this within the scope of their classrooms. This is a bold claim and could take its own volume to fully investigate. There is certainly evidence to the contrary, such as the erasure of Black actors and writers who worked with the Group (Butler, 2022, p. 148),[16] not to mention examples of harmful patriarchies that the Method inherited and upheld from the "system" in the way it treated female actors (Malague, 2012). However, difficulties arise with judging these practitioners and their practices by our own period's ethical standards. These Method teachers, as members of a minority community, experienced prejudice through the racism and religious intolerance of their time. But this does not necessarily mean they themselves did not perpetuate prejudices as well, as it is entirely possible for a member of a marginalised group to still be intolerant of others. An example of this within the Jewish community in the early 20th century is the conflict between Jewish people from different immigrant origins, especially when aligning with classist prejudices. A common attitude for enfranchised Jewish citizens arose as prejudice towards what they perceived as impoverished, rural Jewish immigrants who could potentially impact non-Jewish attitudes towards them, and there is some evidence of this prejudice between these teachers when Adler refers to Strasberg as a "shtetl upstart" (Butler, 2022, p. 152).[17] After all, despite their clear positionalities as *othered*, the four Method teachers I am discussing would not necessarily constitute a diverse group of Jewish people today, apart from anything else being all secular Ashkenazi Americans. Despite relatively tolerant intentions then, these teachers' experiences of prejudice may have influenced their own reactions to living as a minority culminating in unintended consequences.

This does not excuse historical harm nor negate any negative impact caused through experiences with these practices today, but it does provide crucial nuance to the conversation in terms of how we can move forward in the actor training community. What I am ultimately attempting to elucidate is that the Method is not necessarily the hegemonic practice it has become known as. I argue that it can therefore offer means to address problematic consequences of this hegemony, ranging from supporting diverse cohorts of actors to combating ideologies such as white nationalism, if the *othered* contexts of the Jewish Method teachers is appropriately considered. Additionally, I wish to posit the Group Theatre as the forge of the Method only and not necessarily its final product. Looking at how these teachers' work evolved over the many decades they taught provides a holistic view of their attitudes on prejudice and intolerance. For example, Clurman's progressive discourse on working towards egalitarian theatre (Clurman, 1946), as well as his support for productions with overt themes dealing with anti-Black racism, such as Paul Peters and George Sklar's *Stevedore*, and John Wexley's *They Shall Not Die* (Chinoy, 2013, p. 195), add a significant understanding of the Method teachers' approaches to race and diversity.

I contend that there are clear differences between homogenised white America and the ethnic experience and positionalities of the Method teachers. One source for this impression is Muñoz's discussions on how white, middle-class taste in America deems performances with "ethnic affect" as inappropriate' (2000, p. 69). Bial goes a step further as pertaining to Jewish interests in conjecturing on white America's rejections of the Method and its teachers:

> Not surprisingly, when we acknowledge the historical link between the American Method and the Yiddish theater, critiques of the Method as unrefined, vulgar, neurotic, or overly emotional begin to sound very similar to the charges leveled by anti-Semites against Jews themselves.
>
> *(Bial, 2005, p. 166)*

To fully appreciate this from the perspective of the Method teachers, we must investigate what happened to their Jewish positionalities, and Jewish-American identity more generally, as the 20th century progressed. Although the prevalence of Jewish people in the performing arts is contestable (see Brook [2017]), there is some merit since, numerically at least, there are many actors, directors, producers, writers and other professionals in both Hollywood and Broadway who are, to one extent or another, Jewish. Bial (2005) explores the many potential reasons for this, ranging from working class immigrant Jews finding the emerging theatre and film industries of America as vehicles for upward mobility, to Jewish predilections for performance and comedy, to a pure accident of geography. I would add that to America's newest Jewish workers, the comparatively open and inclusive nature of the burgeoning entertainment sector in the US in the 20th century must have felt like a more plausible avenue than attempting to "make it" in its Protestant-dominated (and discernibly Judeo-phobic) industries like car manufacturing or agriculture.[18] America's new Jewish immigrants largely left behind experiences of violent persecution, which influenced their ambitions for performance and artistry through both the Yiddish theatre that reminded them of "the old country" and the new medium of film which firmly established them in their new, relatively safer home in America: "Here they met less virulent but mounting antisemitism, fueled by their largely lower-class immigration, which blocked their rise in more established industries and shunted them into what was then a lowly, if not wholly disreputable, motion picture business" (Brook, 2017, p. 4).

Despite arguably "reasonable" representation in theatre and media, Jewish experience has not translated into Jewish artists' work in a way that one would expect, leading to conversations now in the 21st century about authentic Jewish representation and casting (for example, see Liebman, 2022). Most examples of Jewishness in media are, at best, the butt-of-the-joke or, at worst, harmfully stereotypical. David Zurawik offers one possible explanation for this:

'Too Jewish' is an expression that echoes all too loudly across the history of Jewish characters on network television in its use – most often by Jewish programmers and network executives – as a tool to distort, disguise, or altogether eliminate depictions of Jewish identity from American prime-time television.

(2003, pp. 5–6)

Essentially, American Jews adopted a stance of self-policing the Jewishness of their work, targeting it at the white American masses either in a way that wasn't "too Jewish", or in a way that "being Jewish" was the schtick. Even seemingly "Jewish" television shows faced challenges, such as Fran Drescher's *The Nanny* (broadcast on CBS in the United States from 1993 to 1999) where she had to fight tooth and nail to keep her leading character Jewish: "They didn't want to have Jews playing Jews in a starring role" (Drescher quoted in Goldman, 2020).

Whilst it is easy, and to some extent fair, to group these discussions along with similar contemporary treatments on casting, once Drescher's phrase has imprinted on your mind, it seems to come true an awful lot even today (see, for example, Baddiel's 2022 article "Why Don't Jews Play Jews" on the casting of Helen Mirren, a non-Jewish actor, as Israeli Prime Minister Golda Meir).

At this point, I want to make a brief connection between this theme of erasing Jewish identity in the acting industries and the antisemitic trope of Jewish control. I argue the intersection of these two concepts is relevant to how Jewish actor trainers are perceived. Without delving in great detail into the literature, there is a lineage from thousands-of-years-old conspiracy fantasy antisemitism (Freeman, 2021, pp. 51–61) to harmful falsehoods about Jewish control of the media, particularly Hollywood. These myths have consistently existed in various forms since the inception of these industries (see Brook [2017] once again for a concise history and analysis). I argue that the perpetuation of harmful and racist stereotypes has affected the Method teachers' perceptions of themselves as Jewish-Americans and dialogue about the Method. Such bias has enabled seemingly innocent dialectic about Jewish prevalence in the training of actors and the wider acting industries to develop, at least in part, from anti-Jewish attitudes. If further conversations are to be had amongst actor trainers and acting students concerning the lives, writings and practices of these Jewish visionaries, then sufficient understanding and appreciation of these racialised histories should be required.

There was also a sociological factor at play for the Method teachers that involved how Jewish immigrants to America acculturated into the dominant society. Eric H. Cohen (2010) breaks down acculturation and the main strategies an ethnocultural group employs to join a wider society. One of these responses is assimilation, where an ethnocultural immigrant group does not maintain their heritage, culture and identity, but does build relationships with other groups. This was one of the most common responses for Jewish immigrants to America in the 20th century who significantly reduced their Jewish signifiers whilst becoming more dominantly American, thus reducing their diversity and differences from their society's white hegemony. Freeman (2021, pp. 107–153) extrapolates further and surmises that the antisemitism and rejection Jewish immigrants in early 20th-century America faced from their new non-Jewish fellow US citizens caused many American Jews to acculturate, abandoning large parts of their Jewish culture and peoplehood without ever really gaining full equality due to the prevalence of anti-Jewish prejudice.

This leads me to the provocation that there has been a kind of appropriation of the Method: namely, the Method teachers' Jewish identities were either consciously self-policed or unconsciously assimilated, resulting in those who went on to teach their methods to ignore or possibly even erase the Jewish aspects of their praxes. Essentially, due to the lack of acknowledgement of the original Method teachers' Jewish identities, what is now stereotypically classified as "the Method" is an inauthentic representation of the actor training practices originally taught by these Jewish teachers. As Rosemary Malague indicates, "the single most important factor in this tradition of actor training is the teacher" (2012, p. 188), leading me to consider what is lost when the Method is taught by teachers without the specific Jewish lived experiences of these original four. The implication is not necessarily that acting teachers must have experienced the world in the same way as the originators of the practices they teach; however, such facts must be accounted for especially when problematic and potentially exclusionary results emerge in our institutions. I encourage a conscious resistance against the philosophy of "too Jewish", which erases important elements to the praxes of the Method. Such a phenomenon is not unique to the Jewish community as it has been argued that contemporary culture has homogenised in various ways, particularly due to the vast reach of globalised media industries (see Zukin, 1991; Kellner, 1997; and Lee, 1997 for more on this argument). Theatre industries in general, and, I argue, actor training institutions in particular, have not escaped this model of universalising towards homogeneity. Specific Jewish responses relevant to how these Method teachers' practices were taught and assimilated into the general melting pot of American actor training is perhaps another avenue for further study.

What Are the Implications for the Future of Stanislavsky in Actor Training?

It has been asserted by some working toward anti-racist theatre and performance practices that Adler, Strasberg, Meisner and Clurman belong to the oppressive, culturally white and/or "default" acting methods that fail to address diversity or inclusion in their construction or application. Through assimilation and other negative reactions to experiencing as *other*, the Method may have become hegemonic by the advent of the 21st century, but I argue that it did not start as this, nor was it intended to be as homogeneous or even as harmful as some have experienced it. These teachers' positionalities as "ethnically Other" (Bial, 2005, p. 57) were crucial in the formation of their methods, as well as the specific Jewish ethno-religious codes embedded in their work.

The Method teachers' authentic ethnic identities were downplayed or outright erased both during their lifetimes and afterwards. Whilst it would certainly be inaccurate to claim that actor training in the US and beyond has secretly been diverse or inclusive all along, I argue (acknowledging and, in some way, attempting to invert antisemitic tropes of secret Jewish conspiracy) there was an unaccredited undercurrent to these teachers' work wherein their positions as *othered* in a white Anglo-Saxon and Protestant/Catholic-American society influenced their practices in ways that could potentially contribute to contemporary discussions on race, racism and similar matters for actor training. Therefore, it is important to acknowledge that Clurman and Meisner were children of immigrants fleeing persecution, that Strasberg was himself an immigrant and that Adler grew up and learned her trade amongst the Yiddish immigrant culture. They demonstrated a way to adapt Stanislavsky's "system" by engaging with their ethnic, religious, cultural, racial and even linguistic minority perspectives. They developed discernibly Jewish approaches to their teaching, including from their emotional vibrance, to interpreting text and to contention within the teacher-student (or sometimes even student-student or teacher-teacher) relationship. Today's actors and acting students can be inspired in these approaches to Stanislavsky's teachings, following in these Jewish Method teachers' footsteps by embracing their perspectives and identities as key in their interpretations of canonical actor training systems.

These approaches may also aid in wider decolonisation projects many higher education and actor training institutions are attempting to develop in recent years through combating prejudice in the form of erasive antisemitism, which comes with celebrating Jewishness within the origins of the Method. The effect of this should be to honour the positionalities and specific lived experiences of future generations of actors and their teachers. We all have the right to be in these classrooms and work in these industries without having to erase our identities or conform to archaic conceptions of homogeneity. These teachers did not hide their Jewish ethno-religious backgrounds and likely did not want their students to do so when they read, interpreted or practiced the methods of those who came before them. Even though these specific teachers are no longer with us, their practices are in the form of what is termed "the Method". 21st-century acting teachers do not need to mimic these teachers, but we can be inspired by their approach to their Jewish positionalities and fully embrace our own experiences and backgrounds in our praxes. Adler, Strasberg, Meisner and Clurman interpreted the works of Konstantin Stanislavsky without diminishing their Jewishness. They experienced the world as *other* but often used (consciously or unconsciously) that experience to inform their approaches to practice and art. Therefore, when 21st-century actors learn and use these practices, there is value in emulating the inclusive philosophy I argue was formative in the Method's development, thus addressing a silencing of diverse voices in actor training that has taken place throughout the last hundred years.

Notes

1 The Group Theatre was an experimental theatre production company founded in New York in 1931 by Harold Clurman, Lee Strasberg and Cheryl Crawford. It was set up to challenge what these three (and others) viewed as a lack of creativity and art in American theatre. It operated for ten years with varying success, but was highly influential in the development of the performing arts industries and helped launch the careers of several influential theatre and film practitioners, including Stella Adler, Sanford Meisner, Clifford Odets, Robert Lewis, Elia Kazan and John Garfield.
2 Lord Sacks was Chief Rabbi of the United Hebrew Congregations of the Commonwealth from 1991 to 2013 (Office of the Chief Rabbi, 2016). As Chief Rabbi for most of my childhood and early adolescence as a practising Jewish person in the tiny Jewish community of Glasgow, he was formative in my early understandings of Judaism and identifying as Jewish.
3 Historian David Nirenberg (2013) takes this a step further and argues that core values within Western/Christian, West Asian/Muslim and later secular ideologies were established as oppositions to imagined concepts of Jews and Jewishness.
4 Dara Horn (2021) expands on this by exploring examples of anti-Jewish prejudice in all corners of the world, including East Asia and the Americas.
5 Referencing that by 2020, whilst most Jewish-Americans categorise their Jewish identity as a religious one, an increasing number also largely define themselves as non-practicing religiously (Pew Research Center, 2021).
6 In his book *Jews Don't Count*, Baddiel references his families' experiences of persecution at the hands of the Nazis and used this to reflect on his Jewish identity: "I'm an atheist and yet the Gestapo would shoot me tomorrow. Racists who don't like Jews never ask the Jew they are abusing how often they go to the synagogue" (2021, pp. 40–41).
7 According to Caplan (2018), these are: Harold Clurman, Lee Strasberg, Stella Adler, John Garfield, Howard Da Silva, John Randolph, Clifford Odets, Morris Carnovsky, Sanford Meisner, Anna Sokolow and Lee J. Cobb.

8 Chekhov himself was allegedly somewhat Jewish, having a Jewish mother but a non-Jewish father, and so Chekhov's own relationship to his Jewishness is potentially worthy of future enquiry.

9 And other Moscow Art Theatre practitioners including Boleslavsky, Meyerhold, and Vakhtangov (Chinoy, 2013).

10 "*Tanach*" is an acronym for the three main sets of texts in Judaism, the *Torah* (Hebrew Bible, literally "Instruction" or "Law"), *Nevi'im* (Prophets) and *Ketuvim* (Writings).

11 The oldest surviving *Tanach* is the Leningrad Codex of the Masoretic Texts. Also confirmed by the Dead Sea Scrolls which, despite over 1,000 years of difference, lines up almost perfectly with the Masoretic Texts (Baker, 2022).

12 Writing "G-d" comes from the Jewish tradition not to write out the name of the Divine, even in English. This originates in the prohibition against erasing G-d's name (see *The William Davidson Talmud*, Shavuot 35a) and highlights the value of text in Jewish practice.

13 Clurman relates a story of a student of the group theatre (specifically a student of Meisner) standing up to their "old time" director's instruction by asking, "Why?" To which the director responded: "Don't ask me any of those arty Group Theatre questions" (Gonsalves and Irish, 2021, p. 16).

14 The Tzemach Tzedek was Rabbi Menachem Mendel (1789–1866), the third Rebbe of Chabad, a branch of Hassidic-Judaism founded in the 18th century.

15 The Baal Shem Tov was Rabbi Israel ben Eliezer (1698–1760), a Jewish leader and mystic who founded the Hasidic movement.

16 It is worth noting that, even at the time, some members of the Group spoke out against their treatment of its Black associates.

17 This issue is also explored in the context of the Jewish communities of Vienna in the early 20th century in Tom Stoppard's 2020 pseudo-biographical play *Leopoldstadt*.

18 For example, car magnate Henry Ford was a virulent antisemite who, in 1921, published the first English-language translation "of [the] long-discredited *Protocols of the Elders of Zion* (concocted by Czarist agents in 1905 and purporting to document a Jewish conspiracy for world domination)" (Brook, 2017, p. 5).

References

Adler, S. (1999) *Stella Adler on Ibsen, Strindberg, and Chekhov*. Edited by B. Paris. New York: Alfred A. Knopf, Inc.

Adler, S. (2000) *The Art of Acting*. Edited by H. Kissel. New York: Applause Books.

Baddiel, D. (2021) *Jews Don't Count*. London: TLS Books.

Baddiel, D. (2022) "Why don't Jews play Jews? – David Baddiel on the row over Helen Mirren as Golda Meir", *The Guardian*, 12 January. Available at: www.theguardian.com/film/2022/jan/12/helen-mirren-golda-meir-maureen-lipman-david-baddiel-row-jews-bojack-horseman?fbclid=IwAR1tvF13yO-gNg_F9q8t7u Q-E1WlOiS2J3TMWppiXOth4K0SYJySW12_-zw (Accessed 31 July 2022).

Baker, M. (2022) *Oldest Bible Manuscripts*. 4 March. Available at: https://youtu.be/TvmAaXUKkco (Accessed 23 December 2022).

Bial, H. (2005) *Acting Jewish: Negotiating Ethnicity on the American Stage & Screen*. Ann Arbor: The University of Michigan Press.

Birnbaum, P. (1988) *Encyclopaedia of Jewish Concepts*. New York: Hebrew Publishing Company.

Brook, V. (2017) "Still an Empire of Their Own: How Jews Remain Atop a Reinvented Hollywood", in V. Brook and M. Renov (eds), *Casden Institute for the Study of the Jewish Role in American Life Annual Review*, Volume 14. West Lafayette: Purdue University Press.

Butler, I. (2022) *The Method: How the Twentieth Century Learned to Act*. New York: Bloomsbury Publishing.

Buxbaum, Y. (2006) *The Light and Fire of the Baal Shem Tov*. London: Bloomsbury.

Caplan, D. (2018) *Yiddish Empire: The Vilna Troupe, Jewish Theater, and the Art of Itinerancy*. Ann Arbor: University of Michigan Press.

Cesarani, D. (2021) *The Left and the Jews, the Jews and the Left*. London: No Pasaran Media.

Chinoy, H.K. (2013) *The Group Theatre: Passion, Politics, and Performance in the Depression Era*. New York: Palgrave Macmillan.

Clurman, H. (1946) *The Fervent Years: The Story of the Group Theatre and the Thirties*. London: Dennis Dobson Limited.

Cohen, E. (2010) "Impact of the Group of Co-migrants on Strategies of Accultura-tion: Towards an Expansion of the Berry Model", *International Migration*, 49(4), pp. 1–22. doi:10.1111/j.1468-2435.2009.00589.x.

Cohen, L. (ed.) (2010) *The Lee Strasberg Notes*. Abingdon: Routledge.

Cohen, L. (2019) *A Concise Introduction to: Lee Strasberg*. Digital Theatre +. Available at: https://edu.digitaltheatreplus.com/content/guides/lee-strasberg (Accessed 31 July 2022).

Drescher, F. in Goldman, A. (2020) "The Originals #6 Fran Drescher" [Podcast]. *Los Angeles Magazine*, 28 April. Available at: https://www.lamag.com/culturefiles/fran-drescher-the-originals/ (Accessed 17 November 2021).

Freeman, B. M. (2020) "Erasive Antisemitism – Naming a Subcategory of Antisemit-ism", *benmfreeman.medium.com*, 20 September. Available at: https://benmfreeman.medium.com/erasive-antisemitism-cc71bf7259bb (Accessed 31 July 2022).

Freeman, B. M. (2021) *Jewish Pride: Rebuilding a People*. London: No Pasaran Media.

Gallico, P. (2015[1938]) *Farewell to Sport*. Reprint. New York: Open Road Integrated Media, Inc.

Gonsalves, A. and Irish, T. (2021) *Shakespeare and Meisner: A Practical Guide for Actors, Directors, Students and Teachers*. London: Bloomsbury.

Green, E. (2016a) "Are Jews White?", *The Atlantic*, 5 December. Available at: https://www.theatlantic.com/politics/archive/2016/12/are-jews-white/509453/ (Accessed 31 July 2022).

Green, E. (2016b) *"Jews and the Social Construction of Race"*, *The Atlantic*, 5 December. Available at: https://www.theatlantic.com/politics/archive/2016/12/jews-whiteness/622676/ (Accessed 9 October 2022)

Halbertal, M. (1997) *People of the Book: Canon, Meaning, and Authority*. London: Harvard University Press.

Horn, D. (2021) *People Love Dead Jews: Reports from a Haunted Present*. London: W. W. Norton & Company.

Jacobson, Y. Y. (2016) *Give Me Truth: What Is the Value of Truth in Today's World?* Available at: https://www.theyeshiva.net/jewish/2839/essay-behaaloscha-give-me-truth (Accessed 16 October 2022).

Jewish Virtual Library (2022) *Vital Statistics: Jewish Population of the World (1882 – Present)* Available at: https://www.jewishvirtuallibrary.org/jewish-population-of-the-world (Accessed 11 December 2022).

Kellner, D. (1997) "Critical Theory and Cultural Studies: The Missed Articulation", in J. McGuigan (ed.) *Cultural Methodologies*. London: Sage Publications.

Kissel, H. (ed.) (2000) "Afterword", in S. Adler, *The Art of Acting*. New York: Applause Books, pp. 262–271.

Laytner, A. (2004) *Arguing with God: A Jewish Tradition*. Lanham: Rowman & Littlefield Publishers.

Lee, M. (1997) "Relocating Location: Cultural Geography, the Specificity of Place and the City Habitus", in J. McGuigan (ed.) *Cultural Methodologies*. London: Sage Publications.

Liebman, L. (2022) "Who Gets to Play Jewish? Hollywood is long past the days of 'write Yiddish, cast British' – or is it?", *Vanity Fair*, 27 April. Available at: https://www.vanityfair.com/hollywood/2022/04/jewish-characters-jewish-actors-casting (Accessed 11 December 2022).

Lunfield, H. (1929) *American Jewish Year Book*. Edited by H. Schneiderman. Philadelphia, PA: The Jewish Publication Society of America.

Malague, R. (2012) *An Actress Prepares: Women and "the Method"*. Abingdon: Routledge.

Malague, R. (2021) *A Concise Introduction to Sanford Meisner*. Digital Theatre +. Available at: https://edu.digitaltheatreplus.com/content/guides/a-concise-introduction-to-sanford-meisner (Accessed 31 July 2022).

Meisner, S. and Longwell, D. (1987) *Sanford Meisner on Acting*. New York: Vintage Books.

Muñoz, J. (2000) "Feeling Brown: Ethnicity and Affect in Ricardo Bracho's *The Sweetest Hangover (and Other STDs)*", *Theatre Journal*, 52(1), pp. 67–79.

Nirenberg, D. (2013) *Anti-Judaism: The Western Tradition*. London: W. W. Norton & Co.

Office of the Chief Rabbi (2016) *History of the Chief Rabbinate*. Available at: https://chiefrabbi.org/history-chief-rabbinate/ (Accessed 9 October 2022).

Oz, A. and Oz-Salzberger, F. (2012) *Jews and Words*. London: Yale University Press.

Peck, D. (ed.) (1997) "Jewish American Identity in Literature – Historical Background", *Society and Self, Critical Representations in Literature*. Available at: https://www.enotes.com/topics/jewish-american-identity-literature-15 (Accessed 12 December 2022).

Pew Research Center (2021) *Jewish Americans in 2020*. Available at: https://www.pewresearch.org/religion/2021/05/11/jewish-americans-in-2020/ (Accessed 11 December 2022).

Sacks, J. (2000) *Radical Then, Radical Now*. London: Bloomsbury Publishing.

Sacks, J. (2021) *The Power of Ideas: Words of Faith and Wisdom*. London: Hodder & Stoughton.

Stanislavski, C. 2003[1938] *An Actor Prepares*. Edited by E. Reynolds Hapgood. Reprint. New York: Routledge.

Stella Adler Studio of Acting (2014) *Stella Adler: Awake and Dream! from "American Masters*. 16 August. Available at: https://www.youtube.com/watch?v=4Yo4BLH87YY (Accessed 8 December 2022).

Strandberg-Long, P. (2018) "Mapping Meisner – how Stanislavski's system influenced Meisner's process and why it matters to British Drama School training today", *Stanislavski Studies*, 6(1), pp. 11–19.

The Rabbi Sacks Legacy (2018) *The Way of Identity: On Being a Jew (Ten Paths to God | Unit 1) | Rabbi Jonathan Sacks*. 23 March. Available at: https://www.youtube.com/watch?v=YadhEpDpAsc (Accessed 8 December 2022).

The William Davidson Talmud (Koren-Steinsaltz). Available at: https://www.sefaria.org/Shevuot.35a.1?lang=bi (Accessed 16 February 2023).

Ward, E. (2017) "Skin in the Game: How Antisemitism Animates White Nationalism", *The Public Eye*, Summer, pp. 9–15. Available at: https://politicalresearch.org/sites/default/files/2018-10/PE_Summer2017_web.pdf (Accessed 30 October 2021).

Zukin, S. (1991) *Landscapes of Power*. Berkeley, CA: University of California Press.

Zurawik, D. (2003) *The Jews of Prime Time*. Hanover, NH:University Press of New England.

7

THE INTRACULTURAL PROJECT

Creating an Inclusive Rehearsal Room Beyond Stanislavsky

Kristine Landon-Smith and Dominic Hingorani

This chapter is an edited version of a scripted conversation between two international artists that served as one of two keynote presentations at the Stanislavsky and Race symposium in November 2021.

DOMINIC HINGORANI: One of the jobs of the academic or researcher in the field of performance-making is to uncover, understand and make visible methodological innovations in practice. I am delighted to be sitting with Kristine, who I have had the good fortune to know not only as a friend and mentor, but also as an award-winning director and the creator of an innovative inclusive rehearsal methodology which I have had the privilege not only of writing about, but also observing at first hand. As a researcher, I was lucky enough to be able to spend time in Kristine's rehearsal room, but it is exactly because we have an immediate need to address the issue of "race" and actor training that events like this symposium are vital as a means to share practice and engage with constructive solutions. In this respect, Kristine has developed a coherent, accessible and transferable praxis that is a vital part of this urgent debate. It is also important for us as practice-as-researchers to map and create a critical context for such work. This debate on race, representation and inclusion in performance, of which Kristine's work is an extremely important part, comes out of a particular historiography of performance in the UK.

We know where we want to go in terms of creating a rehearsal room that engages with difference, but in order to understand how we may get there, it is perhaps worth spending a moment recognising where we have come from. I would suggest that the stage is a reflection of how we understand ourselves as a nation. If so, how do we find a methodology that enables us to tell *all* of the stories of ourselves to each other? It is

DOI: 10.4324/9781003330882-11

worth reiterating the key moments from post-war Britain to the present time to understand why we are here and, more importantly, where performer training needs to go. The disclaimer from me is there is no level playing field in terms of "race and ethnicity" in the arts because we are still imbricated in colonial histories and discourses staged quite clearly in the current culture wars. Post-war migrations of Commonwealth countries, notably including India, Pakistan and the Caribbean, are exemplified in the arrival of the Windrush generation of 1948. To evidence my earlier comment on the effects of enduring racist colonial thinking, we only need to look at the scandal in 2017 when it emerged that hundreds of that Windrush generation have been wrongly detained, deported and denied legal rights as a result of racist policy. Of course, the presence of people of colour in the UK historically pre-dates this, but I want to use as a jumping-off point for this discussion a key publication in relation to the debate on theatre, race and ethnicity the arts in Britain ignores – *The Arts of Ethnic Minorities in Britain* (1976). For the first time, an official document espoused the view that "ethnic arts" should not be regarded as an exotic extra outside of British theatre, but should be understood, fostered and funded as though they were a part of British theatre. Whether this has been the case is a moot point as Arts Council England (ACE) is still having to make the creative case for diversity, and we are discussing today not only how that has been applied to those arts, but also, crucially in this discussion, to those *artists*.

Indeed, we are seeing the emergence of new political signifiers such as "Global Majority", which operate to contest the exclusionary and discriminatory practices of the centre. Such signifiers have historiographical antecedents such as the construction of "Black" in the 1980s operating as a positive political signifier for both Asian and Afro-Caribbean communities at that time, not, as postcolonial theorist Stuart Hall points out, "because they were culturally, ethnically, linguistically or even physically the 'same', but because they were treated as the 'same' (i.e., 'non-white' or 'other') by the dominant culture" (2020, pp 74–75).

Such modes of collective resistance are one of the reasons institutional discriminatory modes of exclusion have been made visible and we have seen the emergence of extraordinary playwrights, theatre companies, directors, creative producers and, of course, actors from Global Majority backgrounds in post-war UK. While there is obviously a great deal further to go in terms of representation, we have not seen anything like its equivalence emerge in relation to a performer training that recognises, takes account of and celebrates the cultural diversity of Global Majority performers on the UK site.

However, we need to also learn lessons from our past. While signifiers can be political loci of resistance, they can also paradoxically lead to a reductive ghettoisation and exoticism that turn inward and re-marginalises groups into an ethnic cul-de-sac of separation. The problem we have is that we need to create an inclusive performer training that recognises, marks and is inscribed by difference.

I regard Kristine's practice as a vital and creatively constructive way ahead for all of us as performance makers to decolonise one of the last bastions of discrimination in our world – the rehearsal room. Kristine, what brings you here to the Stanislavsky symposium and where did your journey to this practice start?

KRISTINE LANDON-SMITH: I am so delighted to be part of this important conversation. I am not a Stanislavsky scholar, but I began my long enquiry into actor training almost as a reaction to my own Stanislavsky training and my experience as an actor in the UK over 15 years, where the *lingua franca* of the rehearsal room was predominantly Stanislavsky. So I am going to speak very personally about how and why I began to craft an alternative to Stanislavsky. I also want to talk very specifically about where the Stanislavsky training and methodology was not able to provide me with the conditions to work in where I felt I could thrive by being able to bring my unique identity as an integral ingredient to the making of any work.

I and many other colleagues globally are exploring this question: what does it really mean to bring yourself into a room, your *whole* self into the room, where that whole self is not only welcomed, but also considered as a vital ingredient in the making of a work? How does one shape a pedagogy that is broad enough to support each and every actor equally in the collective? Kaja Dunn, Nicole Brewer, Pamela Jikiemi, Sharrell D Luckett, Amy Ginther, Broderick Chow, Lisa Peck, Daron Oram, Chris Hay, Gail Babb, Dominic, and Siiri and Jay are among many who are constantly interrogating this question and, therefore, asking whether a Stanislavsky methodology is still fit for purpose, and whether by offering approaches that, in the main, are rooted in Eurocentricity, we are providing a curriculum broad enough to serve the diverse body of students in our rehearsal rooms.

My own interrogation into the Stanislavsky method and methods flowing from Stanislavsky began in earnest when I was working with my company Tamasha. Tamasha is a company I co-founded in 1989 with my colleague Sudha Bhuchar to address the lack of stories of the South Asian diaspora being told with a contemporary practice approach on the British stage. I am of mixed heritage, Indian and Australian, and Sudha is Punjabi. In the year 2000, we set up a training wing within our organisation where we trained actors, directors, writers and designers. I ran all the acting workshops and, while hosting actors from a variety of backgrounds and heritages on a daily basis, I observed that so many of these actors felt a sense of paralysis and fear when they came to the floor, particularly with a text from the mainstream canon of work. Actors did not have a sense that their individual and specific "being-in-the-world" could play a part in the making of a piece of work. I had witnessed this earlier in the many education programmes I ran at Tamasha with my colleague Sita Brahma-chari in secondary schools, and there, too, I saw a complete disavowal and lack of engagement with the cultural contexts of the students in the drama classroom. These experiences had a profound impact on me, and they proved to be the catalyst for my intracultural theatre practice that I have been developing over some years.

Today, I find I have an even greater sense of urgency with this work as I still see actors struggling in spaces where differences are ignored rather than nurtured, and where leaders often lack a language that can help their actors investigate the richness of their own background, and, moreover, lack a methodology that allows them to bring these to bear on the acting challenges their actors are facing. This is also of great significance for the audiences we are working with today who also need to feel that the intracultural context is brought into the meaning and expression of new or traditional texts – we are living in a globalised world in which intracultural meaning plays an ever greater role.

DOMINIC HINGORANI: I think it is fascinating that even though at this stage you were a practitioner rather than an academic researcher, the approach is the same. You identified a problem – importantly, a problem only really visible in the practice space – and then set about through a series of methodological experiments over time to find a solution. In this way, I am very interested to also frame this conversation across practice and the academy – as part of the project of myself and many colleagues in both spaces – since occupying both is to make porous the borders between them. Your work also demonstrates the power of praxis. We want to change not only the stages in terms of inclusion, access and representation, but also, crucially, de-colonise the academy, pedagogy and training institutions such as conservatoires.

You have rightly referenced how your work engages with postcolonial thinkers such as Indian academic and practitioner Rustom Bharucha, and his idea of "intra-cultural" practice that is so central to your methodology is the recognition and crucially active *engagement* with "difference". I would like to take this point a little further and say that – to draw on postcolonial theorist Homi Bhabha – the importance of the performance of what he would call "counter-narratives" to contest homogenous constructions of the nation, which excludes diversity and your approach of intracultural actor training, is one such manoeuvre:

Once the liminality of the nation space is established, and its signifying difference is turned from the boundary outside to its finitude 'within', the threat of cultural difference is no longer a problem of 'other' people. It becomes a question of the otherness of the people as one.

(Bhabha, 1994, p. 150)

DOMINIC HINGORANI: Your approach recognises difference as a vital and creative tool. However, it is also the job of the actor to be someone else, to engage in a journey into otherness, to recognise the limits of their own cultural horizons. How can we keep the two in play?

KRISTINE LANDON-SMITH: Yes, I'd like to pick up on the reference to Rustom Bharucha, who first alerted me to this idea about playing with difference within one's own space rather than looking to play with difference only across national boundaries. Bharucha proposes intraculturalism as "a meeting and exposure of differences within seemingly homogenised identities and groups" (1996, p. 116). He advocates the importance of interacting "*through* one's difference constituted as it is through social and cultural specificities, angularities, quirks, imperfections, and limitations" (Ibid.).

So what does this mean and what does it look like in terms of working with the actor, and helping each and every actor understand the validation of self within a culture which may often feel homogenous and hierarchical? The first step is to assist actors to come to self. To have a pedagogy around coming to self. As I stated previously, in my early explorations I found that performers faced great difficulties breaking free of a perception that the specifics of their own being-in-the-world did not have a place or function when working on the floor in rehearsal or on stage. Instead, performers often felt they should always start with a kind of neutrality in order to reach for certain parameters to do with the world of the play, and that they should follow a methodology that did not call for individuality. I believe that this approach has largely been received through a combination of a "rigid" teaching of Stanislavsky combined with an institutional culture that has called for "neutral" as a starting point. And that neutral is always directed by the hegemony of the institution, which makes exploration and discovery of something more inclusive that embraces pluralism very difficult. This, for me, seems to have stood in the way of allowing performers to find an authentic expression of their unique cultural contexts on stage and has stalled the pace of change.

I am always amazed to witness students not used to using their own vernaculars in readings of texts and hardly ever utilising other languages-in the professional space - that they may or may not speak fluently. They prioritise a sort of measured, even-sounding English that for them approximates to something they think might sound like a version of what it is to be an actor in the mainstream, an actor worthy of conservatoire training, an actor who may be considered for casting by the National Theatre. I describe this in my writing as "mimicking the centre".

So from those early workshops in 2000 at Tamasha, I gently began to encourage actors to use everything that they had in their make-up as they came to the floor. This was the beginning of a multi-vernacular, multi-linguistic practice, potentially broad enough to embrace the pluralistic identities in our 21st-century training and rehearsal rooms.

Yeah, I'm whitening it up. I say that because, because my whole thing was to show you what I think an actor is and that's how I'll portray it [...] so I will talk like this because they'll all accept me like that.

(Student in training 2014)

I've always felt a bit like the 'token Asian' on the course, and this made me feel quite 'othered' particularly in terms of the curriculum. When I received this play and my casting I was terrified – I really didn't want to speak Mandarin [...] But by having this safe space created, and this celebration of other cultures and experiences, I slowly became a lot more comfortable speaking Mandarin, and by extension, being Asian. I realised my peers didn't disdain my 'otherness', but thought it was fantastic that I was different. Being comfortable being me while performing is such a new experience and I'm very grateful for it.

(Student in training 2021)

DOMINIC HINGORANI: I think it is wonderful to capture these reflections and see how powerful it is for these actors to be creatively acknowledged in the rehearsal room. It seems the key aspect of your approach for me is the recognition that "white" is an ethnicity – because through that conceptual manoeuvre you radically open up a space of play that enables "difference for all" but simultaneously makes visible and de-centres "whiteness" from the centre. Crucially, to me, it enables you to look even further at intersectionality – embracing the myriad aspects that make us all unique, different, and worth telling stories about – so that geography, class, sexuality, gender and race are embraced in the room. It also starts to understand the lived complexities of power relations that exist in/through individuals, and at the same time decentre and interrogate notions of privilege. In this way your approach celebrates difference as opposed to diversity, which suggests as a term the "separation of totalised cultures that live unsullied by the intertextuality of their historical locations" (Bhabha, 1994, p. 34). A white, working class northern woman does not bring the same experience into the room as a white, middle class gay man.

KRISTINE LANDON-SMITH: Yes, "white" is an ethnicity and is an integral part of the intracultural project. A white student can also feel a pressure not to bring their unique identity to the floor because of socioeconomic factors, sexuality, gender identity: anything that an actor or student feels may not be asked for. And here we come to the question of how to hold a sense of self whilst exploring the fiction.

So where students have somehow felt that their unique identity is not of value, they tend to "mimic the centre". In improvisations, for example, exploring the "Real I" students can bring a truncated version of themselves – code-switching – to present a version of themselves which they feel is being asked for, which they feel may be more palatable to the institution. Stanislavsky likened the "Real I" to when the actor comes to the stage as herself, with her words and actions bearing the imprint of her own personality. The "Dramatic I" was described by Stanislavsky as something that would look and sound as human as the "Real I", but would, in fact, be created behaviour; something that looks like life, but is organised in a way to make an audience believe in the events presented. The "Real I" was important to Stanislavsky as he believed in the presence of the actor's self as the foundation on which to build a performance, stating that truth in performance emanated from the actor, and it was the sharing of the actor's inner soul or inner self which gave the feeling of truth or authenticity. But Stanislavsky's judgement on authenticity and those teaching Stanislavsky are often judgements that can only offer a very narrow version of authenticity, and thus, I think this has become very problematic in the context of today.

In all Stanislavsky's writings, *there is no mention whatsoever of one's own idiosyncratic detail, one's own historical narrative and cultural context, and how this finds a position within the creation of a character.* While Stanislavsky advocated using one's own emotions in order that one can find something that resembles authentic human behaviour on stage, there was no provision for incorporating the actor's own cultural context in this process. So regarding the "Real I" and the "Dramatic I", I feel it is as though Stanislavsky privileged the fictionalised character rather than the artist creating the fiction. He advocated for an intangible belief in the make-believe, which, in so doing, in my opinion, necessitates an erasure of unique qualities and potentialities as the actor subjugates herself primarily to the fixed circumstances of the play.

I don't believe that this erasure of difference was maliciously intended. I think the Stanislavsky method and the adapted teachings of Stanislavsky over a number of decades promoted what Rustom Bharucha would term as a "naïve acceptance of an innately human universality": Bharucha goes on to say, "that in the assumption of a shared universality there can be a total erasure of participants' ethnicities in favour of their universal human identities, creativities and potentialities: all distinctions are erased" (2000, p. 35). And, as I have said before, we need to consider the universality that is proposed: it is a universality that is invariably cast in a white, patriarchal, heterosexist image. So, the universality, or the neutral, if you like, is never politically neutral and is a very narrow version of truth and authenticity.

This is what I have been trying to untangle and understand in my research as I have worked to create a methodology that speaks back to practices that erase individuality and difference. In short, discriminatory practices that do not speak to the reality of a global world in which we all mix with our unique heritage.

We had a group that were from all over the world; We had an American, a Korean, a Canadian, Australians [...] So we would look at the Stanislavskian approach or the Strasbergian approach, or the Meisnerian approach, or a little bit of Suzuki or Butoh. But there was never ever a moment where, um, cultural context was ever sort of broached as a subject.

(Student in training 2013)

KRISTINE LANDON-SMITH: So moving from the "Real I" to the "Dramatic I", the Stanislavsky "system" held no guidance for me around how to incorporate pluralistic cultural identities in the crafting of a work for performance and how to hold a sense of self while merging with a fictional character. My intracultural methodology prescribes exercises that encourage the "Real I" before any exploration of the text begins, and then seeks to make a bridge between the actor's identity and the world of the play. Even once text work begins, the "Real I" is preferred over the "Dramatic I" in my approach. The "Dramatic I" can cloud the ability of the actor to be present on stage, and one has to be very aware of this critical point in training and rehearsals where when moving to text, moving to the "Dramatic I", the actor can fall to ground zero again and experience a complete loss of the value of their unique identity as an integral part of the ingredients for the work. This for me is the critical stage of any rehearsal.

So in my work I question the necessity of the distinction itself of "Real I" and "Dramatic I", finding it not helpful. I am suggesting that, in actor training, in order for every actor to feel a validity in their unique being, the emphasis should remain with the "Real I". I must add that I have always found this notion of the real person merging with a fictional character impossible to understand. In my early years as an actor, I struggled with the idea of character. I never understood what it meant to "merge with character", "to live the fictional circumstances of someone else." I always thought, "Whatever happens, it is always going to be me on the stage, my voice coming out of my mouth, my feet standing on the ground and my ears listening." No one in those early years of training and working could explain to me how to hold one's sense of self when moving to a text, when moving to fictional settings.

Later in my career, I found support in the work of Philippe Gaulier. Instead of encouraging working through the "Dramatic I", Gaulier says, "When you know Falstaff, when you know the writings of Rabelais, when you know great tragedy – all these marvellous things – I try to say to that person, [the actor] you are higher, you are funnier, you are bigger" (cited in Rea, 1991, p. 13). Gaulier insists on privileging the actor over the character by suggesting that the iconic character of Falstaff, or a great comic work such as one written by Rabelais, is only the starting point for the actor. The actor should not be in the shadow of these imaginings. The actor should rather use them as source material and create from there. The development of my intracultural methodology draws on the work of Gaulier where the actor has to work from within themselves rather than paying attention to exercises and techniques that sit outside of who they are. Gaulier encourages actors to find their pleasure to play something, rather than their pleasure to try and become something they are not. The actor always knows they are having pleasure as themselves in playing something, pleasure to wear a red dress, pleasure to play a death scene, pleasure to play looking out of a window – the actor does not lose sight of their own pleasure in playing these things, and in so doing they are extremely alert to their unique creativity and potentiality that they can bring to this endeavour.

So whilst Gaulier has perhaps become a controversial figure because of his reputation of working from a *via negativa* approach, berating the artist for what she is not rather than praising her for what she is, I took from Gaulier this idea about me the actor being as important as the text – *above* the text even – and that my unique being was in fact a critical ingredient in the making of a work or the execution of an exercise. This is when I really began to understand how to craft a methodology where the actor could also be the expert in the making of a work, and their uniqueness could be placed firmly at the centre.

So I am now going to show a short video of how this works in practice. This is an excerpt from a workshop I ran in 2013 from The National Institute of Dramatic Art in Australia, working with students across different years in collaboration with four actors from Tamasha in the UK through video conferencing. The excerpt shows me working with two students, working across that sense of "Real I" and moving to text and the "Dramatic I". I go back and forth and back and forth until the actor gets a real sense of holding the "Real I" when she moves to text. At the end of the excerpt are some reflections from the two facilitators of the session.

The following is an edited transcript of the video, which begins with Kristine asking Participant 1, who is of Ethiopian heritage, what monologue she has chosen to explore, which is revealed to be from the play A Raisin in The Sun *by Lorraine Hansberry.*

KRISTINE LANDON-SMITH: *What is the character saying?*
PARTICIPANT 1: *She's talking about why she wants to study medicine.*
KRISTINE LANDON-SMITH: *Who is she talking to?*

PARTICIPANT 1: *To her African boyfriend.*
  (Kristine points to Participant 2 who is South African.)
KRISTINE LANDON-SMITH: *Aha! Here is the African boyfriend. Is he impressed?*
PARTICIPANT 1: *Yes. Yes.*
KRISTINE LANDON-SMITH: *Okay, let's have a look. You're going to do it with your text.*
PARTICIPANT 1: *Without my African dialect?*
KRISTINE LANDON-SMITH: *Let's see how you're doing it first and we'll work from there.*
PARTICIPANT 1: *(speaking in an American accent as described in the original text) When I was very small, we used to take our sledges out in the wintertime, and the only hills we had were the ice-covered stone steps of some houses down the road. We used to fill them in with ice, make them smooth, and slide down them all day. It was very dangerous.*
KRISTINE LANDON-SMITH: *Okay, very nice! Let's have a play around and see what working from your Ethiopian heritage might bring us. So you're an African college student telling your African boyfriend that you'll be back in a year or so because you're going to college. In other words, wait for me or don't wait for me, right?*
  (Kristine turns to Participant 2.)
  Okay, so you're impressed, but might be thinking "God, you will come back, won't you?"
  (Turns to Participant 1)
  And you might act like, "We'll see!"
PARTICIPANT 1: *(speaking how an Ethiopian woman might speak in English) When I was very small, we used to take our sledges out in the winter …*
KRISTINE LANDON-SMITH: *Okay, but let's do an improvisation first, not the actual text. Improvise the scenario.*
PARTICIPANT 1: *Okay.*
  (Participant 1 begins improvising in Ethiopian language)
KRISTINE LANDON-SMITH: *You can do it in English with an Ethiopian accent, not in the actual Ethiopian language.*
PARTICIPANT 1: *(improvising in English with an Ethiopian accent) You know I will be back for you. You can wait for me, but you know I have many things I want to accomplish in my life. You are not a priority, but I think you are a very handsome man. I could see how, you know, you could maybe be my husband one day.*
PARTICIPANT 2: *(improvising in his South African accent) I think maybe you're going to meet someone else where you are going.*
PARTICIPANT 1: *Nooooooo, not me, huh?*
PARTICIPANT 2: *Mmmm.*

PARTICIPANT 1: *I want you to wait for me, huh? Will you wait for me?*

PARTICIPANT 2: *I don't think my heart can do that. You're so beautiful. Someone will catch you somewhere else.*

PARTICIPANT 1: *Nooooooo. No. My heart belongs to you. But you must prove your worth, huh? You better not hang around with Cuckoo Vouley.*

PARTICIPANT 2: *Don't worry. I won't talk to her.*

PARTICIPANT 1: *I see you talk to her.*

PARTICIPANT 2: *No, you are my one and only.*

PARTICIPANT 1: *I saw you talk to her at the train station, huh? I better not hear anything. I got people watching you, huh?*

PARTICIPANT 2: *That was the last time. You know that.*

PARTICIPANT 1: *Ahh … You better not be lying to me.*

PARTICIPANT 2: *I don't lie to a beautiful girl like you.*

PARTICIPANT 1: *Ahh … You think I am beautiful, huh?*

PARTICIPANT 2: *You're smart, too. What more can I ask for?*

PARTICIPANT 1: *You know you are pretending.*

PARTICIPANT 2: *My mother will be a happy ma.*

KRISTINE LANDON-SMITH: *Okay. And now you can go to the text, as the character with an American accent, and he's talking back to you.*

PARTICIPANT 1: *(speaking English in an American accent) When I was very small, we used to take our sledges out in the wintertime …*

KRISTINE LANDON-SMITH: *(instructing Participant 2) And you come back. Stay in the scene and feed in.*

PARTICIPANT 2: *(speaking English in an American accent) That's beautiful.*

PARTICIPANT 1: *And the only things we had was the ice-covered stone steps of some houses down the road.*

KRISTINE LANDON-SMITH: *(instructing Participant 1) And now you're going to do it with an Ethiopian accent.*

PARTICIPANT 1: *(speaking English in an Ethiopian accent) And we used to fill them in with ice and make them smooth and slide down them all day.*

PARTICIPANT 2: *Eh … (He laughs.) That's great.*

PARTICIPANT 1: *It's very dangerous, you know, far too steep.*

PARTICIPANT 2: *Did you get hurt anytime?*

PARTICIPANT 1: *And, sure enough, one day a kid named Rufus came down too fast and hit the sidewalk.*

KRISTINE LANDON-SMITH: *Good. And now in an American accent. Same woman.*

PARTICIPANT 1: *(speaking in an American accent): And I remember standing there looking at his bloody open face …*

KRISTINE LANDON-SMITH: *And now in an Ethiopian accent.*

PARTICIPANT 1: *(speaking in an Ethiopian accent): … thinking that was the end of Rufus.*

PARTICIPANT 2: *Did you call an ambulance or anything?*

PARTICIPANT 1: *But the ambulance came.*

PARTICIPANT 2: *Ah.*

PARTICIPANT 2: *They took him to the hospital, fixed up his broken bone, sewed it all up. And the next time I saw Rufus he just had a little line down the middle of his face.*

PARTICIPANT 2: *And then you went back and started skiing down there again. Is that right?*

PARTICIPANT 1: *(Sighs.) I never got over that.*

KRISTINE LANDON-SMITH: *Now a bit of an American accent.*

PARTICIPANT 1: *(speaking in an American accent) What one person can do for another.*

KRISTINE LANDON-SMITH: *And now Ethiopian.*

PARTICIPANT 1: *(speaking in an Ethiopian accent) Fix up the problem. Make them whole again. I thought it was the most wonderful thing in the world. I wanted to do that. I think it is the one concrete thing that human beings could do for one another, you know. Fix up the problem, make them whole again. That was truly being God.*

KRISTINE LANDON-SMITH: *Okay, excellent. Really excellent work. Should we open it out to our observers?*

OBSERVER 1: *I think what I am observing is the absolute specificity of choice when you're dropping down into a place where you feel more culturally comfortable. I'm seeing that in praxis. And what I mean by praxis is the idea of theory and practice coming together. So at those last moments in the scene, you were using the actor's choices as a crystal, and as you rotated the crystal, there were lots of different entry points. But one of them is the most specific, which is where the actor sits culturally. What is fascinating to observe is the specificity of choice.*

(Observer 1 speaks to Participant 1)

Your voice dropped down into the character, your body changed.

(Observer 1 speaks to Kristine)

I'm constantly seeing those little moments of praxis in this work that affirms the theory that where you feel most comfortable – culturally – is the door we need to unlock. I think they are more generous choices, more specific choices, but also fundamentally more interesting and engaging choices. So that's what I'm noticing as you move from the theory that you present to a practice of layering, allowing actors to go to a place where they're feeling more comfortable culturally.

KRISTINE LANDON-SMITH: *Thank you. I like the way you've linked the theory and the practice.*

(Kristine turns to Observer 2)

Did you want to share anything?

OBSERVER 2: *Yes. There's something that struck me today. I kept on writing in my notes about depth: "Now the actor, now the voice, and now the*

*body movement – is free." I'm thinking about what happens when you,
Kristine, take the actor to a place which is closer – culturally closer. And
closer to memories the actors can find from their everyday life. What
happens instantly is the performance becomes deep. But this depth is not
only a question of the subject or the character. I see something like a
well. You can drop your bucket down and pull loads of nuances and
elements out, so the performance immediately has a hundred shades.*

DOMINIC HINGORANI: Thank you for sharing that excerpt, Kristine. I think,
for me, what is noteworthy in this video is the performance politics
articulated between actor and director. Firstly, the power relations
between actor and director, which are often hierarchical, especially in
text-based work, are transformed to something much more democratic.
The director has to explicitly accept the limits of their own cultural
knowledge and "play" with where the actor is. In short, the director is
implicated "in play" as much as the actors; Bharucha says, "To work with
an acknowledgement of imperfect knowledge could be the surest way of
securing the trust of one's collaborators" (2000, p. 70). I might suggest
this is an intracultural directing approach as well as actor training methodology. Kristine, could you comment on the work we have just seen?

KRISTINE LANDON-SMITH: I believe drawing on the cultural specificity of the
actor positions them as equal experts in the room. The improvisation
shows this – no one else in the room could have crafted that specific improvisation. It also shows the critical importance of diversity in training in terms
of the make-up of the cohort. These actors were in different years, and the
male actor, Participant 2, was the only Black actor in his year, so he had
never in his training played opposite another Black actor. I could sense how
his observing year group was very moved to see him in this scenario.

I usually set up an improvisation which foregrounds a vernacular other
than an even-sounding English. The possibility of the multi-linguistic is also
there, but I didn't choose to utilise it as the improvisation in English took off
so quickly. So I, too, have to think very quickly, work on my feet in the same
way I am asking the actor to. My use of language – "African girl, African
boyfriend" – places the heritages of the actors firmly in the room, but I could
have improved my language to "Ethiopian girl, South African boyfriend",
which reflected more accurately the heritages of the actors.

The massaging and practising of that point of moving from an improvisation where the "Real I" is fully present to text where the actor begins
to get a sense of how to hold the "Real I" as they merge with the
demands of the text is of tremendous importance.

DOMINIC HINGORANI: Your response to the video exemplifies for me the
importance that we all remain "reflective practitioners", and the importance
of praxis, i.e., the integration of theory and practice in the rehearsal room. In
this respect we see you are allowed to be the artist in the room – playful and

present – but also critically objective and able to simultaneously evaluate, analyse and critique your methodological practice. The video also serves as a microcosm demonstrating the huge amount of work you have done in this area developing your approach. It is also a route to finding constructive answers to address and re-set the discriminatory power relations and practices that currently exist and permeate our rehearsal and training spaces. Your practice – to me – offers an *inclusive* way forward to artistically, creatively and methodologically explore cultural questions of representation, difference and authenticity in training and performance institutions.

KRISTINE LANDON-SMITH: Yes, I believe within these intracultural negotiations lies the possibility of a shift in the power dynamic in an institutional setting. With these actors as the experts, the audience and the institution have to step towards them. I think through engaging and playing with the multifarious cultural identities that inhabit our rehearsal and training rooms, new interpretations will evolve, and work shaped by the dynamics of an intracultural ensemble will start to emerge. This is one way to affect change: developing work on a consistent basis that is a truly reflective representation of society today and inclusive of the myriad of stories that exist.

Being able to share and tell my ancestors' stories, my grandmother's, my mother's and my own experience into a safe environment in both the rehearsal room and on stage was a key part for me and my journey of helping unlock my true self […] I was just being myself: […] the actor who happens to be Australian Aboriginal, African American and Native American Indian.

(Student in training 2013)

Being able to work with my own identity, with my language, Hebrew, was an incredible thing that helped me do a lot of deep soul searching and realise how much my identity means to me […] this project was food for my Hebrew like water is vital to a plant.

(Student in training 2021)

DOMINIC HINGORANI: It's been wonderful having this discussion with you, Kristine. I would like, in closing, to draw together the key ideas and concepts that, for me, underpin your work and the aims of the intracultural actor training methodology you have created. I believe the work:

- recognises the pressure on the actor to "mimic the centre"
- encourages creative engagement through "play" with "difference"
- re-centres power relations to reposition the actor as an "expert in the room"
- re-focuses Stanislavsky's "system" on to the "Real I"
- engages with the cultural context of the actor as a route into character

● fosters a rehearsal room underpinned by a multi-vernacular/multi-linguistic inclusive practice

And, finally, I'd like to add one last thing you haven't mentioned, but I have witnessed in your rehearsal rooms and heard through testimonies from many actors. It's how you create a space that promotes "the pleasure to play" – and what more can we ask for our actors?

References

Bhabha, H. K. (1994) *The Location of Culture*. London: Routledge.

Bharucha, R. (1996) "Under the Sign of the Onion: Intracultural Negotiations in Theatre", *New Theatre Quarterly* 12(46), pp. 116–129.

Bharucha, R. (2000) *The Politics of Cultural Practice: Thinking through Theatre in an Age of Globalisation*. London: Athlone Press.

Hall, S. (2020) "The Work of Representation", in K. Prentki and N. Abraham (eds), *The Applied Theatre Reader*. London: Routledge, pp. 74–76.

Rea, K. (1991) "Play's the thing for good actors", *The Times*, 24 June, p. 13.

A REFLECTION ON THE INTRACULTURAL PROJECT

Mabuhay as an Act of Resistance

James Cooney

Since I was a teenager, I was fascinated by the story of Hamlet. The existential questions and the constant overthinking resonated with me as an angst-ridden young man who often felt "out of joint" with his time and place. I was surrounded by friends, some of whom I still have over 20 years later – "their adoption tried, grapple them unto thy soul with hoops of steel" (Shakespeare, 2008, 1.3: 65–66) – but on some level I always felt a little different.

I just couldn't put my finger on why.

Fast forward to 2016 and I am at The Royal Shakespeare Company playing Rosencrantz in a production of *Hamlet*. This was the first time at the RSC that the title role was played by a Black actor. The production had gone down well with audiences and critics alike. One critic for a national newspaper praised the "predominantly black ensemble" supported by a "white Rosencrantz and Guildenstern" (Billington, 2016). And in an instant, like an actor playing the ghost of Hamlet's father, I had been whitewashed. The difference I felt at school had a finger put right on it. To paraphrase Hamlet, God had given me one "self", and they made my "self" an "other".

My name is James Cooney. And yes, I may *seem* white, but I identify as mixed-race. Why? Well, because I am. I know not *seems*.

My name *could* have been James Macul Cooney, incorporating the name of my mother, Lucilyn Gesalan Macul, daughter to Lucena Sanoy Gesalan. By Filipino tradition, children adopt both of their parents' family names. However, I was born in England in 1989, where double-barrelled names were traditionally seen as "posh". My white, working class, northern Manchester dad certainly didn't fancy that, and so James Cooney was born and Macul was hidden away. Assimilation for me began at birth.

Like many mixed-race people and second-generation immigrants, I have often struggled to know where I belong. Who am I supposed to be? Or not

DOI: 10.4324/9781003330882-10

supposed to be? That is the question. When am I British and when am I Filipino? And if I am "half", when and where am I "whole"? The critic's review, not of my work but of my racial identity, reawakened the emotional burden I had carried for so long. How am I supposed to be my "self" when that "self" doesn't fit the expected narrative? I struggled once again to know where I belonged.

This experience of not belonging is one I have encountered as an acting student and as an actor trainer. As a student, my ethnic and racial identity was one that rarely came up in conversation, and when it did, my "racial ambiguity" was seen as a strength to capitalise upon in an industry that values the ability to transform. I learned how to "soften" my northern accent and speak RP,[1] how to "walk properly" because, according to the Head of Acting in my undergraduate course, I clearly hadn't learned how to do it when I was younger. We were encouraged to work against our "tells", or signs that we were relying on our personal habits rather than transforming into the "character". The curriculum was clear: neutrality equals good acting.

And yet, confusion would abound when I was also encouraged to be "myself", to hone my individuality and practice "authenticity". I would nod along, an expert in assimilating, pretending it all made sense, because if there's one thing I had learned was to not question the status quo. It would only bring me difficulty. I was studying at a highly competitive and prestigious drama school, surely they knew what was best for me. Just do as they say and, eventually, you will belong. This is what "the good immigrant" knows to do.[2]

However, that day of belonging never came. I was the more deceived. In the quest to belong, I was hiding parts of myself. I was nervous of being "authentic" because in doing so I would be harming my chances of work.

I wasn't on a quest to belong. I was on a quest to fit in.

The leading shame and vulnerability research professor Brené Brown defines "true belonging" as follows: "True belonging doesn't require you to change who you are; it requires you to be who you are" (2021, pp. 156–157).

Much like performing in Shakespeare, actor training in the UK is fraught with historical expectations and aesthetic "standards". These expectations can be a barrier to the experience of belonging – especially for actors/students who have traditionally been marginalised from rehearsal/training spaces – by forcing people to conform to a predetermined and unspoken (but well known) standard. The fascinating question for me is how these standards and expectations developed and how we might be able to dismantle them in our quest for belonging. The seemingly widespread adoption and dissemination (a dissemination which is often misrepresented and lost in translation) of Stanislavsky's "system" is a significant moment in the development of actor training and in defining acting standards. I will leave it to other much more knowledgeable writers to detail exactly how this adoption happened in UK drama school training, but I can speak to its impact upon me and my experience of using it as a student and working actor.

One impact on my training was the way in which the "system" encouraged a clear distinction between "the brain" and "the body". Whilst Stanislavsky may have moved away from his early table work to a more embodied "active analysis" of the text, my initial experience of the "system" began with "objective analysis". The text became a kind of artefact that the actor would "mine" for clues by reading the text and highlighting the "facts". This kind of table work is still often prioritised in my experience in professional rehearsal rooms today. During the rehearsals for *Hamlet*, for example, we spent a full *two weeks* of rehearsal sitting around tables paraphrasing Shakespeare into contemporary English, as well as identifying the present and historical facts of the text. I am not saying that this process is bad for "there is nothing either good or bad, but thinking makes it so" (Shakespeare, 2008, 2.2: 260–261). However, it encourages a certain ideology: our *intellectual response to the text* is of primary importance. Trust *the brain* more than the body.

I would argue that this ideal of trusting the brain over the body is a particularly white, Western and patriarchal ideal. It is precisely this ideology which has been used for millennia to oppress and control. In the process of colonisation, indigenous people are taught not to trust their bodies, and that rationality and logic are of primary importance. My experience of the "system" resonates with this ideal. Even the name – the "system" – implies a mechanical approach to acting, one in which you can find the "right" answer to the problem if you think hard enough. As a student actor, I actually appreciated this mechanical approach. It meant I could get the right answer and "pass". But, ultimately, this process further encouraged me to separate brain and body and perpetuate an ideology which can be used to oppress. An example of this would be an exercise in which a director would ask us to say the transitive verb we planned to use before speaking a line. If what we said did not "make sense" for the scene or what we played did not match the verb, we would be heavily criticised.

Similarly, the widespread adoption of the "system" in UK actor training has had the effect of creating a clear hierarchy in training/rehearsal rooms. My understanding of Stanislavsky's early work is that it was particularly hierarchical. The long rehearsal periods where he would carefully craft exactly how each "beat" of the play would look and be performed suggests a man who considered theatre the medium for the writer and director rather than the actor. The director was the *subject* and the actors were his *objects*. This hierarchy and separation of authorship persists in rehearsal rooms today, where the creative team are distinct from the cast. In some cases, productions are marketed using the name and reputation of the director and their particular style of production. If a certain actor doesn't *conform* to that directorial aesthetic, they risk their chances of not getting the job. Like the prioritising of the brain over the body, the training/rehearsal room is often led by a singular voice whose intellectual choices are prioritised over others. In my experience of the "system" in training, this voice is that of the trainer, passing judgement over whether the actors are doing "good work" or not. Invariably, this judgement is imbued with a white, Eurocentric and heteronormative aesthetic, even if the trainer does not identify with these descriptors. I know that I, as a mixed-race British Filipino, still find myself uncritically adopting this aesthetic because it's what I have learnt to mimic or because I think it's what I assume a predominantly white, Eurocentric and heteronormative audience want. This hierarchical approach constantly and consistently reproduces itself in the hope of maintaining power and control. In some ways, I don't blame the teachers, trainers and directors I've had for using the "system", especially when it requires an extraordinary amount of energy to disentangle yourself from its clutches once it has taken hold.

It is therefore all the more crucial that the work of Kristine Landon-Smith and her intracultural theatre practice are given a platform and experienced. It is my belief that her work can not only facilitate the development of skill in acting, but also move students towards an experience of belonging. It did exactly that for me when I experienced one of her classes. At the beginning of the class, we sat in a circle and were given a list of prompts. These included our full name, the names of our parents, the name of a significant ancestor, a body of water near where we grew up and a famous landmark near where we were born. Kristine invited us to share our answers to these prompts and also invited answers in another language if it was available to us. In doing so, I was being invited to bring more of myself to the rehearsal room. There was an understanding that I, the *actor*, and I, the *person*, are impossible to separate. No matter what the play or project, it is me and my body, brain and cultural context that will be in the space, so to try and keep parts of myself at the door is a fool's errand.

Kristine's practice, from this first exercise to working on a text-based scene, placed *me* as the expert of me. The usual hierarchical structure had been flattened. Suddenly I was in a position where I had a voice. I was encouraged to be seen and heard in the room and not assimilate into some kind of homogenous group of people. I wasn't there to please the director/teacher and waste energy questioning whether I was doing right by them or not. Instead, we were peers who were going to do some work together, playing different roles, none more important than another. In providing this framework, I could be fully present in experiencing the work and practising my skills as a performer.

I don't think I was alone. I felt like the other people in the room were experiencing something too. There was an energy in the room amongst the actors which now is difficult to describe – so I won't. Not because I can't, but because by attempting to name everything, we would be falling back into modes of existence akin to the "system". Again, the "system" persists!

Travelling to the Philippines as a child, I would arrive at the airport with signs saying "*Mabuhay*". I always figured this meant "Welcome" in Filipino. Like all languages, it was a way of saying, "You belong here". However, "*mabuhay*" originates from the word *buhay*, meaning "life". To welcome one another, Filipinos wish each other a "good life".

I often open actor training sessions I facilitate by saying "*Mabuhay*" to immediately introduce a different cultural perspective into the English-speaking rooms I work in. But in a world which ultimately ends with the absence of life, to wish another *buhay*/life can be seen as a form of resistance.

I am desperate for LIFE. Life is fascinating, it is unique and it is uncontainable. What strikes me is how often I wish to observe life in a play lasting two hours and 15 minutes with an interval so I can go and get a drink. But LIFE is not as predictable as that. If, like Hamlet, I want art "to hold, as 'twere, the mirror up to nature" and reflect "the very age and body of the time its form and pressure" (Shakespeare, 2008, 3.2: 23–25), then I am committed to encouraging life in the actors. But life is not something any of us can control. And that frightens us.

One of the lasting legacies of the "system" was to codify the elements involved in the process of acting performance. This articulation of the process has no doubt had great benefit to people looking to improve their skill as an actor. But rigidly following the "system" can block the elements of life which it hopes to unleash. Through her intracultural theatre practice, Landon-Smith has found ways for the actor to bring not just any life to their work, but their *own* life. By inviting the actor to bring their whole self, their whole being, their whole cultural context, intracultural theatre practice can breathe life into a system which has the capacity to quash it.

Remember: *mabuhay*! GOOD LIFE!

Notes

1 Received Pronunciation (RP) is traditionally considered to be the standard form of British English pronunciation based on educated speech in southern England.
2 The "good immigrant" refers to the idea that immigrants are welcome to the country they move to as long as they behave and contribute to society. If not, then they should be sent back to their country of origin. The term was used for a collection of essays called *The Good Immigrant* edited by Nikesh Shukla, published via crowdfunding in the UK in 2016.

References

Billington, M. (2016) "Paapa Essiedu is a graffiti prince in RSC's bright tragedy", review of *Hamlet*, directed by Simon Godwin. *The Guardian*, 23 March. Available at: https://www.theguardian.com/stage/2016/mar/23/hamlet-review-paapa-essiedu-rsc-tragedy (Accessed 1 February 2023).
Brown, B. (2021) *Atlas of the Heart*. London: Vermilion.
Shakespeare, W. (2008) *Hamlet*, edited by J. Bate and E. Rasmussen. Basingstoke: Macmillan.
Shukla, N. (ed.) (2016) *The Good Immigrant*. London: Unbound.

8

STANISLAVSKY, ROSE MCCLENDON AND REPARATIONS

Whiteness, Professionalization and Reframing Amateurism in the Theatre of the United States

Amy Steiger

In 1935, famed Broadway actor Rose McClendon, a Black woman, published a letter to the drama editor in the *New York Times* titled, "As to a New Negro Stage." In it, she announced the establishment of the Negro People's Theatre to develop a Black-run program of social realism and create a structure that would train and nurture a "long line of first-rate actors" (McClendon, 1945, p. 136). She believed it would "create a tradition that would equal the tradition of any national group." In an essay about Black actor training in the United States before the rise of Stanislavsky's "system", Monica White Ndounou places McClendon in the legacy of "a rich history of Black actor training grounded in careful study of craft, cultural expression, artistry, history, and lived experiences." Ndounou goes on to emphasize that, while Stanislavsky is celebrated as the progenitor of American actor training, "Black Americans have historically participated in actor training and have influenced acting technique in the United States" (2018, p. 124). McClendon, whose work was instrumental in the development of what were then called the Negro Units of the Federal Theatre Project, is rarely, if ever, cited as an important name in the history of actor training in the United States within predominantly white institutions. Her relative absence from canonical histories is emblematic of the need for a deliberate process of reconciliation and reparations for the harms of our theatrical and national past and present. An important part of that process is dismantling the structures and systems that have encouraged the celebration of white artists in the realm of professional theatre and erasure of the contributions of Black, Indigenous, and People of Color (BIPOC) actors who were historically denied resources and relegated to the margins.

Slightly more often, although still not regularly, students are made aware of the work of Hallie Flanagan, the white woman who was made head of the Federal Theatre Project; they are more likely still to learn about Stella Adler.

DOI: 10.4324/9781003330882-12

If they aren't clear about the specifics of Adler's work or her connection with Stanislavsky, they may be aware of her name and legacy. I reference both Adler and Flanagan here because their paths overlapped and diverged in instructive ways, as did their attitudes toward theatre's purpose. Both women – racialized in the United States as white – had resources that allowed them to travel out of the country and study emerging methods of theatre-making in Europe in the early 20th century. Both had encounters with Stanislavsky and other Russian theatre artists that shaped their later work in the United States.

Hallie Flanagan, whose studies took place on a Guggenheim-funded sabbatical from her position as a professor at Vassar College, a pre-dominantly white liberal arts institution, wrote a book about the Russian experiments she admired and became a successful non-commercial theatre artist (Dossett, 2020, p. 4). Because of this, she was tapped to lead the Federal Theatre Project, a division of the New Deal relief programs inten-ded to put people to work after the Great Depression known as the Works Progress Administration (WPA). Charlotte Canning has pointed out in *On the Performance Front* (2015, pp. 4–5) that Flanagan's status as a white woman facilitated her prominent position and the funding she received from the Guggenheim Foundation to travel and learn. Conscious of her own place in history, Flanagan wrote,

> Our whole emphasis in the theatre enterprises which we are about to undertake should be on re-thinking rather than remembering. [...] The theatre must become conscious of the implications of the changing social order, or the changing social order will ignore, and rightly, the implica-tions of the theatre.
>
> *(Dossett, 2020, p. 4)*

Part of the results of Flanagan's "re-thinking" was providing Rose McClen-don with resources, via the WPA, to build a structure that supported the work of Black artists.

In a television interview nearly 30 years later, Stella Adler revealed a similar awareness of the need for change as she commented on the shift toward making theatre in a purely commercial culture in the United States:

> [The American actor is] dedicated, one: to himself; and then: he's dedi-cated, because of that, to the personality that sells [...] and he becomes more and more [...] dedicated to himself and his property. Now, that is impossible in another environment. This is a transitional stage for us in America. The theatre has been a victim of many things – mechanization, the success motive – and now it's coming of age. We also are going to have to [...] be nationally understood as representing America, American ideas. [...] The American actor is going to have to make sacrifices for

that. [...] If not, we are going to be individually successful and not successful as a national cultural symbol.

(Adler in Rainbolt, 1964)

What Adler doesn't address is the presumed whiteness of that star, and the fact that, as it operates within the systems that built and sustain this country, professional theatre is rooted in white supremacy, patriarchy and settler-colonialism. In the intervening half-century since Adler did this interview, it has become clear that the national cultural symbol of the United States *is* understood to be the man she describes: an individual dedicated less to critical thought than to self-interest and unlimited acquisition of personal property and power. And despite her keen class-based analyses, Adler became known as one of the progenitors of *professional* actor training in the United States.

While the paths their careers and legacies took were quite different (tragically, McClendon died at the age of 36), McClendon, Flanagan and Adler all noted that theatre was at a tipping point in their own times and places, and over the past few years, once again, theatre in the United States finds itself in a "transitional stage," faced head-on with the opportunity to make reparations and correct past harms. As Ta-Nehisi Coates phrases it in a follow-up to his essential essay "The Case for Reparations," "virtually every institution with some degree of history in America, be it public, be it private, has a history of extracting wealth and resources out of the African-American community" (2019, para. 2). Often, the perpetuation of that theft in professional theatre relies on an anti-intellectual idea of actors as passively colonized bodies who serve a few people at the top of a hierarchical system. That system thrives on perpetuating a difference between mainstream theatre that is part of a market-driven business and amateur or publicly supported work that often resists the status quo and calls for change.

Within that system, actors have been expected to participate in a set of ideas about acting (and its purposes and processes) derived largely from various interpretations of the work of Konstantin Stanislavsky – interpretations that were developed in a context that promoted, supported and trained white artists while excluding and harming artists who were not white. In this chapter, I trace how Stanislavsky-based practices became aligned with whiteness under the auspices of professional theatre and suggest that any recuperation of Stanislavsky's legacy requires that we amend Adler and Flanagan's calls in the quotations above in the interest of revisiting McClendon's. Theatre has been part and parcel of a North America built by colonizing land and violently stealing labor, life and resources from Black people, Indigenous people, and People of Color. For theatre to become the cultural symbol and guide of a just and equitable nation, theatre artists – especially those of us who have been racialized as white – will have to reckon with our privilege and past and willingly make sacrifices in the form of material and artistic reparations. This begins with structural changes that tear down the pedestals on which historically celebrated white artists have been placed and invite critical examinations of their practices through the lenses of postcolonial and critical race theory.

In a 2019 *HowlRound* article, "Whiteness, Patriarchy and Resistance in Actor Training Texts", I suggested that "A market-driven context often reinforces the illusion that, for actors, dissent and critical thinking are inherently political, and training for professional work should take place outside of politics" (Steiger, 2019, para. 12). To expand on this, here I pose questions about the idea of "professionalization" in the work of Stanislavsky (and others) to make room for imagining new structures that dismantle white supremacy in theatre. Using Palestinian-American postcolonial scholar Edward Said's framing of amateurism as a potentially transformative social position, I consider how acting students in the classroom are, as bell hooks wrote, in a space of "radical possibility" (1994, p. 34). Finally, I highlight how BIPOC artists have suggested making the artistic and material reparations that are a necessary step in generating new models for theatre training in the United States.

Critical examinations of Stanislavsky and his legacy in the United States have been undertaken by scholars and artists for decades. For example, in "Willful Actors: Valuing Resistance in American Actor Training," Kari Barclay points out, through the lens of Sara Ahmed, who writes at the intersection of feminist, queer and race studies, that "a system of economic and social incentives disciplines performers' desires" (2019, p. 126). Barclay outlines a genealogy of Anglo-feminist criticism of Stanislavsky-based training and its attendant toxic hierarchies, reading American actor training through Ahmed's work on "the education of the will" and positing the emerging field of intimacy direction as a way to "encourage actors to honor their resistance and advocate for their pleasure" (Ibid., pp. 125–126). The earlier feminist scholarship with which their work is in conversation, however, often excludes discussions of race.

It is thanks to the history and contemporary practice of resistance among BIPOC artists that systemic white supremacy in professional theatre has been exposed and challenged. In recent years, "We See You White American Theater," a social media campaign calling out racist practices in professional theatre, issued a list of demands in the interest of equity and repair; Nicole M. Brewer and others have developed anti-racist theatre training to change the culture of the field; KO very publicly left a widely acclaimed role in the Broadway production of *Moulin Rouge* after unsatisfactory responses to producer Scott Rudin's history of abusive behavior, saying in an Instagram post, "Building a better industry is more important than putting money in my pockets" (KO, 2021). In the wake of this fervent call for change, re-evaluations of theatre''s practices have recently taken hold among white critics in the popular press. In "Is It Finally Twilight for the Theater's Sacred Monsters?", *New York Times* theater critic Jesse Green notes that Olga Knipper, an original member of the Moscow Art Theatre termed Stanislavsky a "monster" for having berated her so severely. Green suggests that artists in the United States working in Stanislavsky's legacy engaged in abusive behavior that was far more outrageous. Directors and producers, often also teachers and leaders in the field of theatre training, were supported in their "genius" despite bad behavior, continuing to produce celebrated work and never seeing consequences for their actions (Green, 2022, paras. 3–7).

Green raises the question of what we may have lost by giving these men the space they took up for generations, obscuring many artists doing work that was equally brilliant, often without the attendant harm. He holds up James Baldwin and Alice Childress (whose 1955 play *Trouble in Mind*, which only recently had a Broadway run, was about the very subject of race and power in theatre) as playwrights who were sidelined by white producers, pointing out that the Actors Studio "had a race problem it refused to acknowledge" (Ibid., para. 35). While Rose McClendon does list the Group Theatre as among the companies who voiced support for the Negro People's Theatre, Isaac Butler, in his recent cultural history *The Method: How the Twentieth Century Learned to Act*, offers evidence of the overt racism of the Group, pointing out that even with their interest in addressing social problems, they all but ignored white supremacy. He cites Bobby Lewis as revealing that the Group did not invite Black actors to company-building workshops (2022, p. 147). Later, Butler writes that Baldwin's 1964 play *Blues for Mr. Charlie* stylistically "challenges the very notions of authenticity on which the Method rests" and points out that in the Actors Studio Theatre's production, "Cheryl Crawford and Lee Strasberg attempted to smooth out its rougher, more controversial edges to make it more palatable to a white Broadway audience" (Ibid., pp. 297–298). Frank Corsaro, who was to direct it, had requested a rewrite to "soften the depiction of the white characters" (Ibid.). But while the Group are held up as pioneers of the fundamental skills actors need to succeed, any racism in their history is mostly ignored, nor are student-performers always given opportunities to question how white supremacist assumptions might be embedded in the models of production, training tools and rehearsal practices themselves.

Green's essay ends with a hope that "the theater's sacred monsters" might somehow be redeemed, but ultimately concludes that, "it will not be a net loss to the culture if the spaces such men occupied and turned into gilded niches from which to demand obedience and veneration, are vacated now" (Green, 2022, paras. 40–41). I appreciate the suggestion that it is past time to move beyond the "great men" story of theatre history; I also want to suggest here how the *structures* and *systems* within which these individuals worked (and behaved badly) encouraged their continued veneration. In other words, I suggest that the metaphorical spaces themselves, built as they were on a hierarchical and patriarchal blueprint designed by capitalism, white supremacy and colonization, were built to nurture monstrous behavior and discourage resistance. The "industry" has continued to tolerate such behavior well into the 21st century.

The exclusionary practices – if not official policies – of the schools of acting that fed professional theatre practice starting in the mid-20th century reflect a pattern in the post-reconstruction United States that encouraged white Americans to build wealth and social standing through material support from federally funded sources while excluding Black Americans. In a 2020 article entitled, "What Is Owed," Nikole Hannah-Jones points out that while Black people in the 20th century were subjected to overt theft and violence, they were also deprived of the ability to build wealth through various means. In addition, Hannah-Jones cites Ira Katznelson's book *When Affirmative Action Was White* (2005) in her assertion that "white Americans were not only free to earn money and accumulate wealth with exclusive access to the best jobs, best schools, best credit terms, but they were also getting substantial government help in doing so" (2020, para. 42).

Hallie Flanagan, in her capacity as director of the Federal Theatre Project, attempted to pay back some of the resources that supported her own work; thanks to the ideas and work of artists like Rose McClendon, the Federal Theatre Project celebrated and gave resources to new theatre by Black Americans. However, the Stanislavsky-inspired Group Theatre, members of which later established the Actors Studio, seem to have functioned more like the *other* New Deal programs of the federal government, which Katznelson terms "commanding instrument[s] of white privilege" (2005, p. 18). While the Actors Studio was established as a not-for-profit laboratory for professional actors (Manolikakis, n.d.), it was undoubtedly a predominantly white institution. The emergence of the Method as the foundation for actor training in the United States positioned white artists to be trained in the processes and systems that allowed them entry into and longevity in professional careers, while work that was geared toward social transformation was marginalized and deprived of material support. Especially after World War II and the emergence of the congressional House Un-American Activities Committee (HUAC), which investigated and blacklisted artists assumed to be communist and stripped programs like the Federal Theatre Project of funding, theatre that was critical of the white supremacist and patriarchal status quo was often relegated to amateur or "experimental" status, and thus pushed to the margins.

Professionalization and the Politics of Actor Training in the United States

Currently in the United States, artists from the Global Majority (as well as artists with disabilities and of marginalized genders) have questioned professional practices in commercial and professional not-for-profit theatre institutions. Thanks to social media campaigns rooted in anti-racist activism and to non-profit publications like *HowlRound* (organized as a collective and dedicated to global citizenship and equity) there are growing conversations around race, gender, accessibility, resistance and critical thinking in actors' work and training. As Brewer stresses in her *HowlRound* essay "Parents of Color and the Need for Anti-Racist Theatre Practices",

> Knowing that the roots of the theatre industrial complex are overwhelmingly capitalist, racist, patriarchal, and ableist – a sentinel of white feminism and staunch advocate of meritocracy – provides a wider framework for organizations to begin to effect the necessary long-lasting change that will have considerable impact [...].
>
> *(Brewer, 2019)*

But earlier in the 21st century, many acting teachers were still representing actors as passive and uncritical, laying the groundwork for white supremacist and patriarchal ideas that continue to go unquestioned when the main goal in training is understood to be preparation for entering a market or industry (rather than, say, anti-racist practice or preparing to change the field, engage with their communities to solve problems or be spiritual leaders, etc.) For example, the 2005 annual training issue of *American Theatre* included a panel discussion entitled "How Does Your Garden Grow? Conversations With 6 Actors Who Teach." The majority of artist/teachers given a platform here are not from the Global Majority, reflecting a positional bias in favor of white teachers even as the panel represented acting as a marginalized profession. The moderator of the panel, David Byron, introduces the conversation by pointing out that in the United States, drama departments at universities are typically granted less financial support and have fewer tenured professors than other departments, and connects this problem to the way actors are viewed in this country (Byron, 2005, p. 34).

The disempowerment of actors has a long and complex history, but it is clear in this panel how it is perpetuated in the early 21st-century United States, and how that disempowerment intersects with colonialist and patriarchal structures. Byron asks the actor/teachers, "Is the actor a proactive, creative force, not only on the stage, but in society as a whole?" (Ibid., p. 37). Marian Seldes replies that she doesn't "see the actor as a person who can influence and make a change. We are absolutely the servants of the writer" (Ibid.) Floyd King echoes her sentiment:

> We're the interpreters. It's not *our* words, it's not *our* thoughts, it's not *our* principles that we put up there on the stage. It's the playwright's. If we're doing our job right, that's what we're serving. If anyone's going to change the world, it's going to be a playwright.
>
> *(Ibid., pp. 37–38)*

These ideas make me wonder how and why these teachers feel the need to downplay the actor's social role to their students. Why does it seem virtuous, even necessary, for actors to be at someone else's service?

In response to Gary Sinise's opinion that "In the scheme of things, you know, there are more important things than acting," F. Murray Abraham – whose father was a refugee who fled famine in Syria – pipes in with, "It's the most important thing in the world!" He continues, "I think acting is definitely subversive. There's an anarchic quality to acting that people envy and lash out at. Actors represent a danger to society." Fiona Shaw, who was born in Ireland, responds, "I don't think that good acting is polemical, but I do think that the choices the actor makes are, of course, political" (Ibid., p. 38). Abraham and Shaw – the two members of this panel who have connections with marginalized and colonized populations – make clear through their comments that it is not simply "common sense" for teachers to represent actors as passive, apolitical instruments. Doing so reproduces the hegemonic *status quo*. Teaching students to recognize how they are positioned to resist the racist practices of what Brewer terms the "theatre industrial complex" (Brewer, 2019) reframes their goals and helps to lay a new foundation for theatre practice. They may question the assumed authority of men like Stanislavsky and the rules that have been derived from his work, and in doing so open up the possibility for non-hierarchical processes and thinking.

In *The Politics of American Actor Training* (Margolis and Tyler Renaud, 2010), several authors bring to light that training methods and the institutions in which they are taught and learned exist within a network of cultural and historical circumstances that relegate student/teacher relationships, learning outcomes, curriculum and assessment, etc. From these essays, one gets an impression that students of acting in the United States are beholden to their role supporting a consumer economy and have primarily utilitarian goals. But many of the authors call upon teachers to draw out the potential for critical thinking in the acting classroom. Jonathan Chambers argues that approaches based on Stanislavsky's "system" reflect and produce a humanist agenda. He also points out that while Stanislavsky's work began in a Europe where the shared experience of a "social democratic form of humanism" held sway, work like Strasberg's in the United States took hold in a historical environment that celebrated the capitalist value of the "*private* rights of each individual." But in Chambers' classroom, historicizing methods of acting emphasizes critical thinking over simple technical knowledge (2010, p. 37). Chandrasan points out that the colonialist introduction of European and American theatre training in India supplanted a rich native tradition: "the American system of theatre pedagogy has resulted in what we might call 'rampant professionalism,' uprooting the Indian theatre activist from his sense of immediacy and context, instilling Westernized sensibilities and aesthetics in place of Indian ones ..." (2010, p. 50). Chandrasan calls for a return to Indian forms of training in the interest of creating an actor, "who is politically and culturally conscious" (Ibid., p. 58). The focus of Leigh Woods's article is the institutional constrictions on training, and while she points out the strong benefits of theatre education in a liberal arts context, she suggests that pre-professional theatre programs do students a disservice by necessitating a technical specialization in performance (2010, p. 66). To overcome the de-emphasis on "cognate studies of drama," she invokes ancient traditions of theatre and calls on teachers to honor these ancestors, "especially the ones who took their motives from civic life" (Ibid., p. 76). Overwhelmingly, *The Politics of American Actor Training* points to "professionalization," and the various implications of that process, as the key to understanding how American students of acting define their work.

This problem was acknowledged in professional as well as scholarly circles in previous decades, but only recently in a way that supported real change. In the same issue of *American Theatre* cited above, Robert Brustein writes that as soon as "an actor starts thinking of the profession as 'the business' then it is inevitable that he or she will be more preoccupied with material rewards than with artistic satisfactions" (Brustein, 2005, pp. 46–48). He highlights a significant dilemma still facing actors in the United States who seek training. Many BFA and MFA programs call themselves "professional actor training programs", and actors intending to immerse themselves in "the business" of acting choose these, while performance studies and other academic graduate programs, as well as liberal arts-based undergraduate programs, encourage the ongoing scholarly study of performance alongside theatre practice. Shannon Jackson's study *Professing Performance* (2010) and Simon Shepherd and Mick Wallis's *Drama/Theatre/Performance* (2004) grapple with the long history of institutional distinctions between the academic study of theatre, drama and performance and the *practice* of those arts, both within and outside of the academy. Both trace the lineage of the field of performance studies, which initially defined itself in opposition to theatre studies, through theorists and practitioners in the 1960s, 70s and 80s whose work began in non-commercial, "amateur" spaces for audiences who not only tolerated, but also embraced their inability to fit into marketable ideas of what actors ought to be. But this dichotomous "insider/outsider" structure obscures the intellectual and scholarly investigations actors undertake in professionally oriented programs as much as it ignores the institutional and material limitations that constrain scholars in academic theatre programs.

The position of students in contemporary institutions of higher education in the United States is a fraught one, then, given that the goal of any degree is now often considered to be utilitarian and "professional" rather than driven by curiosity, complexity or pleasure. Students studying theatre are also educational consumers making a clear material sacrifice for a degree and tend to seek an outcome that will help them professionally and materially despite the precarity of the field. It's not a stretch to say that many students in American universities have been educated in a transactional environment where they feel the need to do things "correctly" rather than to stir debate, to ask hard questions, to think critically about the material offered.

I currently teach at a public liberal arts college in the United States, and the expressed purpose of a liberal arts education includes critical thinking, written and oral communication, information and cultural literacies, interdisciplinarity and problem solving – all things theatre artists engage in even when they are not points of emphasis in training. It seems to me a liberal arts context is an excellent place to challenge the parameters of the field, to take risks, to talk about the purpose and history of theater and how it contributes to the bodies of knowledge in other fields (as Hallie Flanagan did in her years teaching in private liberal arts institutions). In recent years, however, even public institutions, including the one where I work, have introduced more and more curricular requirements connected with professional goals. Again, this is understandable – the financial investment to attend college in the United States is a considerable one, and people want a material return on that investment to avoid drowning in debt. But I often lament what this increased commitment to feeding existing markets and industries – the theatre industrial complex– means for our students.

With or without this recent emphasis on professional skills, liberal arts programs within predominantly white institutions continue to fall short when it comes to anti-racist practice. In their 2020 essay for *HowlRound* entitled "How Liberal Arts Theatre Programs are Failing Students of Color," Miranda Haymon articulates the ways liberal arts colleges have failed to achieve the radical re-imagining required for theatre curricula to achieve goals of equity and inclusion. They describe how they were personally required to take on extra labor to provide support for students of color as a visiting artist in more than one liberal arts theatre program, and outline ways to account for the harm students and faculty of color experience in those programs (2020, paras. 6–7). Their suggestions include re-imagining the theatrical canon, hiring faculty of color and guest artists and inviting them in before programming decisions are made, and including *students* of color in planning processes. They also discuss the need for *professional* mentorship. As Hayman notes, "As young theatremakers of color continue to choose a liberal arts education, the theatre departments that house these artists will have to engage in discourse about how pedagogy, practice, and opportunity have been part of the problem" (Ibid., paras. 10–12).

As I think through this problem as a white professor in a liberal arts program, I grapple with how the goals and rules of "professional" work serve white supremacist and colonialist systems. How many of the rules and systems of professionalism are intertwined with whiteness, white supremacy and colonialist thinking, emerging as all these things did with modernity, industrialization, capitalism and colonization? How does thinking of theatre as an "industry" or "business" align with whiteness and limit the possibilities for anti-racist work, resistance and complexity for students of acting? As I understand it, some permutation of Stanislavsky's work is still fundamental to many rehearsal practices in the United States. Where professional mentorship is a goal, it seems important to teach students those skills to help them succeed in the field. But when the Industry remains, to varying degrees, patriarchal and racist, training student actors to use "industry standard" tools unquestioningly is troubling. As teachers of theatre consider how we need to revise our curricula, I suggest including in those curricular revisions an interrogation of the idea of professionalization and a critical examination of the "market".

Reading Stanislavsky through the Lens of Edward Said's Intellectual "Amateur"

I am also informed in my thinking by Edward Said's *Representations of the Intellectual* (1996), in which he suggests that postcolonial resistance relies on being in a position outside a professional institution. While students of theatre – including Stanislavsky's students – work within educational institutions, they are not yet fully beholden to the rules of acting as a career, aligning them in some ways with Said's radical intellectuals. Said defines professionalism as having a focus on what in one's work, "is considered to be proper, professional behavior – not rocking the boat, not straying outside the accepted paradigms or limits, making yourself marketable and above all presentable, hence uncontroversial and unpolitical and 'objective'" (1996, p. 74). His antidote for this is, then, "amateurism":

> [...] someone who considers that to be a thinking and concerned member of a society one is entitled to raise moral issues at the heart of even the most technical and professionalized activity as it involves one's country, its power, its mode of interacting with its citizens as well as with other societies. In addition, the intellectual's spirit as an amateur can enter and transform the merely professional routine most of us go through into something much more lively and radical; instead of doing what one is supposed to do one can ask why one does it, who benefits from it, how can it reconnect with a personal project and original thoughts.
>
> *(Ibid., p. 83)*

Inspired by Said's postcolonial framework, teachers of acting might consider how their students are in an important position having not yet entered a market or industry, and encourage them to think of themselves as embodied public intellectuals positioned to question and potentially transform the parameters of the field.

For example, with regard to Stanislavsky, Sharon Marie Carnicke points out that he "willingly embraced anything that would illuminate acting and drama" (Carnicke, 1998, p. 13), but only certain aspects of what he studied became commodified, especially later in the United States, as "the" craft of acting within professional contexts. We might encourage students to ask what was lost – in addition to the Method of Physical Action or Active Analysis – when an intellectual exploration of various kinds of plays and philosophies regarding how to embody them became Stanislavsky's "system"? What conditions turned the "system" into an object associated with one person instead of a mode of inquiry shared by a company of actors, writers and artists? And how does the commodification of the "system" as a solid set of professional rules serve to reinforce a racist and patriarchal system?

Carnicke's article in *The Politics of American Actor Training* points out that the Russian versions of Stanislavsky's written texts were very different from the edited versions translated by Elizabeth Reynolds Hapgood and published in the US, and that the differences were largely ideological (2010, pp. 15–30). In *Stanislavsky in Focus*, Carnicke's close analysis of factors that influenced what came to be understood as the "system" in the United States points out that there are not only linguistic differences, but also cultural ones that need to be acknowledged when reading Stanislavsky's work (1998, p. 9). Stella Adler also pointed this out, as she encouraged her students not to read Stanislavsky's books: "They'll make no sense to you, because they were written for a different place and time" (Adler, 2000, p. 13). Declan Donnellan, in his introduction to Benedetti's more recent and complete translation of these texts, writes, "for much of the last century Stanislavsky was communized and capitalized to taste" (Donnellan, 2008, p. xii).

A close reading of both the Benedetti and Hapgood translations reveals a representation of students who are decidedly amateur. Hapgood translates the initial chapter of *An Actor Prepares* as "The First Test" (Stanislavski, 1961, p. 16), while Benedetti calls it directly "Amateurism" (Stanislavski, 2008, p. 5), with the first translation suggesting more of a technical assessment, and the latter possibly reflecting the classroom as a laboratory outside of the professional realm and slightly closer to Said's definition. For the students represented in these texts there is a goal of finding a path away from amateurism, but the definition of "professional" seems to be a perfection of craft unrelated to commercial gain. While these students explore key artistic questions, though, a need to learn the proper behavior within their field also makes them beholden to certain rules.

The Benedetti translation includes a preface that Hapgood's adaptations left out in which Stanislavsky is careful to distinguish serious actors' use of his "system" from the use of it by those who are only interested in "professionalism" of a commercial sort. He excoriates the latter, saying that the "system" in that case is only "of use to their career, for money, for the status of these artistically boring, talentless people. They will give themselves out to be my pupils. Don't believe them. They are the worst enemies of art" (Stanislavski, 2008, *An Actor's Work*, pp. 26–27).

The teacher Torstov's words reflect Stanislavsky's thinking at key points in both English translations of the texts. In both the Hapgood and Benedetti, the second chapter deals with acting as an "art" as opposed to "mechanical" acting or, in the Benedetti translation, "Acting as stock-in-trade" (Ibid., p. 16) implying something simply done for the sake of business. The Hapgood translation refers to these pressures as "professional stimuli," and states that they influence the actor to use "stereotyped methods" to please the public (Stanislavski, 1961, *An Actor Prepares*, pp. 29–30). The Benedetti translation is more extensive in this section regarding the job of the actor, echoing the complexity and difficulty Said sees in the job of the public intellectual:

> The theatre, because it is public, because of the element of display in it, is a double edged sword. On the one hand it has an important social mission, but, on the other, it attracts people who want to exploit it to make a career for themselves. These people profit from the ignorance of some and the depraved tastes of others, they resort to favouritism, to scheming and other means that have nothing to do with creative work.
> *(Stanislavski, 2008,* An Actor's Work, *p. 35)*

He goes on, however, as Said does when discussing the intellectual, to point out that these categories of people are only theoretical and the actor's work can never be reduced to one or the other – there is great "art" in professional work sometimes, just as there is uninspired acting in work that is not professionally oriented (Ibid.).

Stella Adler, as discussed elsewhere in this volume, was raised in the traditions of Yiddish theatre and later Stanislavsky's "system". After the 1950s, Adler's generation of teachers had conflicting stances toward "politics", in part because of their history with HUAC. Like others of her Group Theatre colleagues, Adler was actively pursued by the FBI for many years. Many of the early Group members gravitated toward leftist theatres and politics in the 1930s. The predominantly white Actors Studio, however, "like many performing arts institutions of its era, thought of itself as color-blind, apolitical, focused solely on matters of artistic quality, as if such a thing were possible" (Butler, 2022, p. 307). Adler, on the other hand, offers advice to actors that does not shy away from the important political and social work of theatre to capitulate to the market. In her first lecture from *Stella Adler and the Art of Acting*, Adler points out that when she was young, expectations were different: one did not audition, for example, so presumably there was less need to "market" oneself. Deep interest in the theatre was a more significant requirement (2000, p. 10). Adler also claims that a middle-class audience bears responsibility for the American actor's anxiety about success and money. She writes,

> This middle-class way of thinking (Norm) becomes a straitjacket for the imagination. The dread of criticism, money madness, stage fright, unusual

shyness, star-dreaming, and character clichés are impositions made by the public. To be an artist you must overcome these obstacles.

(Adler, 1988, p. 8).

Again, adding a lens of race to Adler's class analysis reveals that the "middle class" or "Norm" imposing these rules is also presumed to be white.

Adler suggests that actors must maintain their independence from an ethos of marketability. She emphasizes that

> Arthur Miller wants to teach morality and justice. So it was, so it is, and so it ever shall be. These are the subjects of theatre. If they aren't your subjects it's not too late to arrange for a tuition refund.
>
> *(Adler, 2000, p. 30)*

She also calls on student actors to devote an hour to "amateur" work for every hour they devote to making money. Again, what Adler's class-based analysis doesn't consider is the long history of relegating work by Black Americans specifically, as well as Indigenous people and POC artists more generally, to the status of resistant "amateur," neither compensating nor even acknowledging their labor or ideas. That needs to be corrected if we wish to explore the full artistic legacy of Stanislavsky-based work in a contemporary cultural and historical context.

Beyond the "Professional"/"Amateur" Binary

Said echoes Adler when he writes,

> Every intellectual has an audience and a constituency. The issue is whether that audience is there to be satisfied, and hence a client to be kept happy, or whether it is there to be challenged, and hence stirred into outright opposition or mobilized into greater democratic participation in the society.
>
> *(Said, 1996, p. 83).*

He positions his amateur intellectual as an outsider whose job is to question rather than perpetuate the status quo, and points to Stephen Dedalus in James Joyce's *Portrait of the Artist as a Young Man* (1916) as an example of a man who, as a product of a colonial environment, learns to resist before he can become a true artist. Such artist/intellectuals, as represented in 19th and 20th century literature, are fiercely independent, "not meant primarily to fortify ego or celebrate status. Nor are they principally intended for service within powerful bureaucracies and with generous employers" (Said, 1996, p. 2). At the same time, Said recognizes the change between the late 19th century and the material pressures within social structures of the late 20th century when he was writing.

Stanislavsky and Adler displayed a modernist contempt for art as commerce, but as we take up their work now, is it possible to "de-professionalize" acting curricula in order to re-introduce critical thinking and anti-racist practice, and celebrate complexity, pleasure, spirituality, intellectual engagement and community rather than preparation for a "trade?" Or can we do both at once? Can we work changing the rules of the "trade" into what we teach in the classroom even with the pressures to prepare students for work in the industry? One can see the seeds of an idea in Stanislavsky's and Adler's work that student actors occupy a liminal position both within and outside of theatre institutions that allows for the possibility of speaking truth to power and imagining possible changes.

As I suggest in "Whiteness, Patriarchy and Resistance in Actor Training Texts", "The naturalization of binaries and hierarchies is one of the ways whiteness and masculinity maintain institutional dominance" (Steiger, 2019). In what ways does white supremacy also rely on maintaining a binary between work that is "professional" and that which is "amateur" in order to privilege the former? In *American Theater in the Culture of the Cold War: Producing and Contesting Containment*, Bruce McConachie recognizes that the image of a container with an inside and outside was among the pervasive capitalist metaphors in the culture of the mid-20th century United States. Citing cognitive theorist Mark Johnson, he writes:

> If, as Johnson states, 'we understand categories metaphorically as containers (where a thing falls within the container or it does not), then we have the claim that everything is either P (in the category-container) or not-P (outside the container).' Thinking with containment as a matrix, in other words, results in either/or propositions that can lead to a 'hardening of the categories' in everyday life.
>
> *(McConachie, 2003, p. 8)*

For Said, the 19th-century intellectual was always an individual who stood *outside* of any group, nation or interest; but do 21st-century artist/scholars need to be beholden to the entrenched binary silos if we accept that those categories often serve as instruments of the hierarchies invented by patriarchy and white supremacy? Can we think in terms of postcolonial hybridity to undermine the structures that support patriarchal dominance and white supremacy in theatre training?

Moving into the 21st century, an increased complexity is evident in Anna Deavere Smith's *Letters to a Young Artist* (2006). Deavere Smith is a Black woman artist working in the United States, and while she acknowledges that commercial culture infuses everything in this country, she expresses a belief that student artists can work within that culture and still maintain a sort of amateur "outsider" status. "You can't base your self-esteem on how well your work is selling or how well it's received," she writes, "We live in business; we live in commerce; it's the air we breathe. But let's take commerce out of it" (p. 28). Deavere Smith defines the people who are responsible for paying the artist's salary as "The Man," and notes that although "The Man" has power, the artist also has some power and choice (Ibid., p. 42).

In Anna Deavere Smith's writings, the social position of the student actor is embraced as one of great potential, as its productive amateurism allows for the possibility of questioning the commercial status quo while maintaining a practical understanding of material reality. She suggests that actors can recognize their power from within the system and, eventually, leverage that power to think critically about the morality and purpose of the system, and potentially change it.

American Theatre and Reparations

As Ta-Nehisi Coates writes,

> And so we must imagine a new country. Reparations – by which I mean the full acceptance of our collective biography and its consequences – is the price we must pay to see ourselves squarely [...] Reparations beckons us to reject the intoxication of hubris and see America as it is – the work of fallible humans.
>
> *(2014, para. 141)*

Theatre is certainly the work of fallible humans who are implicated in colonialist discourses in enormous ways in the United States, and the industry's systems have a monstrous history, including the ongoing practice of stealing labor, life and artistry from BIPOC artists. How do we approach reparations? Because we live within the systems and structures of capitalism, it is troubling that I – a tenured white theatre professor with unearned privilege – would call for "de-professionalization" now that BIPOC artists are finally attaining positions of power and being properly compensated for their work. Discussing artists' work as merely cultural "gifts" in the system as it exists ignores the material realities of life under racial capitalism, and the myth of the struggling artist needed to end long ago.

So as we consider structural shifts, there needs to be a period of rebalancing the scales and giving back what was stolen in very practical ways – not only compensating artists for their work but giving them generations of back pay, both monetary and artistic. During the uprisings in 2020, many organizations, scholars, journalists, activists and artists across disciplines began discussing material reparations for the descendants of enslaved people and taking seriously the movement to return Indigenous lands in the United States to Indigenous people, and it is essential to continue to listen to these calls and organize ongoing, concerted programs of action. For theatre organizations, educators and artists this includes not just material compensation, but also a

reconsideration of the long-standing structures that led us to venerate Stanislavsky as the patriarch of actor training and leave out the contributions of,
for example, Rose McClendon. Again, *HowlRound* offers a rich compendium
of writing suggesting ways to approach this problem, and much has been
written on the subject in recent years across many disciplines.

By way of general monetary restitution, the Brookings Institution, a non-
profit organization that researches public policy, has compiled some key possibilities: free tuition and student loan forgiveness, tax relief and grant grants
for buying homes or starting businesses are among them (Ray and Perry,
2020). This is viable in the context of theatre in various ways. In the 1920s,
Hallie Flanagan was the recipient of a subsidy through which she encountered
first-hand the work of Stanislavsky, Meyerhold and others, bringing those
techniques back to her students at Vassar, a predominantly white private liberal arts institution. Similarly, Stella Adler and Harold Clurman traveled to
Europe to experience new forms of training. White artists receiving support
were participating in a colonialist attitude that associated progress with European modernity, an attitude that reproduced structures celebrating both the
work of men, like Stanislavsky, who were racialized as white, and the structures that placed those men in positions of unquestionable power.

In a contemporary context, why not establish a fund to subsidize international travel for BIPOC theatre students who wish to study methods rooted in
non-European cultures? Or fellowship funds to support actors in their critical
examination of Stanislavsky or faculty's development of college curricula
rooted in the work described in Sharell D Luckett and Tia Shaffer's *Black
Acting Methods*, one goal of which is to "honor and rightfully identify Blacks
as central co-creators of acting and directing theory by filling the perceived
void of Black acting theorists" (Luckett and Shaffer, 2017, p. 2), or Brewer's
anti-racist theatre work? Or donate research time and money to scholars who
explore the contributions of people from the Global Majority who have been
left out of the history of North American actor training, as Monica Ndounou
has done? White leaders, educators and artists might consider Hallie Flanagan's later use of her position to distribute funds to Black artists a model and
find ways to redistribute time, space and money to support the explorations of
BIPOC artists, whatever that work may be.

Reframing history and recuperating the work of Black and Indigenous
artists as central rather than marginal to the history of actor training is part of
the process of reparations and relies on understanding "amateur" work differently. The artists in the WPA's Black units were professional in the sense
that they made a living creating theatre, but they were publicly supported
with federal money. Even so, many of them were also resisting and questioning the systems that kept their communities oppressed. This reframing allows
us to turn slightly Stanislavsky's disrespect for *individuals* who used his work
to make money – "they are the worst enemies of art" – and focus on how the
structures of profit-driven hierarchies are enemies of public health and justice.

An ongoing system of reparations would celebrate and take action to fund the work of BIPOC artists who have been demanding and creating ethical work-spaces centered on mutual care that reconsider the rules and structures of professional behavior. It would allow artists to make a living while creating work rooted in risk, experimentation, collaboration and joy. Theatre leaders might also consider ways to support work that itself makes reparations the focus of its content. For example, in "Ceding Power: On Reparations in the Arts," Nicole J. Caruth highlights "Reparations 365," which is "an ongoing series of performances, workshops and discussions around the topic of dis-tributive justice for Black Americans" sponsored by the JACK performance space in Brooklyn (Caruth, 2020).

Another step toward reparations is acknowledging structural and systemic racism that leads to positioning white artists, usually men, as prominent lea-ders. Kate Dossett suggests that in histories of the Federal Theatre Project, "Black theatrical creativity is often narrated through the lens of powerful white figures who were able to harness it" (2020, p. 75). For example, Jay Plum points out that

> Even the official history of the Negro Units written by the Federal Theatre Project's Department of Information claims that 'guiding the destinations of the Negro Theatre at its inception were John Houseman and Orson Welles.' The history makes no reference to McClendon.
>
> *(Plum, 1992, p. 144)*

What histories had to be suppressed and what sets of rules and processes were in place that set up interpretations of Stanislavsky's work to take hold as the driver of professional training in the US?

It seems essential to examine the requirements of public policy in this regard to uncover hidden biases and overhaul policies. For example, because the WPA was organized as a relief project for workers, the Federal Theatre Project was required to distribute funds in places where professional actors had worked regularly (Dossett, 2020, p. 4), so structurally it worked in favor of "professionals", and the field was biased in favor of white artists through training and opportunities (another way through which interpretations of Stanislavsky's work attained dominance). While planning the distribution of reparative resources to artists previously relegated to "amateur" status, it is important to consider what struc-tural flaws could make administration inequitable and build in processes by which to correct those as they become clear.

Finally, the demise of the Federal Theatre Project came about in 1939, in part because of the emergence of the House Un-American Activities Com-mittee who successfully called for it to be defunded. Through cultural policy, how do we codify artistic reparations to protect support for artists whose labor has gone uncompensated and unrecognized, and make it part of the fabric of the nation in perpetuity?

As part of a commitment to supporting historically marginalized artists creating work that pushes back against the white supremacist, patriarchal *status quo* and proposes new and more equitable systems and ways of working, we must answer these questions with palpable actions before we can build a new Theatre with roles beyond mere professionalization for students of acting. As Kelvin Dinkins, Jr and Al Heartley write in their *HowlRound* essay entitled, "We Don't Want Your Statements, American Theatre,"

> Dismantling white supremacy culture means decentering power, yielding power, and, in most circumstances, having the fortitude to step aside. Please do not claim to undertake this radical endeavor if you are unwilling to sacrifice your positional power and other financial resources in the process.
>
> *(2020, para. 18)*

References

Adler, S. (1988) *The Technique of Acting*. New York: Bantam Books.

Adler, S. (2000) *The Art of Acting*, edited by H. Kissel. New York: Applause Books.

Barclay, K. (2019) "Willful Actors: Valuing Resistance in American Actor Training", *Journal of Dramatic Theory and Criticism* 34(1), pp. 123–141. Available at: Project MUSE. doi:10.1353/dtc.2019.0027 (Accessed: 23 February 2023).

Brewer, N. M. (2019) "Parents of Color and the Need for Anti-Racist Theatre Practices", *HowlRound*, 3 December. Available at: https://howlround.com/parents-co lor-need-anti-racist-theatre-practices (Accessed: 23 February 2023).

Brustein, R. (2005) "Mrs. Worthington's Daughter's Dilemma", *American Theater*, January, pp. 46–48.

Butler, I. (2022). *The Method: How the Twentieth Century Learned to Act*. New York: Bloomsbury.

Byron, D. (2005) "How Does Your Garden Grow? A Conversation with Six Actors Who Teach", *American Theatre*, January, pp. 34–37.

Canning, C. (2015) *On the Performance Front*. Basingstoke: Palgrave Macmillan.

Carnicke, S. M. (1998) *Stanislavsky in Focus*. New York: Routledge.

Carnicke, S. M. (2010) "Stanislavsky and Politics: Active Analysis and the American Legacy of Soviet Oppression", in E. Margolis and L. Tyler Renaud (eds), *The Politics of American Actor Training*. New York: Routledge, pp. 15–30.

Chambers, J. (2010) "Actor Training Meets Historical Thinking", in E. Margolis and L. Tyler Renaud (eds), *The Politics of American Actor Training*. New York: Routledge, pp. 31–45.

Chandrasan (2010) "The Politics of Western Pedagogy in the Theatre of India", in E. Margolis and L. Tyler Renaud (eds), *The Politics of American Actor Training*. New York: Routledge, pp. 46–61.

Coates, T.-N. (2014) "The Case for Reparations", *The Atlantic*, June. Available at: https://www.theatlantic.com/magazine/archive/2014/06/the-case-for-reparations/ 361631/ (Accessed: 23 February 2023).

Coates, T.-N. (2019) "Ta-Nehisi Coates Revisits 'The Case for Reparations'", *The New Yorker*, 10 June. Available at https://www.newyorker.com/news/the-ne

w-yorker-interview/ta-nehisi-coates-revisits-the-case-for-reparations (Accessed: 26 February 2023).

Caruth, N. J. (2020) "Ceding Power: On Reparations in the Arts", *The Ostracon*, 14 August. Available at: https://theostracon.net/ceding-power-on-reparations-in-the-arts (Accessed: 26 February 2023).

Deavere Smith, A. (2006) *Letters to a Young Artist.* New York: Anchor Books.

Dinkins, Jr., K. and Heartley, A. (2020) "We Don't Want Your Statements, American Theatre; or, The Solidarity We Actually Needed", *HowlRound*, 11 June. Available at: https://howlround.com/we-dont-want-your-statements-american-theatre (Accessed: 26 February 2023).

Donnellan, D. (2008) "Introduction", in *An Actor's Work: A Student's Diary.* Translated from the Russian and edited by J. Benedetti. New York: Routledge, 2008, pp. ix–xiv.

Dossett, K. (2020) *Radical Black Theatre and the New Deal.* Chapel Hill, NC: University of North Carolina Press.

Green, J. (2022) "Is It Finally Twilight for Theater's Sacred Monsters?", *New York Times*, 8 June. Available at: https://www.nytimes.com/2022/06/08/theater/men-american-theater.html (Accessed: 23 February 2023).

Hannah-Jones, N. (2020) "What Is Owed: If True Justice and Equality are Ever to be Achieved in the United States, the Country Must Finally Take Seriously What It Owes Black Americans", *The New York Times Magazine*, 30 June. Available at: https://www.nytimes.com/interactive/2020/06/24/magazine/reparations-slavery.html (Accessed: 26 February 2023).

Haymon, M. (2020) "How Liberal Arts Theatre Programs are Failing Their Students of Color", *HowlRound*, 17 June. Available at: https://howlround.com/how-liberal-arts-theatre-programs-are-failing-their-students-color (Accessed: 26 February 2023).

hooks, b. (1994) *Teaching to Transgress: Education as the Practice of Freedom.* New York: Routledge.

Jackson, S. (2004) *Professing Performance: Theatre in the Academy from Philology to Performativity.* Cambridge: Cambridge University Press.

Katznelson, I. (2005) *When Affirmative Action Was White.* New York: W. W. Norton & Co.

KO (2021) "Humanity is more important than my bank account" [Instagram] 14 April. Available at: https://www.instagram.com/p/CNqFSKBFBsj/?hl=en (Accessed: 26 February 2023).

Luckett, S. D. and Shaffer, T. M. (2017) *Black Acting Methods: A Critical Approach.* London: Routledge.

Manolikakis, A. (n.d.). "A History of The Actors Studio". Available at: https://theactorsstudio.org/a-history-of-the-actors-studio (Accessed: 26 February 2023).

Margolis, E. and Tyler Renaud, L. (eds) (2010) *The Politics of American Actor Training.* New York: Routledge.

McClendon, R. (1945) "As to a New Negro Stage", *The New York Times*, 30 June. Available at: https://www.nytimes.com/1935/06/30/archives/as-to-a-new-negro-stage.html (Accessed: 23 February 2023).

McConachie, B. (2003) *American Theatre in the Culture of the Cold War: Producing and Contesting Containment.* Iowa City: University of Iowa Press.

Ndounou, M. W. (2018) "Being Black on Stage and Screen: Black Actor Training Before Black Power and the Rise of Stanislavsky's System", in K. Perkins, *et al.* (eds), *The Routledge Companion to African American Theatre and Performance.* London and New York: Routledge, pp. 124–128.

Plum, J. (1992) "Rose McClendon and the Black Units of the Federal Theatre Project: A Lost Contribution", *Theatre Survey* 33(2), pp. 144–153.

Ray, R. and Perry, A. M. (2020) "Why We Need Reparations for Black Americans," 15 April. Available at: https://www.brookings.edu/policy2020/bigideas/why-we-need-reparations-for-black-americans (Accessed: 26 February 2023).

Reparations 365 (n.d.) https://www.jackny.org/reparations365 (Accessed: 26 February 2023).

Said, E. (1996) *Representations of the Intellectual*. New York: Vintage Books.

Shepherd, S. and Wallis, M. (2002) *Drama/Theatre/Performance*. London: Routledge.

Stanislavski, C. (1961) *An Actor Prepares*. Translated from the Russian by E. Reynolds Hapgood. New York: Routledge.

Stanislavski, C. (1961) *Building a Character*. Translated from the Russian by E. Reynolds Hapgood. New York: Routledge.

Stanislavski, C. (1961) *Creating a Role*. Translated from the Russian by E. Reynolds Hapgood. New York: Routledge.

Stanislavski, K. (2008) *An Actor's Work*. Translated from the Russian and edited by J. Benedetti. London: Routledge.

Stanislavski, K. (2008) *My Life in Art*. Translated from the Russian and edited by J. Benedetti. London: Routledge.

Steiger, A. (2019) "Whiteness, Patriarchy and Resistance in Actor Training Texts: Reimagining Actors as Embodied Public Intellectuals", *HowlRound*, August. Available at: https://howlround.com/whiteness-patriarchy-and-resistance-actor-training-texts (Accessed: 23 February 2023).

Rainbolt, W. (dir.) (1964) *Stella Adler and the Actor*. Los Angeles, CA: KTLA.

Woods, L. (2010) "Degrees of Choice", in E. Margolis and L. Tyler Renaud (eds), *The Politics of American Actor Training*. New York: Routledge, pp. 62–75.

9

I AIN'T STUDYIN' STANISLAVSKY

We Are the Key to Reimagining 21st-Century Actor Training

Monica White Ndounou

I ain't studyin' Stanislavsky.

I initially embraced the "system" when I encountered it in acting classes, workshops and productions, as it happens to be the basis of most of the 1800 college and university training programs throughout the United States (Bernhard, 2014, pp. 472–473). I later found it was not designed with me in mind. As a Black woman from the American south, my people's various intersectional identities have been historically misrepresented on stage and screen. Like many of us who become actors with the keen awareness of this history, I also hoped to make culturally resonant contributions through the craft.

Guided by my own experiences with Stanislavsky-based training and methods in performance, along with discoveries I made upon reading Stanislavsky's *An Actor Prepares* (1942), I learned more about the system, its variations and the many critiques. Upon hearing other Black actors' shared experiences regarding Stanislavsky-based methods, I realized that I needed to make an informed decision about my own process and how I should proceed as an artist and educator. Lloyd Richards,[1] Susan Batson,[2] Baron Kelly[3] and other Black artists and educators have engaged in productive intercultural processes in fruitful conversation with Stanislavsky-based methods used by actors from a range of backgrounds. There are also many other approaches to craft developed by people of African descent. The African Grove Theatre, which launched in 1821 as the first professional Black theatre in the United States, the All-Star Stock Company, as the first Black acting school in the US during the late 1800s, and the countless programs at historically Black colleges and universities and Black theatres from the 19th century to the present, are critical sites for exploring Black American approaches to craft (Peterson, Jr., 1997, pp. 3–6 and 12–13).

DOI: 10.4324/9781003330882-13

Many of the chapters in *Stanislavsky and Race* suggest the importance of inclusion and emphasize a myriad of culturally resonant engagements with and beyond Stanislavsky. Yet, historically, white practitioners present these ideas as a 21st-century phenomenon or one that is not led by Black people and people of the Global Majority. Still, historical and contemporary alternatives developed by Black educators and creators exist. Mainstream programs rarely teach these approaches without the special interest of Black teachers and directors whose work may not be documented as thoroughly as Stanislavsky's or may be recorded in different forms for a variety of reasons.

The blind spots in Stanislavsky's "system" and Stanislavsky-based training are well noted in books by David Krasner,[4] Shonni Enelow,[5] Rosemary Malague[6] and others. Yet I have found some of the most compelling arguments interrogating the system and its variations raised by Black women like writer, actress and director Alice Childress;[7] Hollywood sex symbol and singer Dorothy Dandridge;[8] and actor, director and acting theorist Barbara Ann Teer.[9] Each warned against Stanislavsky-based methods and the popularized techniques that reportedly caused harm to 21st-century Black actors like Michael B. Jordan and Michael K. Williams, the latter of which compelled critically acclaimed actor Courtney B. Vance to call on the industry to provide mental health services for creatives on set.

So I ain't studyin' Stanislavsky. I am much more interested in actively pursuing alternatives developed by Black artists and educators who approach the craft as cultural insiders, recognizing the powerful components of Black cultures and their intersections with craft in training, role selection, preparation, performance, and reception. I am invested in learning and teaching Black cultural traditions, as they expose the hazards and healing of "acting while Black," a term coined by stage and screen actor and director Harry J. Lennix, referring to the craft of acting and the challenges of navigating the industry (Arizona State University, 2008). Drawing from my lived experiences and research including my book, *Acting Your Color: The CRAFT, Power and Paradox of Acting for Black Americans*, this chapter recognizes and appreciates the valuable insights of Black artists, audiences, teachers, and students. As poet, playwright and political activist June Jordan wrote in her "Poem for South African Women": "We are the ones we've been waiting for" (1978). *We* are the key to reimagining 21st century actor training.

Stanislavsky, the "System" and Blackness

Founded in 1901 in Eastern Europe, Konstantin Stanislavsky's system of acting was not developed with Black creatives or with Black narratives. Translated and taught by Richard Boleslavsky in the US,[10] the "system" was reshaped by Lee Strasberg, Stella Adler, Sanford Meisner, Uta Hagen and others. Stanislavsky's "system" and its variations are intended to help all actors achieve realism and consistency in performance. While some of these theories and theorists may be more conducive to intercultural engagement, they do not always address how the process of achieving realism may differ for and impact historically misrepresented people, particularly of the African diaspora; like Black Americans.

What is "real" in Black representation considering the prevalence of historical stereotyping, stereotypical typecasting and normalization of the white gaze? Variations of the same question and answers echo across time. Some answers consider the prevalence of what Pulitzer Prize-winning author, literary critic and educator Toni Morrison, termed the "Africanist presence": a trope in white American literature that utilizes Black characters and culture as a foil for the development of central white characters (Morrison, 1992, pp. 32–33). Others refer to the "fictional double", whose aim, according to literary scholar Debra Walker King is to "mask individuality and mute the voice of personal agency" (King, 2000, p. viii). The Africanist presence and the fictional double frequently appear as the mammy, mulatto, tom, coon, buck, sambo, topsy, sapphire, jezebel, magical negro, etc. (Bogle, 2001). As we are not a monolith, not all people of African descent are sensitive to or haunted by these tropes in the same way. Yet these stereotypes still impact and impress upon audiences and performers within and behind the scenes, which ultimately affect us all.

The Africanist presence and the fictional double, as products of the white gaze, emerge in Stanislavsky's *An Actor Prepares* (1942) but are not sufficiently addressed. In the book, which is written to emulate a student's study of acting with a master teacher utilizing the Stanislavsky "system", the Eastern European, white student preparing to play Shakespeare's Othello in a scene finds it necessary to blacken his face with chocolate cake (and later, makeup) to access the "savage" nature and qualities of Othello. The student is convinced the Moor with royal blood must walk around like a tiger or another animal (Stanislavsky, 1942, pp. 3, 9–10). While the teacher's response to this performance calls out the student for hastily reproducing the external, general characterization of a Black man without considering what Shakespeare wrote and emphasizes the necessity of drawing from lived experiences, the teacher does not name the racist undertones of the approach or offer an in-depth exploration of the ways Black cultural traditions would be a more productive way of adding depth and nuance to the execution (Ibid., p. 27).

For those of us who have experienced predominantly white learning/production environments as the only Black creative or one of a few, we know that the absence of Black people in this scenario is still harmful. The tendency to normalize this treatment of Blackness in training becomes the standard for study and practice coercing Black actors to misrepresent or erase Black culture in voice, movement and emotional expression. This hamstrings Black students', educators' and performers' range of depth and nuance in preparation and performance. It risks their internalizing stereotypes of Black people, cultures, pain and trauma, normalized by the white gaze which can still produce the same negative impacts on Black performers and audiences. Due to the prevalence of white supremacy, institutionalized racism and anti-Blackness, everyone's vigilance and intentional practice is necessary to avoid the same hazardous approaches and outcomes.

The variations of Stanislavsky-inspired training developed by Adler, Strasberg, Meisner and Hagen, among others, also have their blind spots, despite popularity among Black actors who trained with them or have benefited from their methods. In David Krasner's *Method Acting Reconsidered* (2000), actor and educator David Wiles illuminates the burdens of representation thereby exposing the pitfalls of the concept of the fourth wall in the "system" for Black performers, which ignores inherently interactive performance traditions like call and response. *Method Acting and its Discontents* (Enelow, 2015) and *An Actress Prepares* (Malague, 2012) also revisit Stanislavsky-based techniques like emotion memory and their impact on actors, primarily in relation to gender with some consideration of race.

My research for *Acting Your Color* delves more deeply into the racial and cultural implications of many of these considerations, revealing how Black educators and artists have been more likely to recognize such blind spots. The late Broadway director and former Dean of the Yale Drama School, Lloyd Richards; actress and acting coach to the stars Susan Batson; and actor, director and educator Baron Kelly, represent a handful of a multitude of Black artists and educators that have seamlessly infused cultural insights and professional expertise that supplement the blind spots in Stanislavsky-based training. The value of their intercultural engagements with the "system" and related variations cannot be underestimated. Although frequently unwelcome in an educational system and profession that lauds Eurocentric frameworks as the pinnacle, the perspectives of Black artists, students, and educators, are critically necessary to lead the field beyond its arrested development.

Anyone pursuing an advanced degree in acting will do so through the predominantly white lens that dominates, despite the drawbacks of the "system" and related methods. There are no graduate-level programs at historically Black colleges and universities, which may be more likely to include Black history and culture in other parts of the curriculum due to their missions. Artists, Black or otherwise, may never learn of the pitfalls and alternatives to Stanislavsky's "system" and related methods. They may never learn about the training, lives and careers of Black women like Dandridge, Childress and Teer, whose experiences helped me better understand my positionality as a Black woman, actor, director, educator, and writer.

Black People's Shared Experiences Regarding Stanislavsky-based Methods

In her play *Trouble in Mind*, Alice Childress dramatizes a veteran Black actress's encounter with what is not named but appears to be Stanislavsky-based training while working on a Broadway show. As Wiletta Mayer (the Black actress) tries to navigate her character's role in the white-authored production at the center of the play within a play, the stress of the methods and the hostile work environment takes its toll. Wiletta plays a Black mother whose son is lynched in a southern town. Her experiences during the rehearsal with the interracial cast and condescending white director shares many similarities with Dorothy Dandridge's and Barbara Ann Teer's real-life accounts of their experiences in the industry. While Dandridge suffered a career and mental health decline, eventually dying of an accidental overdose, Teer founded her own theatre company and system of acting grounded in African-based spiritual and cultural traditions. Their stories are but a sampling of the countless others in Black actor memoirs, autobiographies, biographies, and interviews, revealing the hazards and potential healing of acting while Black.

In *Everything and Nothing: The Dorothy Dandridge Tragedy*, Dandridge describes "the first attack of my own private plague" following a performance when she "took sick – a sickness peculiar to myself and one that will probably lead to my death one day" (Dandridge and Conrad, 2000, pp. 86–87). She explains, "after the show, I couldn't breathe. I had chest spasms, my legs cramped, my feet and hands tingled. I was unable to talk. I stayed in this contracted fit, doubled up, until I came out of it" (Ibid.). An acquaintance recognized the incident as an "emotional disturbance" and suggested Dandridge get help, which led her into "analysis", or psychoanalysis where she began to examine how her lived experiences, including her mentally handicapped daughter's pain and suffering affected her (Ibid.). Dandridge's performances of characters were frequently the tragic mulatta type, whose stories and traumas often closely mirrored Dandridge's own as a light-skinned, Black woman who desperately sought but was unable to secure sustained love.

As a student of the Actor's Laboratory, Dandridge studied the "Stanislavsky method of acting" and also engaged in a range of other formal and informal strategies for learning the craft including studying other stars, voice lessons and coaching, dancing, etc. (Dandridge and Conrad, 2000, p. 79). Although pioneering as "Hollywood's first African-American Sex Symbol and Screen Legend," none of this prepared Dandridge for the various challenges she experienced with the craft and the industry. Despite her star status, along with Black co-stars Harry Belafonte (*Carmen Jones*), who she reportedly dated for a time, and Sidney Poitier (*Porgy and Bess*), Dandridge was isolated, having very little community. All of this arguably contributed to her emotional disturbance, or "trouble in mind," that eventually ended with her death in 1965.

While becoming an unprecedented star, Dandridge experienced a series of racial and gender-related traumas that she at times re-enacted in many of the scripted scenes she played on stage and screen. Her traumas were frequently intensified by the criticism she faced even while trying to address the shortcomings of the roles she played (Ibid., pp. 200–204). Halle Berry's Emmy award-winning performance of the legendary actress in the 1999 film *Introducing Dorothy Dandridge*, dramatizes Dandridge's struggles behind the scenes. The film demonstrates how the title of sex symbol and screen legend did not save Dandridge from the various hardships she details in her co-authored autobiography, published after her untimely death.

Like Berry's film, Childress's play *Trouble in Mind* paints a revealing portrait of the inner workings behind the scenes and their impact on Black actors, demonstrating the challenges and offering alternatives that go unheeded. Written and staged in 1955, just months after the 14-year-old Black child Emmitt Till was brutally lynched and mutilated in Mississippi by a gang of white men for supposedly whistling at a white woman, the play offers insight into the traumas Black actors can experience working on such material.

Childress dramatizes the complexities of acting while Black, the problems of stereotypical typecasting, lack of alignment with training and the impact of portraying challenging roles or underdeveloped characters and narratives. As part of a mixed cast with a condescending white director, Wiletta endures such distress trying to "justify" actions and behaviors dictated in the play within the play that make no sense within the context of her lived experience as a Black woman from the south. Millie Davis, the only other Black woman in the play, laments the stereotypical typecasting she and the "middle-aged" Wiletta have endured throughout their careers, rattling off a list of all the maid roles they played (Childress, 2011, p. 57). The elderly Sheldon Forrester, a non-confrontational presence throughout, casually exposes the challenges of segregation (yes, even in the north), in his futile attempts to find housing and consistent work, which is not a problem for their white counterparts who happily discuss their housing and job prospects. John Nevins is an idealistic, recent graduate from an acting program who believes the tools of the trade will suffice in his efforts to succeed in the business. Wiletta warns him otherwise. Initially, she encourages him not to tell the white director about his training or give his true opinion of the script (Ibid., p. 54). She explains that Black people are in "show business" not theatre. Her advice served as a form of showbiz training distinguishing between what one learns in school and how the business actually works, especially for Black people. Wiletta later apologizes to John for advising him in this way upon discovering that to play the part truthfully, and "justify" the actions of the characters, she and the others would have to express their true feelings about the script's misrepresentation of Black characters, family and community dynamics. For a truthful portrayal, they would have to explain how the scenarios would play out with Black people.

Childress exposes the impact of misrepresentation in writing coupled with popularized techniques, which leads to the "trouble in mind" Wiletta experiences. Wiletta tries in vain to convince Al Manners, the director, that the poorly written play is unrealistic, particularly the scene in which her character, a Black mother willingly hands over her innocent, Black son to a white mob to lynch him. Drawing from her lived experiences, training, and practice, and quite likely the example of Mamie Till who allowed pictures of her son's mutilated body to be published as an act of protest and resistance, Wiletta explains that a Black mother would never do such a thing so there was no way to "justify" the nonsensical actions. Manners flippantly implies that none of them knows how they would react to a lynching because "we've never actually seen such a thing, thank God … but allow your imagination to soar" (Ibid., pp. 99–100). In that moment, Sheldon reveals that he had, in fact, witnessed a lynching as a child and recounted the haunting memory of the traumatic event. Rather than utilizing the embodied knowledge, professional expertise and cultural nuance the Black actors contributed to the process, Manners ultimately dismisses Wiletta as a troublemaker. In response to her shared concerns, he loses his temper and exposes his racist viewpoints, expressing that Black people cannot control their own narratives or bring any expertise to the process, and even if they did, white audiences would not want to see it (Ibid., pp. 107–111). Paradoxically, Wiletta's refusal to justify a nonsensical narrative led to her dismissal from the project but she remembered her desire to do something grand as an artist (Ibid., pp. 99–100).

Teer's experiences as a Method-trained Black actor who studied with Sanford Meisner, Paul Mann and Lloyd Richards, took her down a similar path. Teer began her career as a dancer. Wanting to use her craft responsibly in non-stereotypical roles, she shifted focus to acting following a knee injury. She had a very successful stage and screen career. Teer is one of the many Black actresses to historically amplify the potential harm of stereotypical typecasting, underdeveloped characters and the use of popularized techniques. She was particularly wary of techniques that encourage the use of emotion memory and other psychologically based methods to convey realism in performance. She understood that what may be "real" in the white imagination could be harmful for Black actors to emulate. Teer warned against the "Magic If" exercise in Stanislavsky-based training. She cautioned against delving too deeply into given circumstances of underdeveloped characters and oppressive narratives, which could lead the Black actor into dangerous psychological and emotional territory due to historical oppression and inequitable access to resources and opportunities (Thomas, 2016).

As a solution to the hazards of acting while Black, Teer eventually founded the National Black Theatre and her TEER: Technology of Soul, which "utilized the symbolism, rituals, and mythology of authentic West African traditions." Her method was designed to shift the Eurocentric, traditional western theatre paradigm from a "self-conscious" art form to "God-conscious" art. The shift centered African-based cultural traditions grounded in the interactive performer-audience relationship found throughout Black culture, especially the Black church. This "Ritualistic Revival" as she termed it, embraced a creative practice and process to make "theatre art that flows from the heart" (Ibid.). Just as Teer actively sought and achieved alternative strategies that speak directly to the most hazardous and harmful aspects of popularized techniques by embracing Black cultures, healthy alternatives for 21st-century actor training, must address harm and focus on healing for the benefit of actors and the evolution of craft.

What We Can All Learn from the Hazards and Healing of Acting While Black

The historical revelations of Dandridge, Childress and Teer combined with the experiences of 21st-century Black actors reveal the hazards and healing of acting while Black are of ongoing, intergenerational concern. For example, Michael B. Jordan and Michael K. Williams reported the cellular trauma that resurfaced in roles that led each into therapy, an important intervention critically acclaimed actor Courtney B. Vance recommends for all actors.

In the 2018 film *Black Panther*, Jordan played N'Jadaka, aka Erik Killmonger, who seeks to avenge the white oppression of his African ancestors and his father's murder at the hands of his uncle, the late king of Wakanda. Pain of the childhood loss of his father along with witnessing violence throughout his life led to Erik's intense isolation. In an interview with Oprah Winfrey, Jordan explained how he got into character:

> I was by myself, isolating myself […] I spent a lot of time alone. I figured Erik, his childhood growing up was pretty lonely. He didn't have a lot of people he could talk to about this place called Wakanda that didn't exist.
>
> *(Schrodt, 2019)*

Jordan dove headfirst into the psychology of the character, but he didn't have an exit plan. He continued,

> Of course it's an extreme version of the African diaspora from the African-American perspective, so to be able to take that kind of pain and rage and all those emotions that Erik kind of represents from being black and brown here in America... That was something I didn't take lightly […]. I didn't have a process. I just did whatever I felt I needed to do or whatever I felt was right in the moment every step of the way […] I didn't have an escape plan, either. When it was all over, I think just being in that kind of mind state … It caught up with me.
>
> *(Ibid.)*

Jordan's story reveals the hazards of acting while Black that Teer warned about with Stanislavsky-based training. Character immersion that embodies the pain and rage of Black experiences by delving deeply into the psychology of the character without an escape plan is dangerous.

Michael K. Williams reported similar complications. Williams rose to fame and landed an Emmy nomination playing Omar Little, an openly gay Robin Hood of the projects on *The Wire*.[11] While Williams succeeded in achieving stardom, the role also aggravated his struggle with sobriety because of its intensity. Williams explains,

> A director calling 'cut' doesn't erase what you're feeling. Your mind feels the fictional the same way it feels the real [...] That's the flip side of getting into a character; you wake up that sleeping beast. I meditate on painful things all day long for a scene and when it's over, it's little wonder I'm tempted to go off and smoke crack.
>
> *(Williams, 2022, p. 15)*

The mind does not know we are acting. Without a concrete method of transitioning out of a character and escaping their world, the mental and emotional strain of portraying "Blackpain"[12] and trauma, is difficult to manage, even without struggles with sobriety.

The clashing of Williams' acclaimed artistry and struggles with sobriety continued throughout the remainder of his life and career. He also earned an Emmy nomination for his portrayal of Freddy, an incarcerated drug addict, imprisoned for life, as he mentors a new inmate on surviving prison in the television miniseries *The Night Of*.[13] For this role, Williams drew upon his nephew's incarceration for a juvenile crime that landed him behind bars for decades. Williams reveals, "The character stirred up so many issues for me that before the shoot ended, after around five years sober, I would cave in on myself" (Williams, 2022, p. 185). Without the support and tools to reconcile the trauma aroused by his methods for a truthful portrayal to honor his nephew's experience, Williams was vulnerable to his addiction.

Recognizing he struggled with addiction before he became an actor, Williams began to explore the patterns that emerged regarding his roles and his relapse when he entered therapy following his turn as Montrose Freeman in *Lovecraft Country* in 2020.[14] Also a critically acclaimed performance, Williams reveals in his memoir the role took him on a journey for which he was not prepared. He explains the role "put me through the wringer, mentally and emotionally," as he played a closeted, gay Black man who survived the 1921 Tulsa Race Massacre. Filmed in Atlanta, where he did not have a support system, Williams relapsed again. He then "got into therapy and Narcotics Anonymous meetings, reconnected with [... his] sponsor, and addressed his] trauma head-on" (Ibid., pp. 232–234). Unfortunately, he lost his battle to addiction and died of an overdose on 6 September 2021.

Upon Williams' death, Courtney B. Vance, his onscreen brother in *Lovecraft Country*, penned a powerful article uplifting the legacy of the actor and the need for mental health care for all actors as part of their creative process due to the hazards of the profession. Vance explained,

Michael talked openly about how certain characters triggered him, which is why it was so important during the filming of *Lovecraft Country* that HBO and the producers understood the importance and value of making sure that Michael got the support and help he needed in real time. There was no waiting until the filming is over, maybe sometime later. It was right then, at the point of crisis. That's a really critical step that our industry needs to always take when a cast member is having a difficult time. We can't do our best work when we're not feeling emotionally strong as human beings.

(Vance, 2021)

While Vance does not blame the system for Williams' death, he acknowledges the toll of role-related triggers on every actor, especially for those dealing with trauma in characters and narratives. His call for industry support of creatives' mental health also applies to the education system, where actors train to professionally engage trauma fueled storylines and/or characters that may trigger them. Having onset or on-campus mental health counselors, not for required use but for easy access, is a step in the right direction.

Intergenerational Black actors and discoveries from interdisciplinary research reveals a range of possible healing solutions to the hazards of the profession. Mental health solutions grounded in Black psychology and sociology, particularly dealing with cultural and cellular trauma, can offer more nuanced support. For instance, sociologist, Dr. Joy DeGruy's theory of post-traumatic slave syndrome (DeGruy, 2017) accounts for how a history of oppression and misrepresentation impacts Black individuals and collectives. Her work combined with psychologist, Dr. Linda James Myers' optimal psychology (Myers, 1993) provides an alternative framework for understanding and addressing Black experiences like post-traumatic slave syndrome triggered in actors like Jordan, Williams and their predecessors. Grounded in African philosophical thought, an Afrocentric or optimal worldview recognizes how people of African descent have a distinct concept of self and experience of time that does not align with the Eurocentric, linear model and emphasis on individualism and competition. On the contrary, an African concept of self recognizes one's interconnectedness with the Ancestors, family, community and the yet unborn. Time is cyclical and ongoing, more like a spiral that can contract and expand, at times collapsing in on itself so that the past, present and future occur simultaneously. This explains how the past and future can bleed so heavily into the present (and vice versa) in preparation and performance of a role. Such occurrences not only reflect the historical moment depicted in the narrative through the character's given circumstances but does so while drawing from the actor's biological and emotional DNA along with the influence of the work environment. Building a mental health plan that takes all of this into consideration can anticipate potential traumas before they occur and offer solutions through processes that draw from cultural practices to confront and reconcile the trauma while acting or postproduction.

We Are the Ones We've Been Waiting For ... We Are the Key to 21st-Century Actor Training

Studying Stanislavsky's "system" and its related processes is a choice and should be an informed one that recognizes the blind spots, the intercultural interventions and the alternative, culturally nuanced approaches available. Safe and brave spaces for teaching, learning, and practicing the craft of acting recognize that Blackness is not the problem; white supremacy, institutionalized racism and anti-Blackness are. The majority of K-12, higher education and their Eurocentric actor training programs fail to teach about Black history and culture and the legacies of slavery and racism consistently and holistically. Historically, Black educators and directors whose work centers Black people and cultures recognize the interdisciplinary approaches to teaching acting are essential. Let us continue to use this gift of second sight to lead the field.

To repair historical harms in actor training, we can continue to draw from historical and contemporary practices of these Black educators and practitioners. Reframing pedagogy and practice by acknowledging the origins of humanity in Africa and the rich histories, cultures and performance traditions is a useful way to explore a craft that essentially concerns what it means to be a human being. A bright future for the field involves curricula in acting theory and practice that center or incorporate study of Black contributions, many of which predate Stanislavsky's "system", along with 20th- and 21st-century theories and practices. Create opportunities for Black and Global Majority students to consistently draw from the wealth of their cultures and traditions so everyone can learn, better understand themselves and the world, and reflect the broadest possible range and depth of humanity in performance.

Black and Global Majority actors, directors, educators and theorists have been doing this uncredited work. It is time we amplify the collective contributions of Black folx[15] rather than sticking to the guru model that has mostly benefit white men and white women theorists. Moving forward, white theorists who are true accomplices will resist the urge to center themselves as innovators where Black, indigenous and Global Majority folx have pioneered. True accomplices will amplify the silenced Black and Global Majority voices who have been minimized and ignored by Eurocentric practices that amplify Stanislavsky and the "system". Together, we will advocate and acquire the resources for Black-led programs and efforts rather than Diversity, Equity, and Inclusion (DEI) initiatives at predominantly white institutions unless those initiatives engage in equitable partnerships with Black-led organizations. For example, The Black Arts Institute at The Billie Holiday Theatre partners with Stella Adler and NYU. The CRAFT Institute, a nonprofit dedicated to curating culturally inclusive ecosystems throughout the world of arts and entertainment, also acknowledges Historically Black Colleges and Universities (HBCUs) as historic academic institutions that have played a major role in the development and evolution of Black actor training yet remain underfunded in comparison to predominantly white theatre programs in academia.

The solutions and healing from the hazards of acting while Black will not be found exclusively in Stanislavsky's "system" or its variations. To continue to seek them there without culturally nuanced intervention is a missed opportunity to learn more about the contributions of Black people and people of the Global Majority. It also risks the potential for transforming 21st-century actor training to reflect the demographics of the nation and the world more accurately using some of the tried-and-true methods of people who explore and engage the craft at the intersections of culture with or without Stanislavsky.

Fixation on Stanislavsky and Stanislavsky-based training without addressing the potential harm of the system and its affiliates in relation to Black people and culture is an occupational hazard we simply cannot afford. Twenty-first actor training programs are only possible when we meaningfully recognize and employ the contributions of Black people to developing acting theories and practices in the United States and throughout the African diaspora. Black educators and artists have historically led the way and we continue to carry on the legacy.

Notes

1 See Carlia Claudine Francis, "Preparing Birds to Fly: Lloyd Richards and the Actor" (2013) on the significant contributions by Lloyd to the field.
2 See *TRUTH: Personas, Needs, and Flaws in the Art of Building Actors and Creating Characters* (2014) by Susan Batson for more about her approach.
3 See Baron Kelly's *An Actor's Task: Engaging the Senses* (2015).
4 See the collection *Method Acting Reconsidered: Theory, Practice, Future* (2000) edited by David Krasner.
5 See Shonni Enelow's *Method Acting and Its Discontents: On American Psycho-Drama* (2015) for a cultural deconstruction of the creation of "the Method".
6 *An Actress Prepares: Women and "the Method"* (2012) details Malague's approach to Stanislavsky-based practice.
7 Childress's 1955 play *Trouble in Mind* depicts in part how Black actors, rehearsing under the purview of a white director, are harmed by the application of elements of Stanislavsky's "system".
8 Dorothy Dandridge was also the first Black woman to be nominated for an Academy Award for Best Actress for her role in *Carmen Jones* (1954).
9 See Lundeana Marie Thomas, *Barbara Ann Teer and The National Black Theatre: Transformational Forces in Harlem* (New York: Routledge, 2016).
10 See Boleslavsky's *Acting: The First Six Lessons* (1933) for an indication of the iteration of the "system" he taught in the US at the time.
11 *The Wire* is an American crime drama television series created by David Simon that ran from 2002–2008.
12 In *African Americans and the Culture of Pain* (2004), Debra Walker King defines Blackpain as "a metaphor of the woundedness and pain that marks the lived experience of Blackness."
13 *The Night Of* is an eight-part American television series originally aired on HBO in 2016. It is based on the 2006 British series *Criminal Justice*.

14 This limited series, developed and produced by Misha Green, premiered on HBO in 2020 and was based on the novel of the same name by Matt Ruff.
15 Folx is a gender neutral term intended to include all groups.

References

Arizona State University (2008) *"Acting While Black" A Conversation with Harry J. Lennix*. 29 October. Available at: https://vimeo.com/2103661 (Accessed: 15 October 2021).

Batson, S. (2013) *TRUTH: Personas, Needs, and Flaws in the Art of Building Actors and Creating Characters*. New York: Webster Stone.

Bernhard, B. (2014) "Training" in D. Rubin and C. Solórzano (eds), *The World Encyclopedia of Contemporary Theatre: Volume 2: The Americas*. London: Routledge, pp. 472–473.

Bogle, D. (2001) *Toms, Coons, Mulattoes, Mammies, and Bucks: An Interpretive History of Blacks in American Films*, 4th edn. London: Bloomsbury Academic.

Boleslavsky, R. 2013[1933] *Acting: The First Six Lessons*, enhanced edn. Brattleboro, VT: Echo Point Books and Media.

Childress, A. (2011) *Trouble in Mind*, in K. Perkins (ed.), *Selected Plays: Alice Childress*. Evanston, IL: Northwestern University Press, pp. 47–114.

Dandridge, D. and Conrad, E. (2000) *Everything and Nothing: The Dorothy Dandridge Tragedy*. New York: HarperCollins.

DeGruy, J. (2017) *Post-Traumatic Slave Syndrome: America's Legacy of Enduring Injury and Healing*, rev. edn. Connecticut: Joy DeGruy Publications.

Enelow, S. (2015) *Method Acting and Its Discontents: On American Psycho-Drama*. Evanston, IL: Northwestern University Press.

Francis, C. C. (2013) "Preparing Birds to Fly: Lloyd Richards and the Actor", Ph.D. thesis. University of Missouri-Columbia. Available at: https://mospace.umsystem.edu/xmlui/handle/10355/83927 (Accessed: 8 September 2022).

Introducing Dorothy Dandridge (1999) [Online] Directed by Martha Coolidge. United States: HBO Pictures (Accessed: 1 October 2021).

Jordan, J. (1980) *Poem for South African Women*. [Online Video] Available at: http://www.junejordan.net/poem-for-south-african-women.html (Accessed: 27 February 2023).

Kelly, B. (2015) *An Actor's Task: Engaging the Senses*. Indianapolis: Hackett Publishing Company.

King, D. W. (ed.) (2000) *Body Politics and the Fictional Double*. Bloomington: Indiana University Press.

King, D. W. (2004) *African Americans and the Culture of Pain*. Charlottesville, VA: University of Virginia Press.

Krasner, D. (ed.) (2000) *Method Acting Reconsidered: Theory, Practice, Future*. New York: Palgrave.

Malague, R. (2012) *An Actress Prepares: Women and "the Method"*. New York: Routledge.

Morrison, T. (1992) *Playing in the Dark: Whiteness and the Literary Imagination*. New York: Vintage Books.

Myers, L. J. (1993) *Understanding an Afrocentric Worldview: Introduction to an Optimal Psychology*. Dubuque, IA: Kendall Hunt Publishing Company.

Peterson, Jr., B. L. (1997) *The African American Theatre Directory, 1816–1960*. Westport, CT: Greenwood Press.

Schrodt, P. (2019) "Michael B. Jordan Saw a Therapist After Playing Villain Erik Killmonger in Black Panther", *Men's Health* (6 February). Available at: https://www.menshealth.com/entertainment/a26208828/michael-b-jordan-therapist-black-panther-killmonger/ (Accessed: 15 October 2021).

Stanislavsky, C. (1942) *An Actor Prepares.* Translated from the Russian by E. Reynolds Hapgood. New York: Theatre Arts Books.

Thomas, L. M. (2016) *Barbara Ann Teer and The National Black Theatre: Transformational Forces in Harlem.* New York: Routledge.

Vance, C. B. (2021) "Courtney B. Vance on Michael K. Williams and Confronting Trauma in Hollywood: 'Therapy Is Essential.'" As told to Richard Newby for *The Hollywood Reporter*, 14 September. Available at: https://www.hollywoodreporter.com/tv/tv-news/courtney-b-vance-michael-k-williams-1235013384/ (Accessed: 11 October 2021).

Williams, M. K. (2022) *Scenes from My Life: A Memoir.* New York: Crown.

INDEX

104–6, 114; ethnicity 109; experiences 100, 105, 113; festivals 110; history 100, 110; identities 99; immigrant communities 100, 102, 107; inheritance 105; interests in conjecturing on white America's rejections of the Method 112; learning 104, 106–7, 110; life 105, 108; liturgical literature 110; Method teachers 101, 104–5, 107, 112, 115; parents 104; people 99–102, 110–12; positionalities 112, 116; predilections for performance and comedy 112; programmers and network executives 113; relationship between emotion and memory 108; secular artists 101; Sephardi communities 102; television 113; theatres 4, 12; traditions 105–6, 110, 117, 119; visionaries 114

Jewish-Americans 101, 116n5; categorising their Jewish identity 112, 116n5; ethno-religious identities as 99; identity 112; and the Method teachers' perception of themselves 113; and racist stereotypes 113

Jewish approaches 110, 115; to memory 110; of the Method teachers 105, 107; to question and argue to gain deeper understanding 107; to Stanislavsky's "system" and teachings 104–5; to teaching 115; to text 104

Jewish identities 101–2, 113–14; and the approach of David Baddiel 100; defined as an ethno-religious group 99–100; erasing of in the acting industry 113; regresses from a complicated "peoplehood" to an apathetic religious denomination 100; secularised 108

Jewish immigrants 100, 102–3, 110; assimilation 114–15, 136; and Method teachers 114; new 112; rejection of 114; rural 111; working class 102

Jewishness 99–101, 103–5, 107, 109, 113, 116–17

Jews 100–3, 105, 108, 112, 116, 116n6, 116; categorising of 101; earliest Judaic traditions 107; light-skinned, white-passing 101; playing Jews in a starring role 113

Jikiemi, Pamela 5, 123
Jordan, June 163
Jordan, Michael B. 163, 169, 171, 174
Joyce, James 154
Judaism 105, 110, 116–17

Kelly, Baron 162, 165
King, Floyd 147
King Lear 26
Kissel, Howard 103
Knebel, Maria 50, 59n6, 64
Knipper, Olga 144
Krasner, David 163

Laban, Rudolf 36
Landon-Smith, Kristine 5, 121–35, 139–40
Latinx 10, 87, 91; actors 91; culture 92; immigrants and their descendants 92; playwrights 85–7; students 92; writers 87
Latinx Theatre Commons 91
learning 19, 23, 44, 67, 70, 94, 97, 105–7, 163, 166, 172; self-liberating process 63, 71; styles 98
Lecoq, Jacques 36
legacies 3, 10, 42, 140–4, 170, 172–3
Lennix, Harry J. 163, 174
Letters to a Young Artist 155
Lewis, Bobby 145
liberal arts theatre program 150
Lilina, Maria 54–5
lineages 15, 23, 113, 149
Longwell, Dennis 99, 108
López, Josefina 94
Lorca, Federico García 92
love 9, 20, 23, 26, 50–1, 53, 74, 90, 96, 108; confession scenes 74; instinctive 58; sustained 166; and the Yiddish theatre 103
Luckett, Sharell 157

MA/MFA Actor Training and Coaching programme 30
Machado, Eduardo 91
Malague, Rosemary 105, 111, 114, 163, 165
Mann, Paul 168
Manolikakis, Andreas 68–70, 74, 146
Mark Taper Forum, Los Angeles 91
MAT *see* Moscow Art Theatre
Mayer, Wiletta 166–8
McClendon, Rose 141–3, 145–6, 157–8, 160–1
McConachie, Bruce 155
media 31, 113, 174
Meisner, Sanford 67, 80, 83–4, 87, 99, 103, 105–6, 108, 110, 115, 163, 165, 168
memories 4, 20, 51, 68–9, 71, 73, 75, 78, 82, 89, 108–10; affective 49, 51,